Mike Holt's Illustrated Guide to

Understanding BASIC MOTOR CONTROLS

Revised Edition

Includes NEC® Requirements for Article 430 - Motors

Mike Holt Enterprises
888.NEC.CODE (632.2633) • www.MikeHolt.com

NOTICE TO THE READER

The publisher does not warrant or guarantee any of the products described herein or perform any independent analysis in connection with any of the product information contained herein. The publisher does not assume, and expressly disclaims, any obligation to obtain and include information other than that provided to it by the manufacturer.

The text and commentary in this book that relates to the *National Electrical Code®* is the author's interpretation of the 2017 Edition of NFPA 70, the *National Electrical Code®*. It shall not be considered an endorsement of or the official position of the NFPA® or any of its committees, nor relied upon as a formal interpretation of the meaning or intent of any specific provision or provisions of the 2017 edition of NFPA 70, *National Electrical Code*.

Mike Holt Enterprises disclaims liability for any personal injury, property or other damages of any nature whatsoever, whether special, indirect, consequential or compensatory, directly or indirectly resulting from the use of this material. The reader is responsible for relying on his or her personal independent judgment in determining safety and appropriate actions in all circumstances.

The reader is expressly warned to consider and adopt all safety precautions and applicable federal, state, and local laws and regulations. By following the instructions contained herein, the reader willingly assumes all risks in connection with such instructions.

The publisher makes no representation or warranties of any kind, including but not limited to, the warranties of fitness for particular purpose or merchantability, nor are any such representations implied with respect to the material set forth herein, and the publisher takes no responsibility with respect to such material. The publisher shall not be liable for any special, consequential, or exemplary damages resulting, in whole or part, from the reader's use of, or reliance upon, this material.

Mike Holt's Illustrated Guide to Understanding Basic Motor Controls, Revised Edition

Third Printing: July 2021

Author: Mike Holt
Technical Illustrator: Mike Culbreath
Layout Design and Typesetting: Cathleen Kwas

COPYRIGHT © 2015 Charles Michael Holt
ISBN: 978-0-9992038-4-2

Produced and Printed in the USA

All rights reserved. No part of this work covered by the copyright hereon may be reproduced or used in any form or by any means graphic, electronic, or mechanical, including photocopying, recording, taping, or information storage and retrieval systems without the written permission of the publisher. You can request permission to use material from this text by either calling 888.632.2633, e-mailing Info@MikeHolt.com, or visiting www.MikeHolt.com.

For more information, call 888.NEC.CODE (632.2633), or e-mail Info@MikeHolt.com.

NEC®, NFPA 70®, NFPA 70E® and National Electrical Code® are registered trademarks of the National Fire Protection Association.

This logo is a registered trademark of Mike Holt Enterprises, Inc.

If you are an instructor and would like to request an examination copy of this or other Mike Holt Publications:

Call: 888.NEC.CODE (632.2633) • Fax: 352.360.0983
E-mail: Info@MikeHolt.com • Visit: www.MikeHolt.com

You can download a sample PDF of all our publications by visiting www.MikeHolt.com

I dedicate this book to the
Lord Jesus Christ,
my mentor and teacher.
Proverbs 16:3

Our Commitment

We are committed to serving the electrical industry with integrity and respect by always searching for the most accurate interpretation of the *NEC*® and creating the highest quality instructional material that makes learning easy.

We are invested in the idea of changing lives, and build our products with the goal of not only helping you meet your licensing requirements, but also with the goal that this knowledge will improve your expertise in the field and help you throughout your career.

We are committed to building a life-long relationship with you, and to helping you in each stage of your electrical career. Whether you are an apprentice just getting started in the industry, or an electrician preparing to take an exam, we are here to help you. When you need Continuing Education credits to renew your license, we will do everything we can to get our online courses and seminars approved in your state. Or if you are a contractor looking to train your team, we have a solution for you. And if you have advanced to the point where you are now teaching others, we are here to help you build your program and provide tools to make that task easier.

We genuinely care about providing quality electrical training that will help you take your skills to the next level.

Thanks for choosing Mike Holt Enterprises for your electrical training needs. We are here to help you every step of the way and encourage you to contact us so we can be a part of your success.

God bless,

Table of Contents

Introduction ix
Scope of *Understanding Basic Motor Controls* ix
How to Use This Textbook ix

CHAPTER 1—INTRODUCTION TO MOTOR CONTROLS 1

UNIT 1—BASIC PRINCIPLES OF MOTOR CONTROLS 3
Unit 1—Introduction 3
1.1 Motor Control Language 4
1.2 Motor Control Basics 8
Unit 1—Conclusion 8
Unit 1—Practice Questions 9

UNIT 2—DEFINITIONS, ABBREVIATIONS, AND SYMBOLS 11
Unit 2—Introduction 11
2.1 Definitions of Control Terminology 11
2.2 Common Abbreviations Used for Electrical Terms and Devices 18
2.3 Standard Symbols 19
Unit 2—Conclusion 20
Unit 2—Practice Questions 21

UNIT 3—COMMON CONTROL EQUIPMENT, DEVICES, AND SYMBOLS 23
Unit 3—Introduction 23
3.1 Auxiliary Contacts 23
3.2 Relays 24
3.3 Drum Switch 25
3.4 Float Switch 26
3.5 Flow Switch 26
3.6 Limit Switch—Mechanical 27
3.7 Limit Switch—Proximity 28
3.8 Limit Switch—Optical 28
3.9 Pressure Switch 28
3.10 Pushbutton Switch 29
3.11 Solenoid 31
3.12 Switch Operations 31
3.13 Temperature Switch 34
3.14 Timing Relay—Pneumatic 35
3.15 Timing Relay with Instantaneous Contacts 35
3.16 Timing Relay—Solid-State 36
3.17 Timing Relay Terminology 36
3.18 Reading a Motor Control Schematic 37
Unit 3—Conclusion 39
Unit 3—Practice Questions 40

CHAPTER 2—MOTOR CONTROLS AND SCHEMATICS 43

UNIT 4—COMPONENTS OF CONTROL CIRCUIT SCHEMATICS 45
Unit 4—Introduction 45
4.1 A Simple Control Circuit 45
4.2 Control Devices with Multiple Contacts 48
Unit 4—Conclusion 49
Unit 4—Practice Questions 50

UNIT 5—MAGNETIC CONTROL 53
Unit 5—Introduction 53
5.1 Electromagnetic Control 53
5.2 Power Sources for the Coil and Control Circuit .. 54
5.3 Coil Applications 55
5.4 Remote Control—Introduction 59
5.5 Lighting Contactor 61
5.6 Feeder Disconnect Contactor with Automatic Control 64
Unit 5—Conclusion 65
Unit 5—Practice Questions 66

UNIT 6—MAGNETIC MOTOR STARTERS 69
Unit 6—Introduction 69
6.1 Magnetic Motor Starters 69
6.2 Other Overload Protection Methods 75
6.3 Auxiliary Contacts 75
6.4 Motor Starter Add-On Accessory Devices 76
Unit 6—Conclusion 76
Unit 6—Practice Questions 77

Table of Contents

UNIT 7—BASIC CONTROL CIRCUITS 81
Unit 7—Introduction 81
7.1 2-Wire Control Circuits 81
7.2 3-Wire Control Circuits 84
7.3 3-Wire Circuit in a Wiring (Connection) Diagram 87
7.4 Multiple Start-Stop Pushbutton Stations 89
7.5 Option of Using a 2- or 3-Wire Circuit in One Diagram... 92
Unit 7—Conclusion 93
Unit 7—Practice Questions... 94

UNIT 8—OVERCURRENT PROTECTION FOR CONTROL CIRCUITS 99
Unit 8—Introduction 99
8.1 Protection for Control Circuits........................... 99
8.2 Common (Tapped) versus Separate Control Circuits... 99
8.3 Control Conductor Sizes 16 AWG and 18 AWG...100
8.4 Control Transformer Protection 102
8.5 Other Standard Control Circuit Overcurrent Protection Arrangements 103
Unit 8—Conclusion 104
Unit 8—Practice Questions.......................................105

UNIT 9—INDICATOR (PILOT) LIGHTS AND ILLUMINATED PUSHBUTTONS....................................107
Unit 9—Introduction 107
9.1 Pilot (Indicator) Lights.....................................107
9.2 Typical Applications for Pilot Lights in Control Circuits 108
9.3 Illuminated Pushbuttons 112
Unit 9—Conclusion 113
Unit 9—Practice Questions.......................................114

UNIT 10—SELECTOR SWITCHES AND TRUTH TABLES 117
Unit 10—Introduction 117
10.1 Truth Tables 117
10.2 Two-Position Selector Switch 117
10.3 Three-Position Selector Switch 118
10.4 Selector Switches—Variations 120
Unit 10—Conclusion 123
Unit 10—Practice Questions.....................................124

CHAPTER 3—REVERSING CONTROLS 127
UNIT 11—REVERSING CONTROLS FOR THREE-PHASE MOTORS...129
Unit 11—Introduction 129
11.1 Reversing Three-Phase Motors.......................129
11.2 Forward and Reverse Contactors 129
11.3 Interlocking Devices 130
11.4 Electrical Interlock for Magnetic Reversing Controls...131
11.5 Combined Interlock Methods for Reversing Starters..134
11.6 Wiring a Reversing Control Pushbutton Station 136
11.7 Wiring a Reversing Control with a Selector Switch...136
Unit 11—Conclusion 137
Unit 11—Practice Questions.....................................138

UNIT 12—REVERSING CONTROLS WITH INDICATOR (PILOT) LIGHTS FOR THREE-PHASE MOTORS 141
Unit 12—Introduction 141
12.1 Adding Forward and Reverse Pilot Lights.......141
12.2 Alternate Pilot Light Connection Points..........142
Unit 12—Conclusion 143
Unit 12—Practice Questions.....................................144

UNIT 13—REVERSING CONTROLS WITH LIMIT SWITCHES FOR THREE-PHASE MOTORS 147
Unit 13—Introduction 147
13.1 Reversing Controls with Limit Switches Used to Automatically Stop a Motor 147
13.2 Reversing Controls—Limit Switches for Automatic Forward and Reverse 148
13.3 Reversing Controls and Limit Switches for Garage Door Applications 150
13.4 Forward-Reverse Control With 2-Wire Circuits 153
Unit 13—Conclusion 153
Unit 13—Practice Questions.....................................154

UNIT 14—REVERSING SINGLE-PHASE MOTORS 157
Unit 14—Introduction 157
14.1 Types of Motors...157
14.2 Reversing Control Circuit 159
14.3 Sequence of Operation 159

Table of Contents

Unit 14—Conclusion 161
Unit 14—Practice Questions 162

CHAPTER 4—CONTROLS FOR MULTIPLE MOTORS 165

UNIT 15—SEQUENCING CONTROL 167
Unit 15—Introduction 167
15.1 Sequencing Control 167
15.2 Controls for Sequencing Multiple Motors 170
Unit 15—Conclusion 173
Unit 15—Practice Questions 174

UNIT 16—MASTER STOP FUNCTION 177
Unit 16—Introduction 177
16.1 Master or Emergency Stop Controls for Multiple Motors 177
16.2 Factory Installed Jumpers 178
16.3 Types of Pushbuttons 178
Unit 16—Conclusion 178
Unit 16—Practice Questions 179

ANNEX A—MISCELLANEOUS REQUIREMENTS 181

UNIT 17—MOTOR AND CONTROLLER DISCONNECTING MEANS IN SCHEMATICS ...183
Unit 17—Introduction 183
17.1 Motor Controllers and Disconnects 183
17.2 Disconnect for Separate Control Circuit 187
Unit 17—Conclusion 187
Unit 17—Practice Questions 188

UNIT 18—MISCELLANEOUS MOTOR CONTROL CIRCUITS 191
Unit 18—Introduction 191
18.1 Combining Devices and Functions for Motor Control Circuits 191
18.2 Control Relay (CR) 191
18.3 Selector Switch Pushbutton 193
Unit 18—Conclusion 195
Unit 18—Practice Questions 196

UNIT 19—MOTOR WINDING CONNECTIONS 199
Unit 19—Introduction 199
19.1 Three-Phase Motors 199
19.2 Dual-Voltage, Nine Lead, Three-Phase Motors 200
19.3 Single-Phase, Dual-Voltage Motors 204
Unit 19—Conclusion 204
Unit 19—Practice Questions 205

UNIT 20—MISCELLANEOUS CONTROL AND SIGNALING CIRCUITS 209
Unit 20—Introduction 209
20.1 Doorbells 209
20.2 Thermostats for Air-Conditioning and Heat ...211
Unit 20—Conclusion 212
Unit 20—Practice Questions 213

ANNEX B—BONUS MATERIAL: ARTICLE 430—MOTORS, MOTOR CIRCUITS, AND CONTROLLERS 215

ARTICLE 430—MOTORS, MOTOR CIRCUITS, AND CONTROLLERS 217

Part I. General 217
430.1 Scope 217
430.2 Definitions 218
430.6 Table FLC versus Motor Nameplate Current Rating 218
430.14 Location of Motors 219
430.17 The Highest Rated Motor 219

Part II. Conductor Size 220
430.22 Single Motor Conductor Size 220
430.24 Several Motors—Conductor Size 222

Part III. Motor and Branch-Circuit Overload Protection 223
430.31 Overload 223
430.32 Overload Sizing for Continuous-Duty Motors 224

Table of Contents

Part IV. Branch-Circuit Short-Circuit and Ground-Fault Protection ... 225
430.51 General ... 225
430.52 Branch-Circuit Short-Circuit and Ground-Fault Protection ... 226
430.55 Single Overcurrent Protection Device ... 229

Part V. Feeder Short-Circuit and Ground-Fault Protection ... 229
430.62 Motor Feeder Protection ... 229

Part VI. Motor Control Circuits ... 231
430.72 Overcurrent Protection for Control Circuits ... 231
430.75 Disconnect for Control Circuits ... 232

Part VII. Motor Controllers ... 232
430.83 Motor Controller Horsepower Rating ... 232

Part IX. Disconnecting Means ... 233
430.102 Disconnect Location ... 233
430.107 Readily Accessible ... 233
430.109 Disconnecting Means Rating ... 234

Part X. Adjustable-Speed Drive Systems ... 234
430.120 General ... 234
430.122 Conductor Sizing ... 234
430.124 Overload Protection ... 236
430.128 Disconnecting Means ... 236
430.130 Branch-Circuit Short-Circuit and Ground-Fault Protection ... 236

Part XIV. Tables ... 237
Table 430.248 Full-Load Current, Single-Phase Motors ... 237
Table 430.250 Full-Load Current, Three-Phase Motors ... 238
Article 430—Practice Questions ... 239

FINAL EXAM ... 241

INDEX ... 257

Introduction

Mike Holt's Illustrated Guide to Understanding Basic Motor Controls

This edition of *Mike Holt's Illustrated Guide to Understanding Basic Motor Controls* textbook is intended to provide you with the tools necessary to understand common basic motor control circuits. The writing style of this textbook, and in all of Mike Holt's products, is meant to be informative, practical, useful, informal, easy to read, and applicable for today's electrical professional. Also, just like all of Mike Holt's textbooks, it contains hundreds of full-color illustrations.

The study of motor controls is an extensive and complicated subject. *Mike Holt's Illustrated Guide to Understanding Basic Motor Controls* is designed to provide a foundation for students who are just beginning to learn about motor controls. It can also be helpful for journeyman and master exam preparation.

Scope of *Understanding Basic Motor Controls*

This textbook, *Mike Holt's Illustrated Guide to Basic Motor Controls*, explains how to read and understand basic motor control schematics. It helps students understand the equipment represented by the symbols in the schematics, and how motor controls are used in practical applications. Most of the circuits and symbols presented in this book represent industry standards. There are frequently variations in the symbols, terminations of wiring, or equipment used by other authors or by manufacturers, depending on the application. Most of the motor control circuits in this textbook were selected to introduce specific basic concepts of motor controls. Keep in mind that there can be many other variations to these circuits. This textbook isn't intended to be a comprehensive study of motor control circuits. It's also important to understand the *National Electrical Code®* requirements associated with motor controls. While the *Code®* has little to do with how a motor control circuit runs, it contains many requirements for the disconnecting means, controllers, wiring methods used to install the control wiring, the installation of equipment, enclosures, and the overcurrent protection for the conductors, and the equipment being installed.

Additional Resource

Article 430—Motors, Motor Circuits, and Controllers, from *Mike Holt's Illustrated Guide to Understanding the National Electrical Code, Volume 1* contains the specific rules for sizing feeder and branch circuit conductors, selecting ground-fault and short-circuit protection, and sizing motor overload protection, control circuit conductors, controllers, and disconnecting means for electric motors.

This text has been added to this textbook as Annex B. These requirements are based on the 2020 *NEC* and you should always consult your *Code* book for current requirements.

You can review Mike's complete line of *Code* products at www.MikeHolt.com/Code.

How to Use This Textbook

Units 1 through 16. Read each unit carefully then answer the questions at the end of each unit. Make sure you read all multiple-choice selections because many questions have more than one correct answer. As you progress through this textbook, you might find you don't understand every explanation, example, calculation, or comment. Try not to become frustrated, and don't get down on yourself. It may be helpful to mark an area you have a problem with and come back to it later.

Annex A and B. Treat Annex A the same as you do each unit. Read each part carefully and answer the questions at the end. Annex B is reference material on *NEC* requirements for motors. Completing the practice questions at the end of this material is optional.

Use of Nominal Voltages versus Motor-Rated Voltages. Common system nominal voltages include 120/240V, 120/208V, and 277/480V, which are the rated voltages of the electrical service to the building or facility [220.5(A)]. Common motor-rated voltages are lower (115V, 208V, 230V, and 460V) and allow for voltage drop from the building service or separately

Introduction

derived system. In this textbook, system nominal voltages will be used when discussing the power supply and wiring system. Motor-rated voltages will typically be used when discussing the actual motor [Tables 430.248 and 430.250].

Cross-References and Author's Comments. Since the *National Electrical Code* ("*NEC*" or "*Code*") contains several rules that pertain to motor controls, this textbook contains a number of cross-references to that document to help you develop a better understanding of how these rules relate to this subject. These cross-references are identified by *Code* article, section, and (if present) subsection numbers in brackets, an example of which is "[220.5(A)]."

> **Author's Comments:** These were written by Mike to help you (the reader) better understand the subject of motor controls by bringing to your attention items you should be aware of.

NEC **Requirements.** You'll notice that all *NEC* text has been paraphrased, as well as some of the article and section titles being different than they appear in the actual *Code*. Mike believes doing so makes it easier to understand the content of the rule, so keep this in mind when comparing this textbook against the actual *NEC*. As you read through this material, be sure to take the time to review the text along with the outstanding graphics and examples provided.

Final Exam. After completing all units and Annex B, take the final exam. As with the unit exams, read all multiple-choice selections because there may be more than one correct answer.

Textbook Errors and Corrections

We're committed to providing you with the finest product with the fewest errors and take great care to ensure our textbooks are correct. But we're realistic and know that errors might be found after printing.

If you believe that there's an error of any kind (typographical, grammatical, technical, etc.) in this textbook or in the Answer Key, send an e-mail that includes the textbook title, page number, and any other pertinent information to corrections@MikeHolt.com.

Companion Videos

One of the best ways to get the most out of this textbook is to use it in conjunction with the corresponding videos. Mike Holt's videos provide a 360° view of each topic with specialized commentary from Mike and his panel of industry experts.

To order your copy of the videos at a discounted price, call our office at 888.632.2633.

Acknowledgments

About Mike Holt Enterprises

Mike Holt worked his way up through the electrical trade from an apprentice electrician to become one of the most recognized experts in the world as it relates to electrical power installations. He was a Journeyman Electrician, Master Electrician, and Electrical Contractor. In 1974, Mike realized there was a need for quality electrical training and opened Mike Holt Enterprises.

Today, Mike Holt Enterprises is the leader in all aspects of electrical training. Mike and his entire staff are dedicated to making the industry safer through training and state-of-the-art products. Mike's background as a struggling student, who dropped out of high school and later went on to get his GED and eventually attend The University of Miami, has helped him understand the needs of his students and the customers using his products. As a result, he has set a standard that all products must be easy-to-understand, focused on the essentials, and include lots of detailed illustrations to help the materials come to life.

What sets Mike Holt Enterprises apart from other publishing companies is that from its very beginning it was created to serve the needs of the electrical community exclusively. Mike has always wanted to make sure that the focus was aimed at meeting the needs of electrical professionals. His books are designed to make the electrical student not only learn the material, but enjoy the process. His DVD programs bring electrical experts from across the country into living rooms and classrooms to discuss the various aspects of each subject.

Mike has realized his vision over the last 40 years of creating a company that takes care of its customers, provides high quality training, and continues to find ways to improve the safety of the industry. This book, *Understanding Basic Motor Controls*, is another example of how Mike Holt Enterprises sets the bar for quality materials.

Mike Culbreath—Author and Illustrator

Graphic Illustrator
Alden, MI
www.MikeHolt.com

Mike Culbreath devoted his career to the electrical industry and worked his way up from an apprentice electrician to master electrician. He started in the electrical field doing residential and light commercial construction. He later did service work and custom electrical installations. While working as a journeyman electrician, he suffered a serious on-the-job knee injury. As part of his rehabilitation, Mike completed courses at Mike Holt Enterprises. and then passed the exam to receive his Master Electrician's license. In 1986, with a keen interest in continuing education for electricians, he joined the staff to update material and began illustrating Mike Holt's textbooks and magazine articles.

He started with simple hand-drawn diagrams and cut-and-paste graphics. When frustrated by the limitations of that style of illustrating, he took a company computer home to learn how to operate some basic computer graphic software. Becoming aware that computer graphics offered a lot of flexibility for creating illustrations, Mike took every computer graphics class and seminar he could to help develop his computer graphic skills. He's now worked as an illustrator and editor with the company for over 25 years and, as Mike Holt has proudly acknowledged, has helped to transform his words and visions into lifelike graphics.

Originally from South Florida, Mike now lives in northern lower Michigan where he enjoys kayaking, photography, and cooking, but his real passion is his horses. Mike loves spending time with his children Dawn and Mac and his grandchildren Jonah, Kieley, and Scarlet.

Special Acknowledgments—I would like to thank Ryan Jackson, an outstanding and very knowledgeable *Code* guy, and Eric Stromberg, an electrical engineer and super geek (and I mean that in the most complimentary manner, this guy is brilliant), for helping me keep our graphics as technically correct as possible.

Acknowledgments

I also want to give a special thank you to Cathleen Kwas for making me look good with her outstanding layout design and typesetting skills and Toni Culbreath who proofreads all of my material. I would also like to acknowledge Belynda Holt Pinto, our Chief Operations Officer and the rest of the outstanding staff at Mike Holt Enterprises, for all the hard work they do to help produce and distribute these outstanding products.

And last but not least, I need to give a special thank you to Mike Holt for not firing me over 25 years ago when I "borrowed" one of his computers and took it home to begin the process of learning how to do computer illustrations. He gave me the opportunity and time needed to develop my computer graphic skills. He's been an amazing friend and mentor since I met him as a student many years ago. Thanks for believing in me and allowing me to be part of the Mike Holt Enterprises family.

Mike Holt Enterprises Team

Technical Editorial Director

Steve Arne

Training Director
AETech Electrical Training Center
Rapid City, South Dakota
www.ElectricianClass.com

Steve Arne has worked as an electrician, electrical contractor, and electrical instructor for 40 years. Nineteen years of his career were spent as a teacher and department head in post-secondary education. Since Steve retired from Western Dakota Tech in 2003, he has provided industry-direct training specializing in continuing education Electrical Code classes and Electrician Exam Preparation classes for Journeyman and Master's level exams.

In 2012, Steve and Deb's son Ryan returned to Rapid City South Dakota to help Steve expand his training business at AETech Electrical Training Center to include a 640 hour full-time pre-employment Apprentice Electrician Training Program. Steve is currently a Board Member of the South Dakota Electrical Commission and serves on the State and Local Chapter Boards of the South Dakota Electrical Council.

Steve worked with Mike Holt as a technical editor and video team participant beginning in 2002, and uses Mike's books in his classes. He is very thankful to have been associated with an industry leader like Mike who has a real heart to help others and provides excellent training products to help students in the electrical industry.

Steve and his wife Deb live in Rapid City, South Dakota where they're both active in their church and community, and love to spend time with their children and grandchildren. The highest priority for both of them is putting God first in both their home and business.

Editorial Team

I would like to thank Toni Culbreath and Barbara Parks who worked tirelessly to proofread and edit the final stages of this publication. Their attention to detail and dedication to this project is greatly appreciated.

Production Team

I would like to thank Cathleen Kwas who did the layout and design of this book. In addition, thanks go to Belynda Holt Pinto, who ran the production for this title. Their desire to create the best possible product for our customers is appreciated.

Video Team Members

Mike Holt, **Steve Arne**, and **Mike Culbreath** (members of the Mike Holt Enterprises Team) were video team members, along with the following highly qualified professionals.

Dennis Carlson

Master Electrician/Electrical Trainer
Rocky Mountain Electrical Training
Steamboat Springs, CO
www.RMETtech.com

Dennis Carlson has been in the electrical trade for over 30 years, and has held the positions of Project Superintendent, Field Engineer, Start-up-Coordinator, General Foreman, Foreman, Journeyman, and Craft Training Manager. He's certified with NCCER as a Master Trainer, and is a professor for Victoria University, Australia

Acknowledgments

as a Master Trainer. In April 2013, he graduated from Salem International University with a Bachelor's degree in Business Administration.

Dennis is a Master Electrician/Contractor licensed in several states, and a member of the NFPA and IAEI. He's trained thousands of electricians in the last 20 years using Mike Holt's material and has been working with Mike for the last 13 years on his Exam Prep courses.

Dennis and his wife, Cindy, live in Steamboat Springs, Colorado, where they're both active in enjoying God's great outdoors, their church, and the community. They have two children, Brandy, a graphics arts designer who lives in Greeley Colorado, and Josh who is an electrical estimator in Denver Colorado. "Life is too short to do only one thing so you have to prepare yourself for the next challenge. Never stop learning and striving to achieve those goals that you have."

Eric Stromberg

Electrical Engineer/Instructor
Stromberg Engineering, Inc.
Los Alamos, NM
www.strombergengineering.com

Eric Stromberg worked as a journeyman electrician, before and during the time he attended college. When he graduated with a degree in Electrical Engineering in 1982, he took a job as an electronics technician. Eric became a licensed fire alarm installation superintendent and spent the next seven years installing and maintaining life safety systems in high-rise buildings.

In 1989, he went to work for Dow Chemical, where he designed power distribution systems for world-class industrial facilities. Eric began teaching *National Electrical Code* classes to engineers in 1997. He received his professional engineering license, for the State of Texas, in 2003 and, in 2005, started Stromberg Engineering.

In 2013, Eric retired from Dow Chemical and now lives in the mountains of northern New Mexico. Eric's oldest daughter, Ainsley, lives in Boston, Massachusetts with her husband Nathan. His son, Austin, is in the Air Force and is stationed at Minot, North Dakota. His youngest daughter, Brieanna, is a singer/songwriter who lives in Austin, Texas.

Dan Webb

Electrical Supervisor
Timber Products Company
Medford, Oregon

Dan Webb has been involved in the wood products industry for over 30 years with over 20 years as an electrician. As a teenager Dan started as a maintenance "shop-boy" helping the millwrights with the day-to-day tasks. He spent the next several years as a millwright and then moved in to the electrical side of maintenance. Dan specialized in process control becoming an integrator in advanced PLC, computer based operator interfaces, shift reporting, and other data acquisition or control processes.

Currently Dan is an Electrical Supervisor for Timber Products Company at the Medford complex which consists of a Hardwood Plywood Plant and a Particleboard Plant. He's also highly involved in the local apprenticeship program as committee chair for the local apprenticeship training council and as an instructor for the related training coordinated by the local community college. Dan is also an Oregon State approved continuing education instructor providing the necessary training required by the Oregon Licensing requirements.

Dan and his lovely wife Cindy enjoy living in the beautiful Rogue Valley of Southern Oregon. He and Cindy are ATV enthusiasts and members of the Oregon Dune Patrol. They also enjoy motorcycling, fishing, and just enjoying the great outdoors.

Dan says that he became involved in apprenticeship and continuing education to give back to the process that has enriched his life and helped him grow his "work-life" into a challenging and satisfying career.

Acknowledgments

Advisory Committee—2009 Edition

Hugh Charles
Electrical Commissioner
Department of Physical Planning
Charlestown, Nevis

Harry Cunningham
Instructor
Independent Electrical Contractors, Inc.
Gibsonton, Florida

Clifford F. Johnston
Electrical Inspector
Gibraltar, Michigan

Don Keathley
Instructor
Russelville Apprentice, Inc.
Russellville, Arkansas

Ronald Taylor
Instructor
Russelville Apprentice, Inc.
Morrilton, Arkansas

Richard M. Vining
Instructor U.S. Army Guided Missile School
Tustin, California

INTRODUCTION TO MOTOR CONTROLS

The subject of motor controls is both complicated and technically challenging. This textbook is designed to provide a foundation for students who're just beginning to study motor controls. It can also be helpful for journeyman and master exam preparation. This introductory chapter contains general information related to motor controls, including definitions, abbreviations, and drawing symbols. It consists of the following units:

Unit 1—Basic Principles of Motor Controls

Unit 2—Definitions, Abbreviations, and Symbols

Unit 3—Common Control Equipment, Devices, and Symbols

Notes

UNIT 1

Basic Principles of Motor Controls

Unit 1—Introduction

This unit discusses the basic concepts of motor control, including "motor control language" and the types of wiring diagrams used.

Motor Control Circuits

Motor control circuits are an effective way to reduce cost by using smaller wire and reduced-amperage devices to control a motor. Imagine trying to wire a pushbutton station for a 100A motor using 3 AWG conductors. Many smaller motors use the same size conductors for both control and power circuits, but as the horsepower increases it becomes impractical to do so, **Figure 1–1**. Motor control circuits are often connected to lower voltages than the motor they control to make it safer for operators and maintenance personnel. A motor control circuit, for the most part, is simply a switch (or group of switches) and a motor. If you keep the word "switch" in mind, it helps keep the intimidating subject of "motor control" in its proper context. For example, the following can be considered motor controls:

A time clock that operates a pool or sprinkler pump is nothing more than an automatic switch. At a preset time, a set of contacts open or close (turn off or on). **Figure 1–2**

An automatic garage door opener uses a radio signal to operate a switch that activates a garage door in much

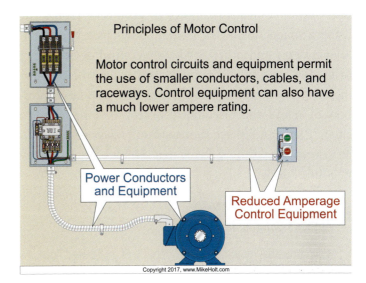

Figure 1–1

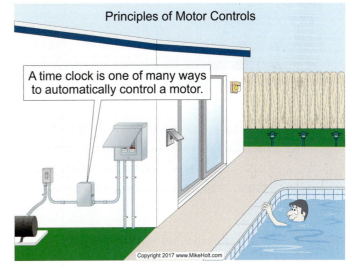

Figure 1–2

Unit 1 — Basic Principles of Motor Controls

the same manner as a typical "up-down" pushbutton station.

Many motors are controlled by computerized control systems, solid-state logic controls, or programmable logic controllers (PLCs). The fundamentals of control systems still apply. The PLC controls an external output based on the logic of a control program, and that output controls the motor or groups of motors by using a magnetic starter, and in some cases additional relays. PLCs and other solid-state control devices were originally invented to provide less expensive replacements for older automated systems that used large numbers of relays and mechanical timers. In some cases, a single PLC can replace thousands of relays resulting in less expensive wiring systems that offer greater flexibility in control designs.

Author's Comments:

- In industrial processes, the control of pressure, flow, speed, temperature, and other items are essential for efficient productivity and safety. Devices such as solid-state sensors, static controls, solid-state relays, and programmable controls can provide very precise control for an industrial process.
- Although the subject of solid-state controls isn't covered in detail in this textbook, the concepts are very similar to other motor controls in that they essentially use switches to control motors.
- Many experts agree that the best way to learn about motor controls is to start with the standard control methods covered in this textbook. This statement also applies when electronic controls are the subject being studied.

Many control circuits include motor overload protection devices. Traditional overload (OL) protectors operate on the relationship between heat and current. As current increases, heat increases. If an overload device is rated 10A, and the current exceeds that rating, the OL device will operate to open the circuit because of the increased heat caused by the current running through it. A magnetic starter or other motor controllers may include overload devices, or they may be an integral part of the motor, particularly with small motors.

Author's Comment: Short circuits and ground faults aren't considered overloads.

There are two basic designs of motor control equipment, NEMA and IEC.

NEMA (National Electrical Manufacturers Association). NEMA is a trade association for manufacturers of electrical equipment and supplies. NEMA standards specify motor horsepower (hp) ratings, speeds, motor frame sizes and dimensions, motor torques, motor starter size ratings, and enclosure specifications.

NEMA-rated products are typically heavy duty, can be used in a broad range of applications, and some starters can be maintained and repaired. For these reasons, they're often more expensive than IEC motor starters. NEMA-rated motors and motor controllers are the type most commonly used in North America.

IEC (International Electrotechnical Commission). IEC is an international standards organization. IEC motor starters are often less expensive, smaller in size, are tailored for specific motor performance requirements, and the selection of the right starter for each application is very important. IEC-rated motor controllers are widely used in Europe and Asia.

1.1 Motor Control Language

Electrical symbols, words, and line diagrams provide the information necessary to understand the operation of motor control circuits. Used together, they create a

Basic Principles of Motor Controls — Unit 1

type of motor control "language" that's used to transfer information and ideas quickly and efficiently.

The symbols in motor control schematics represent devices, power conductors, control conductors, conductor connections and terminals, and sometimes the motor itself.

The words, phrases, and abbreviations in a schematic are generally accepted terms that represent functions, describe actions, and list sequences of operation.

In many cases, the symbols and words have a similarity to the items they represent. The basic types of schematics are shown in **Figure 1–3**. Parts A, B, and C of that figure illustrate three different methods of representing the same control circuit.

(1) Ladder Diagrams (Figure 1–4)

Ladder diagrams are also called "line diagrams" or "elementary diagrams." They're used to represent the function of the control circuit and the associated devices, but don't show the components of the control circuit in their actual positions. As control circuits become more complex, a ladder diagram can be less complicated to read than a wiring or connection diagram. For example, in **Figure 1-4**, notice the set of contacts marked M under the start pushbutton. The M contacts marked 2 and 3 are actually located in the motor starter fairly close to the coil, as shown in **Figure 1–3B**, and the normal physical appearance of these contacts often look as shown in **Figure 1–3C**. (Notice that all three examples of the M contacts are shown with a blue background in **Figure 1–3**.)

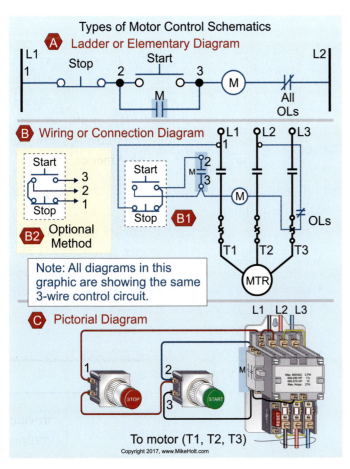

Figure 1–3

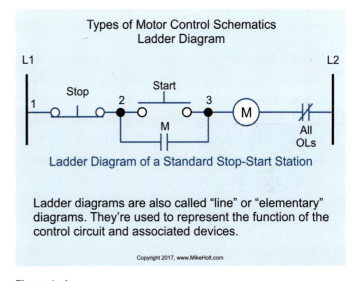

Figure 1–4

The ladder diagrams in **Figures 1–4 and 1–5** illustrates electrical function, showing the M contacts in parallel with the start pushbutton to form what's called a "holding circuit." The physical location of the M contacts isn't shown in the ladder diagram.

Understanding Basic Motor Controls | Mike Holt Enterprises | 5

Unit 1 | Basic Principles of Motor Controls

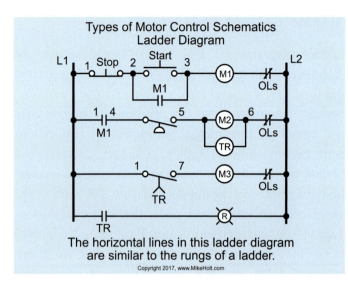

Figure 1–5

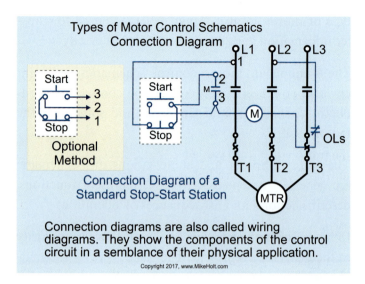

Figure 1–6

Figure 1–5 shows a more complicated version of a ladder diagram. Notice that the horizontal lines in this control circuit are similar to the rungs of a ladder.

> **Author's Comment:** An important point to remember is that schematics show motors and control equipment in the resting, or off state (sometimes called the "shelf" state). Part of the difficulty, when first learning about motor controls, is in understanding how the different components of the control circuit interrelate during the operation of the controls.

(2) Connection Diagrams (Figure 1–6)

Connection diagrams, or wiring diagrams, show the components of the control circuit in a semblance of their actual physical locations. The start-stop pushbutton station is shown more as an actual device in the control circuit wired to a set of contacts marked 2 and 3. In Figure 1–4, the wires on each side of the M contacts trace back to points 2 and 3 on either side of the start pushbutton. The contacts marked M in Figure 1–4 are the same contacts as those marked 2 and 3 in Figure 1–6.

Different manufacturers of control devices, as well as books about motor controls, use different methods of showing the control circuit wiring. For example, in Figure 1–3B1, the control wiring from the start-stop pushbutton station runs to the actual connection points 1, 2, and 3. As the wiring diagrams become more complicated, the optional method shown in Figure 1–3B2 is frequently used to show the connection points for the start-stop pushbutton station. Here, in Figure 1–6, instead of running the control wires to the actual connection point, arrowed lines represent connections to be made by the installer.

> **Author's Comments:**
> - Many times you see plain lines (no arrows) with numbers to indicate connections to be made by the installer. We use both methods in this textbook.
> - Many of the components and symbols used in ladder diagrams and wiring diagrams are the same. In order to make schematics easier to read, some manufacturers combine the two types of diagrams together. Some equipment comes with both ladder diagrams and wiring diagrams.

Basic Principles of Motor Controls — Unit 1

- Remember, ladder diagrams show electrical function and wiring diagrams show the actual components.

It's very common to find different styles of schematics combined in a single wiring diagram. The top part of the diagram in **Figure 1–7** is in the style of a connection diagram, while the style showing the start-stop station and coil is similar to a ladder diagram.

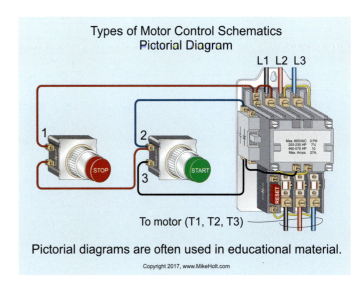

Figure 1–8

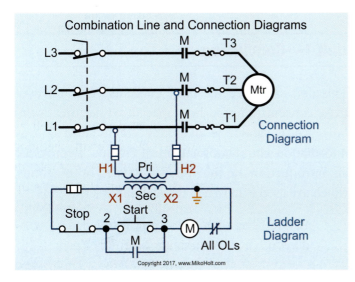

Figure 1–7

(3) Pictorial Diagrams (Figure 1–8)

Pictorial diagrams are often used in educational material and as exploded views or cut-away views in installation and maintenance literature. Pictorial diagrams help students see actual devices and components used in motor control circuits and how they relate to the symbols used in ladder diagrams and wiring diagrams. For example, the start pushbutton we mentioned earlier has wires run to the device that contains the set of contacts M in **Figure 1–4**, and to contact points 2 and 3 in **Figure 1–6**.

Author's Comments:

- Often a hand-drawn diagram of a control circuit constructed in the field helps in understanding how a circuit functions and how to make the necessary connections, especially during the learning process. **Figure 1–9** shows the hand-drawn version of the 3-wire start-stop control circuit shown in **Figure 1–3**. Notice that the stop pushbutton is in series with coil M, and that the start pushbutton is in parallel with M contacts 2–3. The entire control circuit in this example is in parallel between line 1 and line 2. These basic relationships can be found in many control circuits.

- The numbers in this diagram are simply for the aid of the reader and it don't imply that terminal 1 on one device should always be connected to terminal 1 on another device.

Once you understand the terminology and symbols involved in motor control circuit wiring, understanding how it works becomes easier and less intimidating.

Unit 1 — Basic Principles of Motor Controls

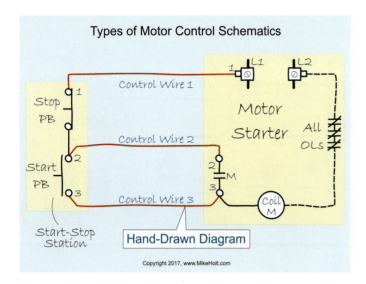

Figure 1–9

1.2 Motor Control Basics

The purpose of this textbook is to introduce the basics of motor controls. Many of the control circuits that are covered are standard control circuits used in many different applications. Each circuit can have several variations and optional devices in addition to those included in the schematics. This textbook won't teach you all of these control circuit variations, but will give you a basic understanding of motor controls, and how to read wiring diagrams and understand the sequences of operation.

When beginning this study of basic motor controls, remember that motor controls are basically different kinds of switches that turn things on and off, both manually and automatically. This may help you keep things in perspective.

There are many good books available for more advanced studies about this subject. Also check with the manufacturers of motor control equipment for educational material and standard motor control circuits.

Unit 1—Conclusion

This unit explained the basic concepts of motor controls, concentrating on how specialized electrical symbols, words, and line diagrams are used to convey information about motor control circuits. It provided an introduction to the following types of diagrams, which are used extensively throughout this textbook:

- Ladder diagrams (these are also called "line diagrams" or "elementary diagrams").

- Connection diagrams (also called "wiring diagrams").

- Pictorial diagrams.

Practice Questions

Unit 1—Practice Questions

Introduction

1. A motor control circuit, for the most part, is simply a _____ and a motor.

    (a) motor
    (b) switch
    (c) feeder
    (d) magnet

2. Many types of overload protectors operate on the relationship between _____.

    (a) heat and current
    (b) the neutral conductor and the earth
    (c) branch circuits and feeders
    (d) voltage and wattage

1.1 Motor Control Language

3. Schematics show motors and control equipment in their "resting" or "shelf" state.

    (a) True
    (b) False

4. Ladder diagrams are also known as _____.

    (a) line diagrams
    (b) elementary diagrams
    (c) pictorial diagrams
    (d) a or b

5. _____ are used to represent the function of the control circuit and the associated devices, but don't show the components of the control circuit in their actual positions.

    (a) Ladder diagrams
    (b) Connection diagrams
    (c) Wiring diagrams
    (d) Pictorial diagrams

6. Connection diagrams are also called wiring diagrams.

    (a) True
    (b) False

7. _____ are used mostly in educational material and as exploded views or cut-away views in installation and maintenance literature.

    (a) Ladder diagrams
    (b) Connection diagrams
    (c) Wiring diagrams
    (d) Pictorial diagrams

8. The motor control circuit shown in **Figure 1–10** is a _____.

    (a) ladder diagram
    (b) connection diagram
    (c) wiring diagram
    (d) pictorial diagram

Unit 1 — Practice Questions

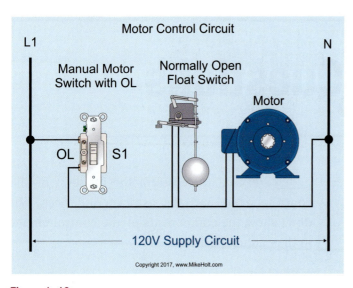

Figure 1–10

9. The motor control circuit shown in **Figure 1–11** is a _____.

   (a) ladder diagram
   (b) connection diagram
   (c) wiring diagram
   (d) pictorial diagram

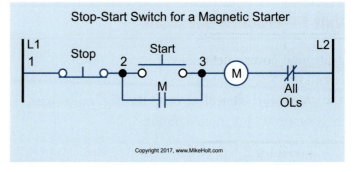

Figure 1–11

UNIT 2: Definitions, Abbreviations, and Symbols

Unit 2—Introduction

This unit covers definitions used in motor control, common abbreviations for electrical terms and devices, and graphic symbols used on motor control diagrams.

2.1 Definitions of Control Terminology

3-Wire Control. See the definition of "Control, 3-Wire."

Actuator. The part of a limit switch that transfers the mechanical force of the moving part to the electrical contacts.

Across-the-Line Starter (Full-Voltage Starter). A device consisting of a contactor and overload relay to start a motor at full voltage and to protect the motor from overload.

ANSI. American National Standards Institute.

Automatic. Self-acting; operating by its own mechanism without human intervention. For example, a sump pump is turned on automatically by a level (float) switch that senses rising water.

Autotransformer Starter. A starter equipped with an autotransformer that serves to reduce the voltage applied to the motor terminals during starting. An autotransformer is a single-winding transformer with multiple voltage taps.

Auxiliary Contacts. Contacts in addition to, and electrically isolated from, the main power contacts which function in unison with the main power contacts.

Bimetallic Overload Relay. An overload relay which resets automatically.

Blowout Coil. An electromagnetic coil used in contactors and starters to deflect an arc when a circuit is interrupted.

Branch Circuit. The circuit conductors between the final overcurrent protection device and the outlet or equipment.

Capacitor. An electric device that stores electrical energy by means of an electrostatic field.

Capacitor Start Motor. A single-phase induction motor with a main winding arranged for direct connection to a power source, and an auxiliary start winding connected in series with a capacitor. The start winding with the capacitor circuit is usually only connected during starting.

Centrifugal Starting-Switch (Rotary Machinery). A centrifugally operated automatic mechanism used to switch a set of contacts after a motor has attained a predetermined speed.

Author's Comments:

- One of the circuit changes usually performed is to open or disconnect the auxiliary start winding circuit of a single-phase motor once the motor has reached approximately 65 to 70 percent of its running speed.
- In the usual form of this device, the part mounted to the stator frame or end shield is the starting switch, and the part mounted on the rotor is the centrifugal actuator.

Unit 2 — Definitions, Abbreviations, and Symbols

Coil. Magnetic coils are made up of many turns of insulated wire. The coil creates a magnetic field when energized. In the case of a relay, or solenoid, energizing and de-energizing a coil is used to cause mechanical motion which can open and close electrical contacts or provide other mechanical operations. Many coils are encapsulated with an epoxy resin or other material to improve the mechanical life of the device.

Combination Starter. A magnetic starter having a manually operated disconnecting means, as well as short-circuit and ground-fault protection, built into the same enclosure with the starter.

Common Control Circuit (Tapped Control Circuit). A motor control circuit tapped from the motor branch circuit. The *NEC* defines this as a "motor control circuit." See the definition of "Separate Control Circuit."

> **Author's Comment:** A motor control circuit can get its power from the branch circuit supplying the motor [*NEC* Article 430, Part VI], or from another source such as a panelboard, in which case it's considered a Class 1 circuit [*NEC* Article 725, Part II]. A Class 1 circuit is often called a "separate control circuit."

Connection Diagram. A diagram showing the electrical connection between the control circuit and the equipment. This type of diagram is also called a "Wiring Diagram."

> **Author's Comment:** A connection diagram typically shows the connection of control devices and the motor. A line or ladder diagram will show mostly the functions of the control circuit instead of the actual devices.

Contact, Electrical. A junction of conducting parts permitting current to flow.

Contacts. Connecting parts that touch each other to complete a circuit, and separate to open a circuit.

Contactor. An electromechanical device for repeatedly establishing and interrupting an electric power circuit.

Control. A device or group of devices that serve to govern, in some predetermined manner, the electric power supply to an apparatus.

Control Circuit (Motor Control Circuit). The circuit of a control apparatus or system that carries the electric signals directing the performance of the controller but doesn't carry the main power current.

Control, 3-Wire. A control function that utilizes momentary contact devices (usually two or more) and a "holding," "seal-in," or "memory" auxiliary contact. An example of a 3-wire control circuit is one that makes use of a start-stop pushbutton station in conjunction with holding contacts.

Controller. A device, or group of devices, that serves to govern, in some predetermined manner, the electric power delivered to the load (such as a motor) to which it's connected. A magnetic motor starter is one type of controller.

Current Relay. A relay that functions or actuates at a predetermined value of current. A current relay may be either an overcurrent relay or an undercurrent relay.

CW, CCW. Clockwise (CW) and counterclockwise (CCW) rotation when viewing a motor from the front end, which is opposite the shaft. Often an arrow showing the correct direction of rotation is stamped on the motor housing.

De-energized. The state of a device with no voltage or current applied.

Delta-Connected. Connection of a three-phase system so that the individual phase elements are connected across the pairs of the three-phase power leads (A to B, B to C, or C to A).

Definitions, Abbreviations, and Symbols — Unit 2

Drop-Out. The voltage, current, or power value that causes the release of a relay.

Electromechanical. A device that's comprised of both electrical components and mechanical components. Relays, solenoids, and circuit breakers are examples of electromechanical devices.

Electronic Overload. A device that has built-in circuitry to sense changes in current and temperature.

Elementary Diagram. A diagram in which symbols and a plan of connection are used to illustrate a control circuit in simple form. These diagrams are also called "Line Diagrams" or "Ladder Diagrams."

Energize. To apply electrical power.

Eutectic Alloy (Solder Pot). An alloy that converts from a solid to a liquid state at a specific temperature, and rapidly returns to a solid state upon cooling. This material is used in some types of motor overload elements.

Float Switch. A switch operated by a float that responds to the level of liquid.

Flow Switch. A control switch that detects the movement of fluid or air.

Fuse. An overcurrent protection device containing a calibrated current-carrying member that melts and opens a circuit under specified overcurrent conditions.

Fuse Element. A calibrated current-carrying member that melts when subjected to excessive current. The element is enclosed by the fuse body and may be surrounded by an arc-quenching medium such as silica sand. Fuse elements are sometimes referred to as "links."

General-Purpose Motor. A motor built with standard ratings, with standard performance and mechanical construction, and designed for general use. Its general ratings are listed for continuous use with a temperature rise rating of 40°C.

Author's Comment: A motor with a nameplate temperature rise rating of 40°C means that the motor is designed to operate so it won't heat up more than 40°C above its rated ambient temperature when operated at its rated load and voltage.

Heat Sink. A mass of metal in physical contact with a device, used to dissipate heat.

Horsepower. The measure of the time rate of doing work (working rate). One horsepower equals 33,000 pound-feet of work per minute or 550 pound-feet per second. Assuming 100 percent efficiency, 746 watts of power will produce one horsepower.

Interlock. A device actuated by the operation of some other device with which it's directly associated to govern succeeding operations of the same or allied devices. Interlocks may be electrical or mechanical. When mechanically interlocked, components are usually electrically interlocked as well.

Interlocking. A control circuit function used to prevent one part of a control circuit from energizing, while another part of the control circuit is energized. For example, interlocking can prevent the forward control circuit from being energized while the reverse circuit is energized. Interlocking is frequently done with relays and auxiliary contacts but it can be done mechanically as well.

Inrush Current. During a full-voltage start, the inrush current is the amount of current a motor needs in order to start properly. This is typically 600 percent of the full-load current or motor operating current.

Inverse Time. The relationship between time and current is inverse. In an inverse time circuit breaker, as the amount of current increases, the time for the breaker to trip decreases.

Unit 2 — Definitions, Abbreviations, and Symbols

Jogging (Inching). Quick momentary and repeated closures of a control circuit applied to start a motor from rest for the purpose of accomplishing small movements of the driven machine.

Jumper. A short length of conductor used to connect two points.

Ladder Diagram. A diagram which shows the function of control devices and circuits rather than the actual equipment or location of equipment. Ladder diagrams are also called "Elementary Diagrams" or "Line Diagrams."

Latching Relay. A relay that can be mechanically or magnetically latched in a given position by one element and released by the operation of either the original or a second element. Loss of operating power won't release a latching relay; operation of the unlatch function is required.

Limit Switch. A switch operated by some part or motion of a power-driven machine, equipment, or other mechanical movement to change the state of the associated electrical circuit.

Limit Switch, Rotating Cam. A rotating cam limit switch is a rotating shaft with adjustable cams used to activate contacts. It can have several sets of contacts. It's typically used with equipment that has a repetitive cycle of operation, such as machine presses.

Line Diagram. A diagram in which symbols and a plan of connection are used to illustrate a control circuit in simple form. A line diagram shows the function of control devices and circuits rather than the actual equipment or location of equipment. Line diagrams are also called "Elementary Diagrams" or "Ladder Diagrams."

Load Center. An enclosure that houses several circuit breakers for the purpose of power distribution. See the definition of "Panelboard."

Locked-Rotor Current. Current carried by the line conductors during motor starting, or with the rotor locked or stationary, and with rated voltage (and rated frequency in the case of alternating-current motors) applied to the motor.

Lockout. A mechanically operated device installed to prevent the operation of a control circuit, disconnect switch, or other device that's used to supply voltage to a circuit or circuits.

Low-Voltage Protection. Applies only to magnetic controls with 3-wire control circuits. In the event of a power loss to a motor, the motor won't automatically restart when power is restored. The motor must be restarted manually.

Low-Voltage Release. Applies to magnetic and manual control circuits that automatically restart 2-wire circuits. When power failure disconnects service, the controller automatically restarts the motor when power is restored without any human interruption.

Magnetic Contactor. A contactor operated by a magnetic coil.

Magnetic Starter. A magnetic contactor incorporating an overload relay used to stop a motor if an overload condition occurs. A magnetic motor starter is often the motor controller.

Manual Control. A control operated by mechanical means, almost always by a human operator. Examples of manual controls are toggle switches, safety switches, foot switches, drum controllers, and so forth.

Motor. A device that converts electrical energy to mechanical work.

Motor-Circuit Switch. A switch rated in horsepower that may include overload protection.

Motor Control Center. A combination of motor starters, motor controls, and motor disconnect switches assembled into one enclosure.

Definitions, Abbreviations, and Symbols — Unit 2

Motor Control Circuit. See the definition of "Control Circuit."

NEMA. National Electrical Manufacturers Association.

NEMA Size. Motor controller rating.

Normally Closed (NC) and Normally Open (NO). The position taken by the contacts of a contactor or relay when the operating coil is de-energized. The terms apply only to non-latching types of devices.

> **Author's Comment:** A normally closed (NC) set of contacts is closed when the operating coil is de-energized. A normally open (NO) set of contacts is open when the operating coil is de-energized. In a magnetic motor starter or relay, it's common for an operating coil to have several sets of NC or NO contacts (or a combination of NC and NO contacts) that allow several different control functions to be activated by the energizing of the coil.
>
> Another way to look at it is that "Normal" can be thought of as shelf position. If a device is taken out of the circuit and put on a shelf, then it will be de-energized and in its relaxed state.
>
> Devices such as a toggle (snap) switch or a circuit breaker don't have normally open (NO) or normally closed (NC) contacts. They're simply open or closed (off or on).

Off-Delay. A device that doesn't start its timing function until the power is removed from the timer.

On-Delay. A device that has a preset time period that must pass after the timer has been energized before any action occurs on the timed contacts.

Overcurrent. Any current in excess of the rated current of the equipment or the ampacity of a conductor. Overcurrent may result from an overload, short circuit, or ground fault condition.

Overcurrent Device. A device operated by excessive current that interrupts and maintains the interruption of current flow in the circuit. See the definition of "Overcurrent."

> **Author's Comment:** Overcurrent protection is typically provided by a fuse or circuit breaker. For motor circuits, overcurrent protection is often divided into ground-fault protection and short-circuit protection that's provided by a circuit breaker or fuse(s), and overload protection which is typically accomplished by a separate overload device.

Overload. Operation of equipment in excess of its normal full-load rating, or a conductor in excess of its rated ampacity that, when it persists for a sufficient length of time, will cause damage from overheating. The *NEC* states that a short circuit or ground fault isn't an overload. See the *NEC* definition of "Overload."

> **Author's Comment:** Overload protection is provided for motors in a number of ways. Some common methods include fuses, thermal sensing devices that are an integral part of the motor, an overload relay in the motor starter, or solid-state overloads in conjunction with current sensing devices such as current transformers (CTs). Short-circuit and ground-fault protection for the motor is generally provided by a circuit breaker or fuse in the branch circuit supplying the motor.

Overload Protection (also called "Running Protection"). Overload protection is provided by a device that operates on excessive current, but not necessarily on short circuit, to cause and maintain the interruption of current flow to the governed device.

Overload Relay. A device that provides overload protection for electrical equipment. The overload relay interrupts the power supply to the load when an overload condition develops.

Unit 2 — Definitions, Abbreviations, and Symbols

Overload Relay Heater Coil. The coil used in thermal overload relays that provides heat to melt a eutectic alloy or operate a bi-metal strip.

Overload Relay Reset. A pushbutton used to reset a thermal overload relay after the relay has operated.

Panelboard. A distribution point containing overcurrent protection devices, and designed to be installed in a cabinet.

Parallel Circuit. A circuit with multiple paths for current flow. See the definition of "Series Circuit."

Pick-Up Voltage or Current. The level of voltage or current at which a device or equipment starts to operate.

Pilot Device. A pilot device directs the operation of another device. For example, a float switch is a pilot device that responds to liquid levels. A flow switch is a pilot device that's operated by the movement of a gas or liquid.

Plugging. Braking by reversing the line voltage (dc only) or phase sequence. The motor then develops a retarding force.

Pneumatic. Filled with, or operated by, pressurized gas. Compressed air or other inert gases are used in pneumatic equipment.

Polyphase. More than one phase, usually referring to three-phase. Two-phase equipment was common at one time, but is seldom used anymore.

Pressure Switch. A pilot device operated in response to changes in pressure levels.

Pushbutton. A switch having a manually operated plunger or button used to actuate the switch.

Pushbutton Station. A unit assembly of one or more externally operable pushbutton switches, sometimes including other pilot devices such as indicating lights or selector switches, in an enclosure.

Rating. A designated limit of operating characteristics based on definite conditions. Operating characteristics such as load, voltage, frequency, and horsepower may be included in the rating.

Relay. A device operated by a change in one electrical circuit to control a device in the same circuit or another circuit. Relays are frequently used in control circuits.

Remote Control. Function initiation or change of an electrical device from some remote point or location.

Remote-Control Circuit. Any electrical circuit that controls any other circuit through a relay or equivalent device. For example, a 3-wire circuit to a start-stop station is a remote-control circuit.

Resistor. A device in which the primary purpose is to introduce resistance into an electrical circuit.

Resistor Starter. A starter that includes a resistor connected in series with the primary windings of an induction motor to furnish reduced voltage for starting. It includes the necessary switching mechanism for cutting out the resistor and connecting the motor to the line voltage after starting.

Running Protection. See the definition of "Overload Protection."

Safety Switch. Enclosed, manually operated disconnecting switch rated by horsepower and current that disconnects all ungrounded conductors.

Schematic. A general term for a diagram. There are several types of diagrams used for motor controls and any of them can be referred to as a schematic. See the definitions of "Elementary Diagram," "Ladder Diagram," and "Line Diagram" as well as "Connection Diagram" or "Wiring Diagram."

Definitions, Abbreviations, and Symbols — Unit 2

Selector Switch. A manually operated switch that uses a rotating motion for actuating a device. It can be used to switch control wiring to allow different functions in one or more control circuits. Example: in one position of a selector switch, control devices are used to stop and start a motor, in another position of the selector switch, the same start device will activate a jogging function.

Separate Control Circuit. A motor control circuit that receives its power from a separate source such as a panelboard. This type of control circuit is considered a Class 1 circuit and must follow the requirements of Article 725, Part II of the *NEC*. See "Common Control Circuit."

> **Author's Comment:** A motor control circuit that receives its power by tapping the branch circuit that supplies the motor is called a "common control circuit" and the requirements of Article 430, Part VI of the *NEC* apply.

Sequence of Operation. A written detailed description of the order in which electrical devices and other parts of the equipment should operate.

Series Circuit. A circuit in which all the components or contact symbols are connected end-to-end (as in a continuous loop), providing only one path for current flow. See "Parallel Circuit."

Short-Circuit and Ground-Fault Protection. The fuse or circuit breaker protecting the branch circuit to the motor generally provides short-circuit and ground-fault protection for the motor and branch circuit.

> **Author's Comment:** Because motors have high-inrush starting currents, the size of fuses and circuit breakers are set high enough to avoid nuisance tripping. Motor overloads, which have a slower trip capacity, are generally provided as an integral part of the motor or added to the motor starter as part of the control circuit. They provide protection at a much lower current level but with a greater time delay to allow the motor to start.

Solenoid. An electromagnet that has an electric coil, is approximately cylindrical in form, and has an armature (plunger) whose reciprocating motion is along the axis of the coil.

Solid-State Relay. A switching device that has no contacts, and switches entirely by electronic means.

Solid-State Timer. A timer whose time delay is provided by a solid state electronic device enclosed within the timing device.

Speed Switch. A speed switch is a pilot device used for detecting speed or the direction of rotation of a motor or driven machinery.

Starter. A device that connects line voltage to a motor through a set or sets of contacts.

Symbol. A generally accepted sign, mark, or drawing that represents an electrical device or component. Legends are sometimes provided that explain the symbols.

Temperature Controller. A control device responsive to temperature changes.

Terminal. A point at which an electrical component is connected to another electrical component. A terminal is also a fitting attached to a conductor or device for convenience in making electrical connections.

Three-Phase. Three individual sources of alternating currents or voltages, 120 degrees out-of-phase with each other, and sometimes referred to as polyphase.

Time Delay. A time-interval function purposely introduced into a circuit.

Time-Delay Fuse. A fuse that will carry an overcurrent of a specified magnitude for a specified time without opening. Current/time requirements are defined in the ANSI/UL 248 *Standard for Fuses*.

Unit 2 — Definitions, Abbreviations, and Symbols

Timer. A device that provides adjustable time periods to perform a function. An Off-Delay Timer controls output following an intentional time delay after the input is de-energized. An On-Delay Timer controls output following an intentional time delay after the input is energized.

Torque. In a motor, torque is the twisting or turning force caused by attracting or opposing magnetic fields that produces rotor rotation.

Transformer. A device used to change ac voltage from one voltage level to another. A transformer can either step-down (decrease) voltage or step-up (increase) voltage.

Transformer, Control Circuit. A transformer used to supply reduced voltage to a control circuit.

Troubleshoot. To locate and eliminate the source of abnormal operation.

Undervoltage Protection. A device that operates on the reduction or loss of voltage, interrupting power to the main circuit.

Voltage Relay. A relay that functions at a predetermined value of voltage. A voltage relay can be either an overvoltage or undervoltage relay.

Wiring Diagram. See the definition of "Connection Diagram."

2.2 Common Abbreviations Used for Electrical Terms and Devices

There's no set standard for abbreviations, but these terms are widely accepted. Variations of the following are usually similar in use and should be fairly obvious. Examples are: TDR for "Time-delay relay," THERM for "thermostat," and so on.

1-Ph	Single-phase
3-Ph	Three-phase
A	Amperes
ac	Alternating current
A/C	Air-conditioning
ALM	Alarm
AM	Ammeter
AWG	American Wire Gage
CAP	Capacitor
CNC	Computer numeric controls
CB	Circuit breaker
CEMF	Counter electromotive force
CKT	Circuit
CONT	Control
CR	Control relay
CRM	Control relay master
CT	Current transformer
D	Down
dc	Direct current
DE	Dual element
DISC	Disconnect switch
DP	Double-pole
DPDT	Double-pole, double-throw
DPST	Double-pole, single-throw
DS	Drum switch
DT	Double-throw
EMF	Electromotive force
F, FWD	Forward
FLC	Full-load current
FLS	Flow switch
FREQ	Frequency
FS	Float switch
FTS	Foot switch
FU	Fuse
FVR	Full voltage reversing
FWE	Furnished with equipment
GEN	Generator
G, GND	Ground
HOA	Hand-off automatic
hp	Horsepower
IC	Integrated circuit
INTLK	Interlock
JB	Junction box
LCD	Liquid crystal display
LED	Light emitting diode
LS	Limit switch
LT	Lamp (Light)

Definitions, Abbreviations, and Symbols — Unit 2

M	Main Line or Motor
MCC	Motor control center
MTR	Motor
MN	Manual
NEC	*National Electrical Code*
NEG	Negative
NEMA	National Electrical Manufacturers Association
N, NEUT	Neutral
NC	Normally closed
NCHO	Normally closed, held open
NCTC	Normally closed, timed closing
NCTO	Normally closed, timed opening
NO	Normally open
NOHC	Normally open, held closed
NOTC	Normally open, timed closing
NOTO	Normally open, timed opening
OL	Overload
OT	One time (nontime)
PB	Pushbutton
PH	Phase
PL	Pilot light (Indicator light)
PLC	Programmable logic controller
PLS	Plugging switch
POS	Positive
PRI	Primary
PS	Pressure switch
R, REV	Reverse
REC	Rectifier
RES	Resistor
RH	Rheostat
S	Slow, or switch
SW	Switch
SEC	Secondary
SV	Solenoid valve
1-Ph	Single-phase
SEC	Secondary
SOL	Solenoid
SP	Single-pole
SPDT	Single-pole, double-throw
SPST	Single-pole, single-throw
SS	Selector switch
SSW	Safety switch
T	Transformer
TB	Terminal board
3-Ph	Three-phase
TD	Time delay
THS	Thermostat switch
TR	Time-delay relay
U	Up
UV	Undervoltage
WP	Weatherproof

2.3 Standard Symbols

Symbols are used to represent different devices, conductors, and connections related to motor control circuits. Tables 1A, 1B, and 1C provide examples of some of the symbols commonly found in motor control schematics. Not all of the symbols found in these tables will be used in this textbook. See **Figures 2–1, 2–2, and 2–3**.

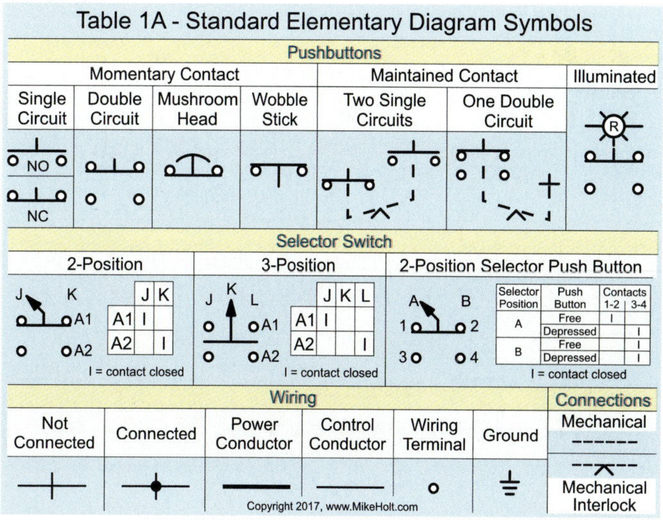

Figure 2–1

Unit 2 — Definitions, Abbreviations, and Symbols

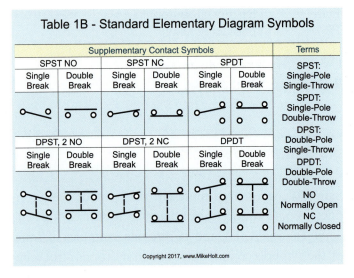

Figure 2–2

Author's Comment: Manufacturers of motor control devices and equipment are an excellent source of information related to symbols and circuits used on motor control schematics. In addition to symbols used on control schematics, manufacturers use additional symbols in their catalogs and other literature to aid in the selection of the type of control devices needed in different applications. Most of this information can be found online. Your electrical supply house is another possible source of information related to the selection and installation of motor control equipment.

Unit 2—Conclusion

This unit explained definitions, abbreviations, and graphic symbols used on motor control diagrams.

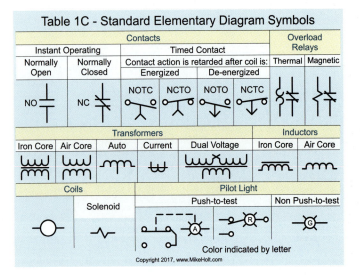

Figure 2–3

Unit 2 Practice Questions

Unit 2—Practice Questions

2.1 Definitions of Control Terminology

1. The circuit conductors between the final overcurrent device and the outlet or equipment is a _____.

    (a) control circuit
    (b) common control circuit
    (c) branch circuit
    (d) parallel circuit

2. An electromechanical device used for repeatedly establishing and interrupting an electric power circuit is a _____.

    (a) contactor
    (b) control
    (c) float switch
    (d) combination starter

3. The circuit of a control apparatus or system that carries the electric signals directing the performance of the controller but doesn't carry the main power current is called a _____.

    (a) control circuit
    (b) service
    (c) feeder
    (d) branch circuit

4. Which of the following item(s) can be considered a manual control switch?

    (a) A toggle switch.
    (b) A safety switch.
    (c) A drum switch.
    (d) all of these

5. A device operated by a change in one electrical circuit to control a device in the same circuit or another circuit is a _____.

    (a) pressure switch
    (b) relay
    (c) resistor
    (d) transformer

6. A manually operated switch that uses a rotating motion for actuating a device is called a _____.

    (a) speed switch
    (b) pressure switch
    (c) safety switch
    (d) selector switch

7. A circuit in which all the components or contact symbols are connected end-to-end (as in a continuous loop), providing only one path for current flow is called a _____.

    (a) separate control circuit
    (b) series circuit
    (c) short circuit
    (d) remote-control circuit

Unit 2 | Practice Questions

8. The point at which an electrical component is connected to another electrical component is called _____.

   (a) an end point
   (b) a terminal
   (c) the clamping point
   (d) the torque setting

9. A device used to supply reduced voltage to a control circuit is called a _____.

   (a) motor control switch
   (b) relay
   (c) limit switch
   (d) control circuit transformer

2.2 Common Abbreviations Used for Electrical Terms and Devices

10. A common abbreviation for a safety switch is _____.

    (a) SS
    (b) SSW
    (c) SAS
    (d) SSP

UNIT 3

Common Control Equipment, Devices, and Symbols

Unit 3—Introduction

This unit covers various types of relays and switches used for motor control applications. It explains each type of control device, summarizes its operation, and shows the symbol(s) used to represent it on motor control diagrams.

3.1 Auxiliary Contacts

Auxiliary contacts are used in addition to, and electrically isolated from, the main power contacts but function in unison with the main power contacts, Figure 3–1. The typical auxiliary contact device shown in Figure 3–1A has one set of normally open (NO) contacts (points 2 and 3), and one set of normally closed (NC) contacts (points 4 and 5).

Auxiliary contacts are frequently used in motor starters. When the coil is energized and the main power contacts are closed, the auxiliary contacts are activated. A normally open (NO) set of contacts will close, and a set of normally closed (NC) contacts will open. When the coil de-energizes and the main power contacts open, the auxiliary contacts will return to their normal open or normal closed position. Remember that the word "normal," when referring to normally open or normally closed, indicates the at-rest position of the contacts when the relay or starter coil is de-energized. Figure 3–2

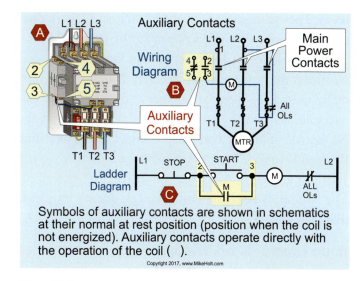

Figure 3–1

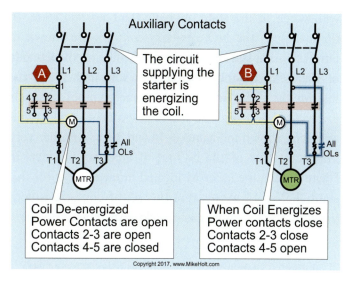

Figure 3–2

Understanding Basic Motor Controls | Mike Holt Enterprises   23

Unit 3 — Common Control Equipment, Devices, and Symbols

An important point to remember when beginning to learn about motor controls is the difference between symbols for auxiliary contacts and symbols for main power contacts. The symbols for both of these are very similar. **Figure 3–1B** shows a common wiring diagram of a magnetic motor starter with both main power and auxiliary sets of contacts. In this example, the main power contacts have no numbers assigned to them. They're in series with the L1, L2, and L3 conductors that supply the main power to the motor (MTR). The normally open (NO) set of auxiliary contacts has terminals marked with the numbers 2 and 3. The normally closed (NC) set of auxiliary contacts has terminals marked with the numbers 4 and 5. Notice that the NC set of auxiliary contacts, 4-5, has a diagonal line through it to indicate the contacts are closed when the starter is at rest, or when the starter coil isn't energized. The NO set of auxiliary contacts, 2-3, doesn't have that diagonal line.

In the **Figure 3–1C** ladder diagram, only the NO set of auxiliary contacts 2-3 is shown. The main power contacts, which aren't shown, will close when the coil is energized, and at the same instant all auxiliary contacts will switch to the state opposite their normal state. In this example, the NO auxiliary contacts are shown in parallel with a start pushbutton. The line on the left side of the contact symbol connects to terminal 2, and the line on the right side of the contact symbol connects to terminal 3. These are the same points (2 and 3) that are being shown in **Figures 3–1A and 3–1B**. Another very important part of the NO set of auxiliary contacts in **Figure 3–1C** is the letter M located immediately over this symbol. The M means that this set of contacts is activated by coil M (shown as a circle with an M inside it).

Author's Comment: A set of normally open (NO) contacts is sometimes called "Form A" contacts. A set of normally closed (NC) contacts is sometimes called "Form B" contacts. Sometimes Form A or B contacts will be represented by simply an "A" or "B" next to the contacts on a schematic.

It's often possible to add an additional set(s) of auxiliary contacts to the magnetic motor starter for additional control, indicating, or monitoring features.

3.2 Relays

Relays are similar in nature to magnetic contactors. A relay is basically a switch that uses a coil to operate one or more sets of contacts, **Figure 3–3**. The main difference is that relays aren't designed to carry the high-current loads that most commercial and industrial contactors and motor starters use.

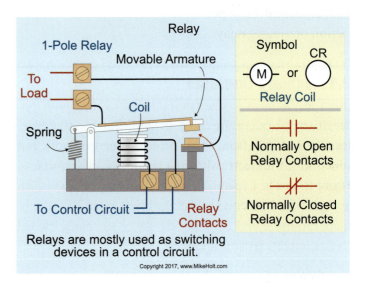

Figure 3–3

Relays come in many different configurations and ratings and are used for many different functions in control and signaling circuits. There are magnetic relays as well as electronic relays. Relays are typically rated 15A or less, but there are some that are rated 20A and 30A. For motor control applications, the relay coil voltages are typically rated between 24V and 600V.

Common Control Equipment, Devices, and Symbols — Unit 3

When the relay coil energizes, it opens or closes electrical contacts, and when the coil de-energizes, the electrical contacts return to their normal positions.

Relays are often used to add more sets of electrical contacts to a control circuit to obtain more switching functions. For example, a set of auxiliary contacts for a motor starter can be used to energize a control relay with multiple sets of electrical contacts. Control relays are also used for sequencing operations, such as master controls for interlocking parts of equipment, as control circuits when it is desirable to electrically isolate control circuits, and for many other functions. Control relays are used in low-voltage wiring for turning on lights and other equipment. Relays can also have timed functions such as time-delay open and time-delay close. See the section on timing relays later in this unit.

In control wiring diagrams, a control relay symbol looks like a coil symbol with a CR (control relay) designation, **Figure 3–4**. The contacts that operate with the control relay are also marked CR. When more than one control relay is used, a number designator is usually added with the electrical contacts marked the same. For example, control relay 2 is CR2 and any contacts that operate with that coil are marked CR2 as well.

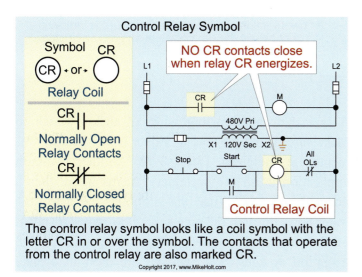

Figure 3–4

Author's Comment: Remember that the control relay coil and the contacts are one device. The ladder diagram in **Figure 3–4** is showing the electrical function rather than the physical device.

Solid-State Relay (SSR). A solid-state relay is an electronic switch, which unlike an electromechanical relay, contains no moving parts. It's sealed against dirt and moisture, and is resistant to shock and vibration. The interior construction of the relay depends on whether it's being used on ac circuits, dc circuits, or a combination of both.

3.3 Drum Switch

A drum switch has a handle which is manually rotated either left or right to change the contacts within the switch. It can be used to make-and-break numerous connections, which allow functions like motor starting, stopping, reversing, and braking to all be done with one device. A drum switch can also be used with magnetic starters and other control equipment.

The number of contacts can vary and some drum switches can have an additional set of contacts added to them. The drum switch in **Figure 3–5A** is being used to reverse a three-phase motor. **Figure 3–5B** is a connection diagram showing where the line and motor leads connect. **Figure 3–5C** is a table showing the internal connections of the drum switch in each of the three different positions.

Author's Comment: Drum switches don't provide motor overload (OL) protection.

Unit 3 | Common Control Equipment, Devices, and Symbols

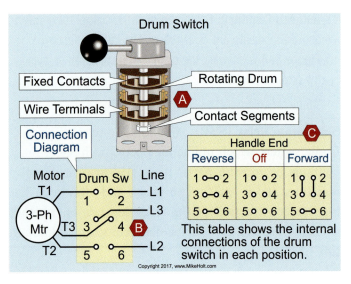

Figure 3–5

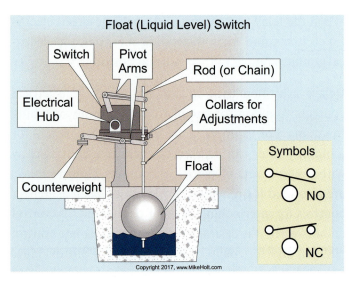

Figure 3–6

3.4 Float Switch

A float switch, also called a "liquid level switch," is generally used to start and stop a pump motor in order to control the level of water or other liquid. Common applications are to automatically fill a tank with liquid, or to control a sump pump, which automatically empties a tank or an area such as a basement of water or other liquid.

The float switch may be mounted on the pump itself or permanently wall- or floor-mounted depending on the application. The float is mounted to either a rod or chain with a counterweight. The rising and falling of the float moves a pivot arm, which is connected to the electrical contacts that open or close the control circuit. **Figure 3–6**

3.5 Flow Switch

A flow switch is operated by the flow of air or liquid. A paddle is used to activate one or more sets of contacts. Flow switches are typically installed in or on air ducts or pipes. **Figure 3–7A**

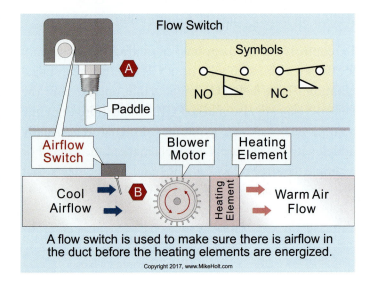

Figure 3–7

A typical installation might use an airflow switch to make sure there's air flow in a duct before heating elements are energized, **Figure 3–7B**. Another common application is on fire sprinkler systems where there's normally no flow. When the sprinklers are activated, water flows through the pipe and a flow switch installed on that pipe is used to activate a fire alarm signal. On irrigation systems, flow switches are used to protect pumps from pumping dry by turning them off if water flow isn't sensed inside the pipes.

26 | Mike Holt Enterprises | *Understanding Basic Motor Controls*

Common Control Equipment, Devices, and Symbols — Unit 3

3.6 Limit Switch—Mechanical

Machinery can be operated automatically using a variety of timers, sensors, controllers, or actuators. For example, limit switches are used in process automation to sense many mechanical situations that are then used to control the motor's function. There are several types and styles of limit switches. There are various types of actuating methods, and different applications, but the basic operation for all limit switches is the same.

Common applications for limit switches include limiting travel (movement), automatic forward and reverse, starting and stopping magnetic starters, counting moving objects, emergency stop, and initiating alarms.

Limit switches operate to open or close electrical contacts when an actuating lever (arm) is operated by an external force, **Figure 3–8A**. The symbols for the electrical contacts in limit switches are a little different in appearance than the contacts in other common devices.

There are two types of normally open contacts, **Figure 3–8B**. The first is a set of regular NO contacts, which function much the same as any other common control device. The second are normally open, held closed (NOHC) contacts that are a set of NO contacts that close when machinery or equipment moves the actuator. The contacts are "held closed" until the actuator is released, then they return to their normally open position.

There are also two types of normally closed contacts. Regular NC contacts, and normally closed, held open (NCHO) contacts, **Figure 3–8C**. The NCHO symbol represents a set of NC contacts that open when machinery or equipment moves the actuator. The contacts are "held open" until the actuator is released, then they return to their normally closed position.

Author's Comment: The operation of the NOHC and NCHO contacts can be difficult to remember. A tip on recognizing NO or NOHC is that the horizontal line of the contact arm for both types is under the right terminal. For NC or NCHO contacts, the horizontal line of the symbol is over the right terminal. **Figures 3–8B and 3–8C**

There are many combinations of contact arrangements, but a standard limit switch usually comes with one set of NO contacts and one set of NC contacts. This type of double-circuit limit switch offers a variety of different connection options. **Figure 3–9A** shows a double-circuit limit switch with the operating lever in the normal position. The NC contacts are closed and the NO contacts are open. **Figure 3–9B** shows that when the operating lever is activated, the NC contacts open and the NO contacts close.

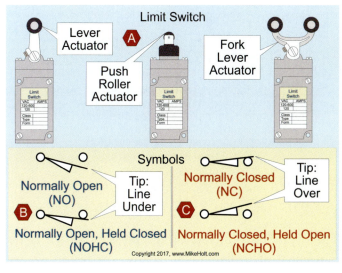

Figure 3–8

Unit 3 | Common Control Equipment, Devices, and Symbols

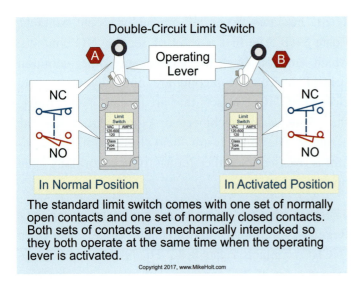

Figure 3–9

3.7 Limit Switch—Proximity

Proximity limit switches (proximity sensor) have no mechanical arms or levers and are able to detect the presence of nearby objects without any physical contact. Proximity switches use methods such as magnetic fields, or capacitive or inductive reactance to sense when objects come close, and then open or close electrical contacts based on the proximity of the objects. A capacitive proximity switch might be suitable for nonmetallic or plastic objects. An inductive proximity switch is used with metal objects.

3.8 Limit Switch—Optical

An optical limit switch is a combination of a sending and receiving unit. It can also consist of a combination sending/receiving unit and a reflector. It works on the principle of an LED that sends short bursts of light to either the receiving unit or the light is reflected back to the sending/receiving unit. Interruption of the light beam activates the control functions. This type of limit switch is sometimes used when detection of very small objects is required.

3.9 Pressure Switch

Pressure switches are used to monitor the pressure of liquids such as water and oil. Pneumatic pressure switches can monitor gases and vapors, including air. A pressure switch can be used as part of a control circuit to control the pressure of the medium being monitored, or to control some other part of a process.

Common applications include air compressors, well pumps and water systems with motor-driven pumps, hydraulic systems, and pressurized lubricating systems. The type of pressure switch selected for an application depends on a number of variables such as the amount of pressure involved and the nature of the liquid or vapor. **Figure 3–10**

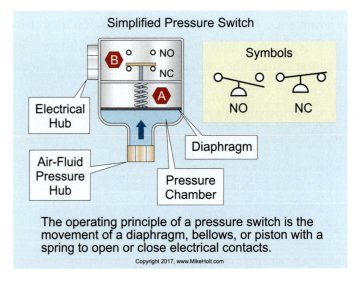

Figure 3–10

The operating principle of the pressure switch is the movement of a diaphragm, bellows, or piston against a spring, **Figure 3–10A**. The setting of the spring determines at what pressure the electrical contacts change state. Many pressure switches have adjustable low and high values that can be set for different applications.

Common Control Equipment, Devices, and Symbols — Unit 3

Pressure switches usually come with a NO set of contacts and a NC set of contacts. These contacts can be either SPST or DPDT. **Figure 3–10B**

A vacuum switch is another type of pressure switch and works on the same principle as other pressure-type switches. However, instead of a pressure chamber, there's a vacuum chamber. The movement of the diaphragm against a spring closes or opens the NO or NC electrical contacts. The symbol used in electrical diagrams is the same. **Figure 3–11**

A NC PB remains closed at all times except when it's being pushed.

Many switching devices will have a symbol printed on them to indicate if a set of contacts is NO or NC. These symbols are shown in the pictorial view of **Figures 3–12 and 3–13** on the side of each switch, between the connection terminals. Another method is the use of clear plastic construction to expose working contacts that allows the installer to see if the contacts are NO or NC.

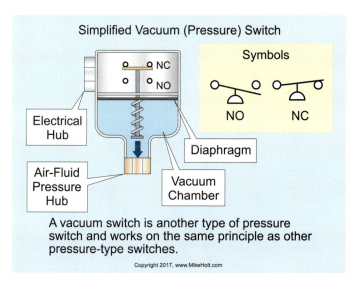

Figure 3–11

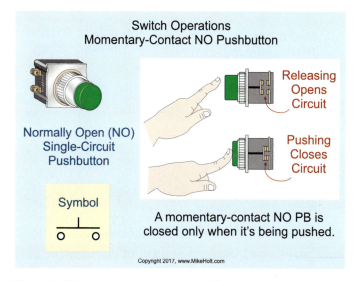

Figure 3–12

3.10 Pushbutton Switch

Pushbuttons (PB) are switches that are pushed to make-or-break contacts rather than moving a handle. Most pushbuttons are the momentary-contact spring-loaded type. This means that the normal position is when the pushbutton is at rest. **Figure 3–12** illustrates a normally open (NO) single-circuit, momentary-contact pushbutton. A NO PB remains open at all times except when it's being pushed. **Figure 3–13** shows a normally closed (NC) single-circuit, momentary-contact pushbutton.

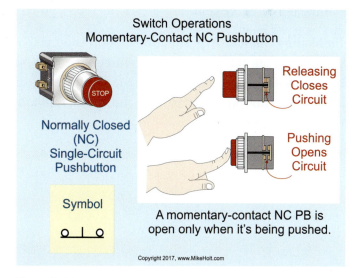

Figure 3–13

Understanding Basic Motor Controls | Mike Holt Enterprises

Unit 3 | Common Control Equipment, Devices, and Symbols

A single pushbutton switch can have additional sets of momentary contacts. The double-circuit pushbutton shown in **Figure 3–14** has one set of NC contacts and one set of NO contacts.

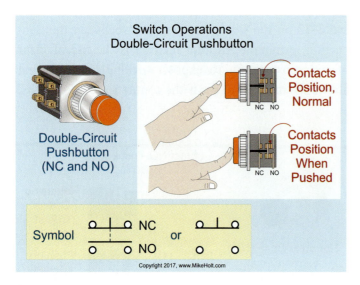

Figure 3–14

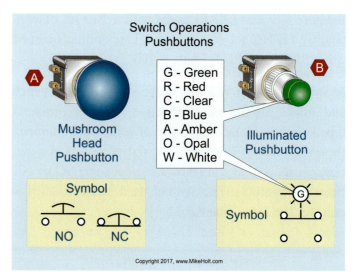

Figure 3–15

There are many other pushbutton configurations. Some have maintained contacts instead of momentary contacts. Some have large mushroom head buttons that are easier to push, **Figure 3–15A**. Pushbuttons can have illuminated buttons, **Figure 3–15B**. The letter in the light symbol indicates the color.

Pushbutton Station. A pushbutton station is an enclosure containing two or more pushbuttons. They can be ordered with legend plates to indicate the function of each pushbutton such as start, stop, up, down, forward, or reverse. **Figure 3–16**

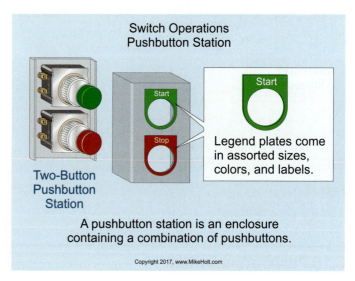

Figure 3–16

Common Control Equipment, Devices, and Symbols — Unit 3

3.11 Solenoid

A solenoid is an electromagnet with a movable plunger, **Figure 3–17**. When the coil is energized, the magnetic field pulls the plunger in. When the coil is de-energized, either a spring or gravity moves the plunger back to its original position. The combination of magnetism and mechanical motion can be made to do useful work and is used extensively in motor control applications. Typical uses for solenoids include remote door locks, doorbell chimes, valves, and electric brakes. Solenoids are also made so the plunger pushes out rather than pulls in, and can be constructed so the plunger is pulled in on one side and pushed out the other side.

Figure 3–18 shows a two-way NC solenoid valve. While the coil is de-energized, a spring holds a disc in the valve seat and there's no flow through the valve, **Figure 3–18A**. When the coil is energized, the plunger is pulled up, which opens the valve, **Figure 3–18B**. Solenoid valves can be used with gases or liquids.

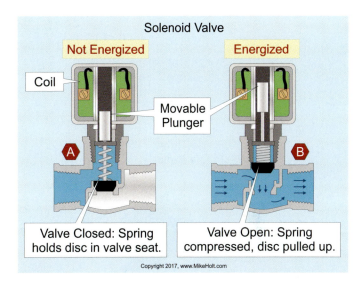

Figure 3–18

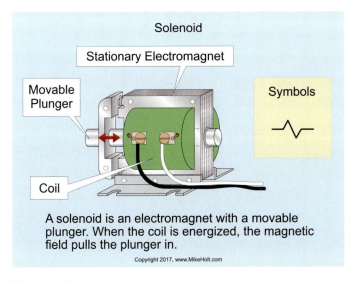

Figure 3–17

Solenoid Valve. In a solenoid valve, the solenoid plunger is connected to a disc or plug-in valve. The movement of the plunger when the coil is energized can be used to either open or close the valve. There are many different types and applications, but the basic operation is the same.

3.12 Switch Operations

Many motor control functions can be related to some form of switch or switching action. Common switch operations used in control circuits are explained below:

Toggle Switch. Toggle switches are manually operated devices. They come in several combinations of switching functions. A standard on-off wall-mounted snap switch used for most lighting outlets is an example of a toggle switch.

Unit 3   Common Control Equipment, Devices, and Symbols

SPST. Single-Pole, Single-Throw. The SP (single-pole) indicates the number of conductors providing power to the switch (such as L1). SP is sometimes referred to as a 1P (one-pole) switch. The ST (single-throw) indicates the number of possible positions for the switch other than Off. Examples of SPST devices are 120V ac snap switches, 120V manual motor switches, or single-pole circuit breakers. **Figure 3–19**

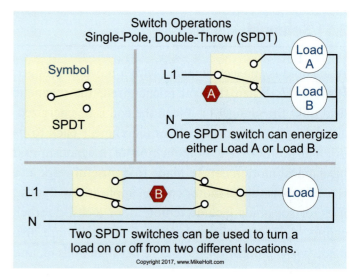

Figure 3–20

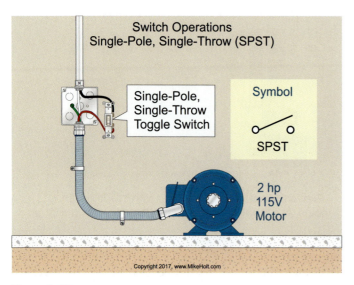

Figure 3–19

SPDT. Single-Pole, Double-Throw. The SP (single-pole) indicates the number of conductors providing power to the switch (such as L1). The DT (double-throw) indicates the number of positions for the switch other than off. **Figure 3–20**

One example of using an SPDT switch is to use one switch to energize one of two different loads, **Figure 3–21**. Another example is using two SPDT switches to turn one load on or off from two different locations, **Figure 3–22**. This is often called a 3-way switch. The "3" refers to the number of conductor terminals in the SPDT switch.

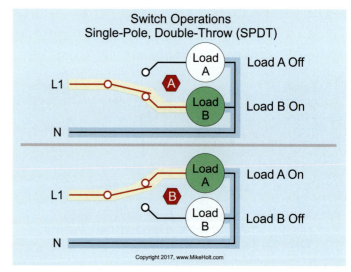

Figure 3–21

DPST. Double-Pole, Single-Throw. The DP (double-pole) indicates the number of conductors the switch will control (such as L1 and L2). The ST indicates the number of possible positions for the switch other than Off. Examples of a DPST device are a 240V toggle switch, which is sometimes referred to as a 2P (2-pole) switch, or a double-pole (2-pole) circuit breaker. **Figure 3–23**

32   Mike Holt Enterprises | *Understanding Basic Motor Controls*

Common Control Equipment, Devices, and Symbols — Unit 3

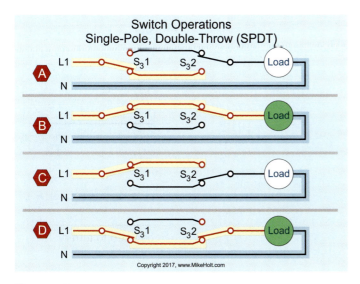

Figure 3–22

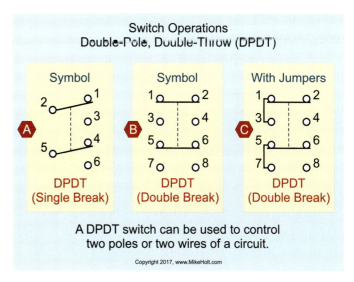

Figure 3–24

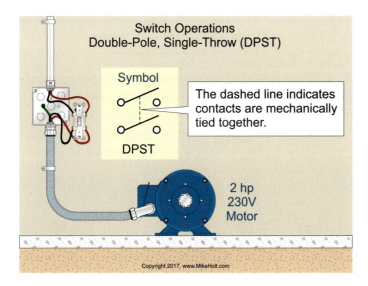

Figure 3–23

DPDT. Double-Pole, Double-Throw. The DPDT single-break switch in **Figure 3–24A** has six terminals while the double-break DPDT switch in **Figure 3–24B** has eight terminals. A DPDT type of switch is sometimes used for a transfer switch.

Another type of DPDT switch is a 4-way switch. It has limited use for motor controls because it comes with limited current ratings. When used with two SPDT (3-way) switches, a DPDT (4-way) switch adds a third location where a load can be turned on and off, **Figure 3–25**. In **Figure 3–25A**, the switch has continuity between terminals 1 and 2, and a second path of continuity from terminals 3 and 4.

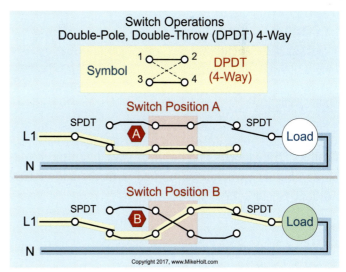

Figure 3–25

Understanding Basic Motor Controls | Mike Holt Enterprises 33

Unit 3 — Common Control Equipment, Devices, and Symbols

In **Figure 3–25B**, the continuity follows the dashed lines so that terminal 1 connects to terminal 4, and terminal 3 connects to terminal 2. This arrangement is rare for motor controls but it does show the DPDT function. A 4-way type DPDT switch can also be used to reverse a single-phase or three-phase motor.

Nonfusible Disconnect (Safety Switch). This type of switch can be used as a manual on-off disconnect for a motor. It's often used with magnetic motor starters. Nonfusible disconnect switches incorporate the use of pivoting knife-blade type contact points that operate from a handle. Nonfusible disconnect switches are typically configured as DPST or 3PST (3-pole, single-throw). **Figure 3–26**

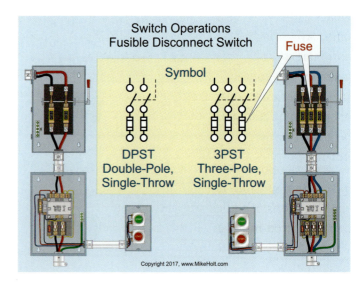

Figure 3–27

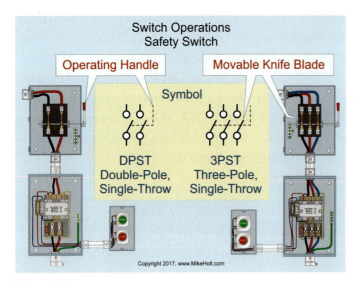

Figure 3–26

Fusible Disconnect. This utilizes the pivoting knife-blade contact principle combined with the use of fuse holders. **Figure 3–27**

3.13 Temperature Switch

A capillary-tube type temperature switch is very similar to a pressure switch. This type of temperature switch has a sensing bulb with a capillary (very small) tube connecting it to a chemically filled bellows. **Figure 3–28**

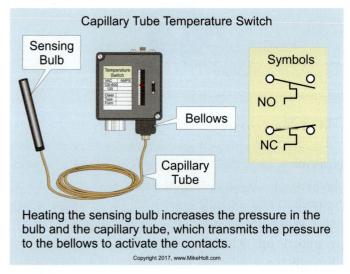

Figure 3–28

Heating the sensing bulb increases the pressure in the bulb, which is transmitted through the capillary tube and increases the pressure in the bellows, which in turn activates the contacts inside the switch housing. When the temperature drops, the pressure decreases. The change in pressure is transmitted through the capillary tube, which allows the contacts to return to their normal position.

When the sensing bulb is used in higher temperature locations, it's filled with liquid. When this type of switch is used in lower temperatures, such as refrigeration equipment or freezers, it's filled with a gas or vapor instead of liquid.

Another type of temperature control is a thermocouple, which uses a temperature sensitive bi-metal strip and usually has a faster response time than capillary-tube types of temperature switches.

> **Author's Comment:** A thermocouple isn't actually a switch. A thermocouple consists of a junction of dissimilar metals that produces a small voltage when heated. That voltage can be used to activate other control devices.

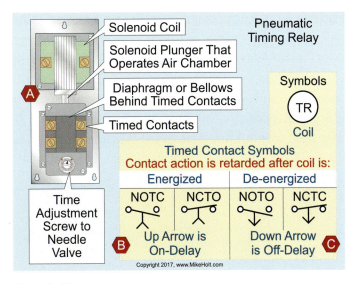

Figure 3–29

3.14 Timing Relay—Pneumatic

The pneumatic timer is a very common type of timing relay, especially for off-delay purposes. It works on the principle of energizing a solenoid (coil with a plunger) over a diaphragm or bellows (air chamber) that includes a needle valve that restricts the air in and out of the bellows. When the relay is energized, the solenoid plunger is pulled up, which opens the bellows. Air enters through the needle valve and slowly fills the bellows. When the bellows or air chamber is filled, one or more sets of contacts are activated. The time it takes for the bellows to fill is adjusted by slightly opening or closing the needle valve. **Figure 3–29**

The contacts that are activated when the solenoid energizes are on-delay and the contact symbol has an up arrow in it, **Figure 3–29B**. When the solenoid coil is energized, the time delay begins for the on-delay contacts. The contacts that are activated when the solenoid coil de-energizes are off-delay and the contact symbol has a down arrow in it, **Figure 3–29C**. When the coil is de-energized, the time delay begins for the off-delay contacts.

A pneumatic timer can be a control device by itself, or it can be an actuating device for a regular control relay.

3.15 Timing Relay with Instantaneous Contacts

Some time-delay relays have a set of instantaneous contacts, or the ability to add a set of instantaneous contacts. These instantaneous contacts operate without any time delay, just like control relay contacts or like an auxiliary set of contacts will operate for a motor starter coil. The standard symbol for a set of NO or NC contacts is used but it's identified by having the same letter designation as the timing relay coil.

Figure 3–30 is a line diagram including a timing relay (TR) controlled by motor starter coil M2. TR has one set of time-delay contacts used to provide a delay in energizing the motor starter 3 (M3) coil. The instantaneous contacts in the same timing relay are used to energize a pilot (indicator) light when the TR coil is energized without any time delay. When the TR coil is de-energized, the pilot (indicator) light goes out with no time delay.

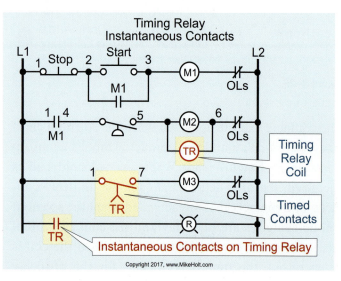

Figure 3–30

3.16 Timing Relay—Solid-State

Perhaps the most common timers used today are solid-state (electronic) timers, as well as timers incorporated into solid-state control equipment and PLCs. The symbols used for solid-state on-delay and off-delay timers are basically the same as those used in mechanical timers, but some manufacturers and textbooks include a diamond shaped outline around the symbol to distinguish it as a solid-state symbol.

3.17 Timing Relay Terminology

Some common contact terminology used with time-delay relays includes:

NOTC. Normally open, timed closing contacts. These are controlled by an on-delay timer and are NO contacts that close at a definite time after the timer control circuit has been energized.

NCTO. Normally closed, timed opening contacts. These are controlled by an on-delay timer and are NC contacts that open at a definite time after the timer control circuit has been energized.

NOTO. Normally open, timed opening contacts. These are controlled by an off-delay timer and are NO contacts that close immediately when the timer control circuit is energized and stay closed until a definite time after the timer control circuit has been de-energized.

NCTC. Normally closed, timed closing contacts. These are controlled by an off-delay timer and are NC contacts that open immediately when the timer control circuit is energized and stay open until a definite time after the timer control circuit has been de-energized.

Many other timing devices are also used in motor controls. Pneumatic timers are widely used in automatic controls, as well as dashpot timers (solenoid operated pistons in cylinders of oil) and motor-driven timers. Many of the operating principles are the same as, or similar to, timing relays.

Common Control Equipment, Devices, and Symbols — Unit 3

3.18 Reading a Motor Control Schematic

Figure 3–31 contains some of the devices and associated symbols covered in this unit used in a ladder diagram of a control circuit. These symbols can also be found in the Tables in Unit 2. Use the symbols legend in the bottom part of this figure to see how symbols are combined to create a schematic. To read schematics, it's important to remember that diagrams are shown in the "at rest" or "shelf" position.

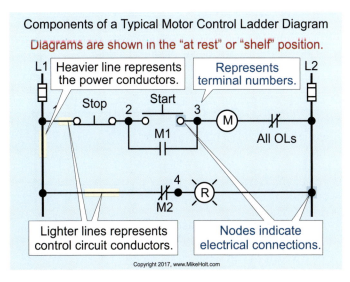

Figure 3–32

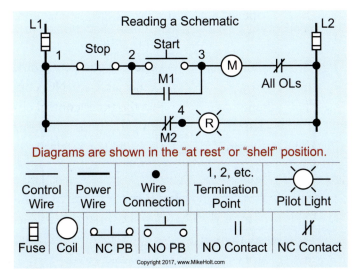

Figure 3–31

Figure 3–32 shows some of the components related to power and control conductors and terminals. The numbers 1, 2, 3, and 4 are showing points where conductors will need to be terminated. Remember that these terminal numbers aren't found on the devices you'll be connecting in the field. They're just used on schematics as reference points.

CAUTION: *The terminal numbers found on a schematic rarely match the terminal numbers found on some wiring devices. Different manufacturers will use different numbering systems. Wiring must always be based on function, not on terminal numbers. We're matching many terminal numbers in this textbook only for the purpose of making it easier for students to learn.*

In Figure 3–33, don't confuse the circle with the M in it with the motor. Since this is a ladder diagram, the actual motor isn't shown. Coil M is the device that closes the power contacts (which aren't shown in a ladder diagram either) of the motor starter. It's assumed that when the coil is energized, the power contacts are closed. You must know that the auxiliary contacts operate when coil M energizes and de-energizes. Auxiliary contacts are typically marked with the same letter as the coil with which they operate.

Understanding Basic Motor Controls | Mike Holt Enterprises   37

Unit 3 — Common Control Equipment, Devices, and Symbols

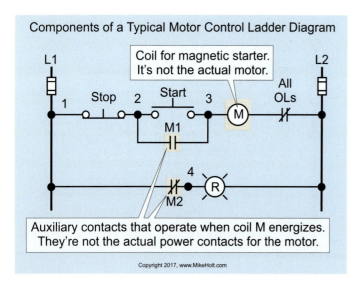

Figure 3–33

Author's Comment: Parent, Child, and Sibling. Many motor control functions are accomplished with sets of contacts that are activated by a coil, such as those found in magnetic motor starters or relays. These devices can have several sets of contacts operated from a single coil. The term "Parent Coil" refers to the coil that operates the group of contacts. The sets of contacts that are activated by the parent coil are sometimes called the "Child" or "Sibling" contacts.

Sometimes the contacts that operate from the parent coil are numbered, such as contacts M1 and M2 that operate with coil M. It's common to have just the letter designator without numbers in the diagram. In that case, the contacts are sometimes referred to with their connection points. For example, contacts M1 in **Figure 3–33** can also be called "M contacts 2-3" because these contacts connect to points 2 and 3 in the control circuit. Contacts M2 can also be called "M contacts 1-4" because these contacts connect to points 1 and 4 in the control circuit. Both methods of identifying contacts will be used in this textbook.

Figure 3–34 points out several symbols representing some the components of a motor control schematic. Schematics frequently use short labels to help identify the function of a device in a control circuit. For example, the word "Stop" is used to indicate what the normally closed pushbutton switch is being used for. The phrase "All OLs" is used to indicate that the normally closed contacts symbol represents the overload protection associated with this control circuit. The letter "R" is used with the pilot light to indicate that a red lamp or lens is required.

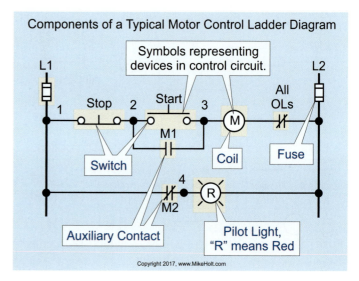

Figure 3–34

Figure 3–35 illustrates one of the learning tools we use in this textbook. The yellow and blue shading aren't found on any control circuits you'll work on in the field. We use this shading to indicate voltage paths to different parts of the control circuit. For example, the yellow shading shows the voltage path between where the control circuit connects to L1 on one side of the start PB, and one side of auxiliary contacts M1 through the stop PB. The blue shading shows the voltage path between where the control circuit connects to L2 on one side of coil M and one side of the pilot light.

Common Control Equipment, Devices, and Symbols — Unit 3

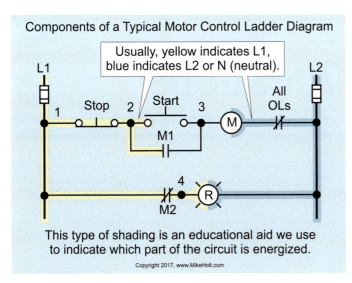

Figure 3–35

Author's Comment: This shading isn't showing the actual voltage through the control circuit. It's just showing the paths required to energize the individual components.

Unit 3—Conclusion

This unit explained various types of common motor control devices including auxiliary contacts, control relays, pushbutton stations, solenoids and solenoid valves, flow switches, pressure switches, limit switches, and timing relays.

Unit 3 Practice Questions

Unit 3—Practice Questions

3.1 Auxiliary Contacts

1. In a magnetic motor starter, when the coil is energized, a normally open (NO) set of contacts will close, and a set of normally closed (NC) contacts will open.

   (a) True
   (b) False

2. In **Figure 3–36**, the auxiliary contacts are indicated by the letter _____.

   (a) A
   (b) B
   (c) D
   (d) M

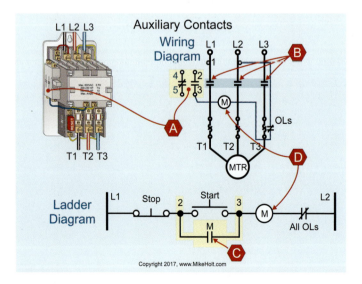

Figure 3–36

3. In **Figure 3–36**, the power contacts in the magnetic starter are indicated by the letter _____.

   (a) A
   (b) B
   (c) C
   (d) D

4. In **Figure 3–36**, the letter D is the _____.

   (a) motor that's energized when the main power contacts close
   (b) overload relay for the contactor
   (c) coil that activates the auxiliary contacts and the main power contacts
   (d) stop-start station

5. In **Figure 3–36**, letter C is indicating a set of auxiliary contacts. Which of the following statement(s) is/are correct.

   (a) This is a set of normally open (NO) contacts.
   (b) The M over the auxiliary contacts indicates that coil M activates the contacts.
   (c) The NO auxiliary contacts have terminal numbers 2 and 3.
   (d) all of these

3.2 Relays

6. For motor control applications, the relay coil voltages are typically rated between _____.

   (a) 0V and 5V
   (b) 24V and 600V
   (c) 277V and 480V
   (d) 600V and 1,000V

Practice Questions — Unit 3

7. In **Figure 3–37**, which of the following statements is correct?

    (a) When the control relay is energized the NC CR contacts open.
    (b) When coil M energizes, the NO CR contacts close.
    (c) When coil M energizes, the NC CR contacts close.
    (d) When the control relay is energized, the NO CR contacts close.

8. In **Figure 3–37**, when the control relay is energized the NO CR contacts close and energize coil M.

    (a) True
    (b) False

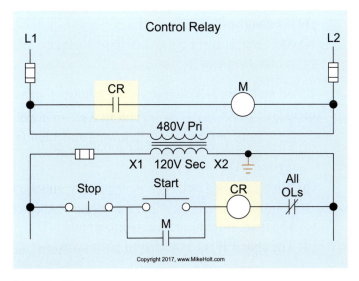

Figure 3–37

3.3 Drum Switch

9. Drum switches provide motor overload (OL) protection.

    (a) True
    (b) False

3.11 Solenoid

10. Solenoid valves can be used with gases or liquids.

    (a) True
    (b) False

3.12 Switch Operations

11. A standard on-off wall-mounted snap switch used for most lighting outlets is an example of a _____.

    (a) temperature switch
    (b) pressure switch
    (c) toggle switch
    (d) transfer switch

3.14 Timing Relay—Pneumatic

12. In **Figure 3–38**, the timing relay controls _____ set(s) of contacts.

    (a) one
    (b) two
    (c) three
    (d) four

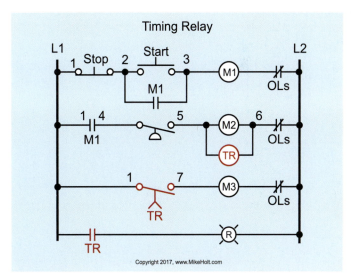

Figure 3–38

Unit 3 Practice Questions

13. In **Figure 3–38**, the timing relay in this ladder diagram has _____

    (a) a set of NOTC contacts
    (b) a set of instantaneous contacts
    (c) a set of NCTC contacts
    (d) a and b

14. In **Figure 3–38**, when the timing relay is energized, a set of normally open, timed closing contacts _____.

    (a) close after a time delay
    (b) open after a time delay
    (c) open instantaneously
    (d) aren't activated by the timing relay

15. In **Figure 3–38**, the timing relay coil is connected to points _____.

    (a) 1-2
    (b) 3-4
    (c) 5-6
    (d) 1-4

16. In **Figure 3–38**, the timing relay contacts with a time delay feature are connected to points _____.

    (a) 1-2
    (b) 3-4
    (c) 5-6
    (d) 1-7

17. In **Figure 3–38**, the device connected to points 4-5 is _____.

    (a) a coil
    (b) a start-stop switch
    (c) an auxiliary contact
    (d) a pressure switch

18. In **Figure 3–38**, the start PB is connected to points _____.

    (a) 1-2
    (b) 2-3
    (c) 3-4
    (d) 4-5

19. In **Figure 3–38**, the device connected to points 1-2 is a(n) _____.

    (a) NC PB
    (b) pressure switch
    (c) coil
    (d) motor overload

20. Based on **Figure 3–38**, which of the following statements is correct?

    (a) There are two sets of NO auxiliary contacts for coil M1.
    (b) There are two sets of NC auxiliary contacts for coil M1.
    (c) The float switch is connected to points 1-7.
    (d) The start PB is connected to points 5-6.

CHAPTER 2: MOTOR CONTROLS AND SCHEMATICS

This chapter covers basic concepts, components, and schematics of motor control circuits. It consists of the following units:

Unit 4—Components of Control Circuit Schematics

Unit 5—Magnetic Control

Unit 6—Magnetic Motor Starters

Unit 7—Basic Control Circuits

Unit 8—Overcurrent Protection for Control Circuits

Unit 9—Indicator (Pilot) Lights and Illuminated Pushbuttons

Unit 10—Selector Switches and Truth Tables

Notes

UNIT 4
Components of Control Circuit Schematics

Unit 4—Introduction

To work on motor controls properly, you must learn to read and understand motor control schematic diagrams. Motor control schematics are different than typical electrical building plans (blueprints). They use different symbols to express different types of information.

Electrical plans typically show the locations of electrical devices and utilization equipment, with the wiring connections between them. But blueprints don't normally show how those components work together; for that, you depend on basic electrical and *NEC* knowledge. By contrast, motor control schematics don't show the physical locations of components, but do illustrate how they actually operate.

4.1 A Simple Control Circuit

Figure 4–1 shows a line-type diagram, **Figure 4–1A**, and a pictorial-type diagram, **Figure 4–1B**, of a single-pole manual motor switch with overload protection feeding a 115V motor. This is a form of manual control. Line 1 (L1) is the ungrounded conductor and N is the neutral conductor.

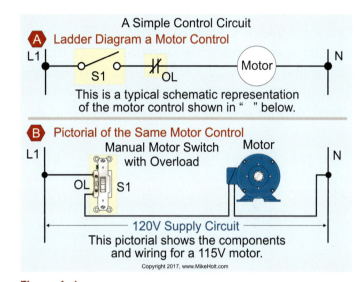

Figure 4–1

Remember that ladder diagrams don't always show the physical location of the motor control devices. In **Figure 4–1A**, notice that switch S1 and the OL on the left side of the motor appear to be two different devices. In this motor control application, the S1 switch provides two different functions for this control circuit. One is the on-off to the motor, and the other is the overload protection for the motor. We know from looking at **Figure 4–1B** that the OL is physically located on the manual motor switch but the **Figure 4–1A** ladder diagram shows the OL and on-off functions separately.

Understanding Basic Motor Controls | Mike Holt Enterprises

Unit 4 | Components of Control Circuit Schematics

Author's Comment: System voltages versus motor rated voltages. The 120V circuit in **Figure 4–1** represents nominal (system) voltage, the 115V represents the voltage rating of the motor. See the introduction of this textbook for other examples of these voltages.

The switch energizes the motor. Either the switch or the OLs located on the switch can de-energize the motor. The toggle switch is a manually operated device, while the OL is an automatically operated device. The OL can be thought of as an automatic switch that operates or opens if the current rises higher than the setting of the OL device. **Figure 4–2**

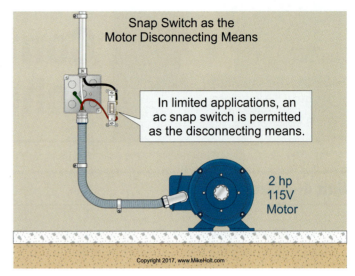

Figure 4–3

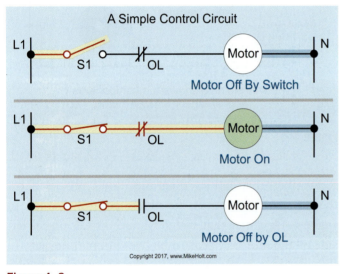

Figure 4–2

Author's Comment: Manual switches are hand-operated mechanical devices. If the switch is closed (motor running) and the power goes out, the motor will stop but the switch will remain in the closed position. When the power comes back on or when the circuit is re-energized, the motor starts again automatically. In some cases, this is a desired function. For example, it may be useful for blower motors, refrigeration equipment, or automatic pumps to restart automatically when power returns, without requiring someone to go back and restart them manually. On the other hand, electrical equipment like lathes, saws, drill presses, and other machinery will pose a danger to persons if they automatically start up after a power failure. Careful consideration must always be given to the selection of devices that start and stop motors and other equipment. This subject will be covered in more detail later in this textbook.

The motor-circuit switch with OL protection shown in **Figures 4–1 and 4–2** is horsepower-rated and normally used with smaller horsepower single-phase motors. In some cases, a regular general-use snap switch (no overload protection in the switch) can be used as a disconnecting means for motors rated 2 hp or less and 300V or less. See 430.83(C) and 430.109(C)(2) of the *NEC*. **Figure 4–3**

Adding an Automatic Control Device

Figure 4–4 shows the same control circuit as **Figure 4–2**, with a float switch added. The manual switch energizes the control circuit and contains the OL protection device. The float switch operates the motor as long as the toggle switch is in the On position and the overload (OL) is closed.

Components of Control Circuit Schematics — Unit 4

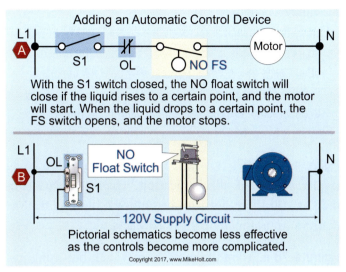

Figure 4–4

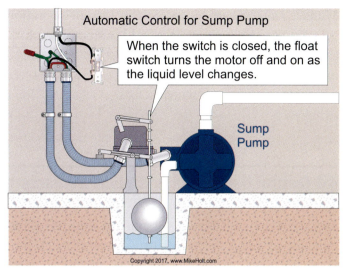

Figure 4–6

Advantages of Ladder Diagrams

Figure 4–4A is the ladder diagram that corresponds to the **Figure 4–4B** pictorial schematic. Although the switch with the OL is physically one device, it's represented as S1 and OL in **Figure 4–4A**. This is very common in motor control circuit diagrams and schematics. **Figure 4–5** shows how the devices in **Figure 4–4** operate. This control arrangement can be used for a sump-pump application. **Figure 4–6**

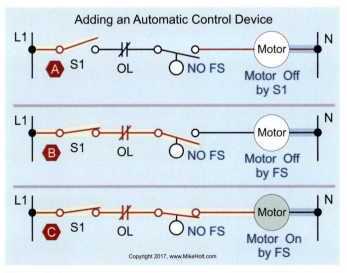

Figure 4–5

Figure 4–5A shows that when S1 is open, nothing will operate. The motor is off even though the OL is closed. The NO FS can't operate the circuit if S1 is open. **Figure 4–5B** shows S1 and the OL closed, and the NO FS contacts open with the pump motor not running. The circuit is considered automatic in this position.

When the liquid rises, the NO FS contacts close, **Figure 4–5C**, and the pump motor runs. When the liquid level drops, the float goes down which opens the FS contacts and the pump motor will stop. If the OL opens for any reason, the circuit will become inoperative and the pump motor will stop.

If the motor is already stopped, the open OL will prevent the pump motor from starting. These functions can't be easily seen when looking at the pictorial diagram shown in **Figure 4–4B**.

As motor control circuits become more complicated, the pictorial type of schematic becomes less effective and is seldom used, while ladder diagrams become more helpful and are used more often.

Unit 4 — Components of Control Circuit Schematics

Manual switching of motors in this type of operation is limited to single-phase, minimal horsepower motors. Some of the other automatic controls that can be used in a simple motor control arrangement include pressure switches, temperature switches, time clocks, and limit switches.

Author's Comment: The float switch's "normal" position is sometimes defined as the state the contacts will be in with no external forces acting on them to actuate the switch. In other cases the "normal" position may be a full tank situation. Be careful to read the manufacturer's notes carefully to understand how this is defined.

4.2 Control Devices with Multiple Contacts

Most switching devices such as float switches, limit switches, or relays come with at least two sets of contacts. This often includes both NO and NC contacts but can be any combination of both. **Figure 4–7** shows how many symbols are simplified and used in a wiring diagram or schematic. Often, only one set of contacts is being used in the motor control circuit so it's very common to adjust the symbol used in the motor control diagram. **Figures 4–7A and 4–7B** show the same control device being used for different applications.

Figure 4–7A shows how just the NC contacts are being used for the tank fill application. The set of NO contacts is still there but isn't being used. It simplifies the diagram to not include those contacts.

Figure 4–7B is using the same float switch, but using just the NO set of contacts for a sump-pump application. Only the set of contacts necessary for the application is shown in the diagram.

Figure 4–8 shows the tank filling application from **Figure 4–7A**. This application can be used with a watering tank for livestock. Now, instead of pumping water out, the same float switch is using the NC contacts to add liquid. As the animals drink the water, the level drops, the NC contacts of the float switch close, the pump motor starts, the water level rises to a certain point, which opens the contacts in the float switch, and turns off the pump.

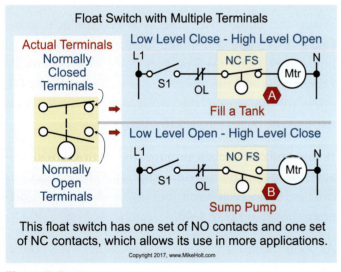

Figure 4–7

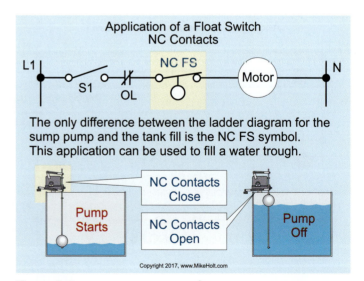

Figure 4–8

Unit 4—Conclusion

This unit introduced the type of motor control schematic called a "ladder diagram" (also called an "elementary diagram" or "line diagram"). It used this type of diagram to illustrate a simple 2-wire control circuit used with small single-phase motors, and a similar circuit with a mechanical automatic control device; in this case, a float switch for controlling a pump.

Unit 4—Practice Questions

4.1 A Simple Control Circuit

1. In some cases, a general-use snap switch can be used as a disconnecting means for a motor rated 2 hp or less.

    (a) True
    (b) False

2. If a toggle switch for a motor is closed and the power goes out, the _____.

    (a) motor will stop when the power comes back on
    (b) motor will start when the power comes back on
    (c) toggle switch will automatically open
    (d) a or c

3. Automatic controls that can be used in a simple motor control arrangement include _____.

    (a) pressure switches
    (b) temperature switches
    (c) time clocks
    (d) all of these

4.2 Control Devices with Multiple Contacts

4. Switching devices such as float switches, limit switches, or relays always come with only one set of contacts.

    (a) True
    (b) False

Practice Questions—General

Note: The following questions can be based on any part of this textbook up through this unit.

5. In **Figure 4–9**, the control circuit is connected to _____.

    (a) L1 and L3
    (b) points 3-4
    (c) L2 and L3
    (d) L1 and L2

6. In **Figure 4–9**, there is(are) _____ momentary-contact pushbutton(s).

    (a) one
    (b) two
    (c) three
    (d) four

7. In **Figure 4–9**, the coil is marked with _____.

    (a) the letter M
    (b) the letter R
    (c) M1
    (d) M2

Practice Questions — Unit 4

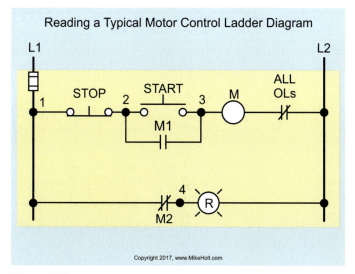

Figure 4–9

8. In **Figure 4–9**, the auxiliary contacts are marked _____.

    (a) M1 and M2
    (b) 3-4
    (c) stop-start
    (d) L1 and L2

9. In **Figure 4–9**, when the start pushbutton is pressed, the _____.

    (a) M coils energize
    (b) NO M1 contacts close
    (c) NC M2 contacts open
    (d) all of these

10. In **Figure 4–9**, which of the following statement(s) is(are) true?

    (a) The heavier lines represent the power wiring (branch circuit).
    (b) The lighter lines represent the control circuit.
    (c) The OLs are connected between the coil and L2.
    (d) all of these

11. In **Figure 4–9**, the letter in the middle of the pilot light symbol represents _____.

    (a) the direction the motor turns
    (b) the color of the pilot light
    (c) which coil activates the pilot light
    (d) the terminal number to which the pilot light is connected

12. In **Figure 4–9**, the normally closed auxiliary contacts M2 are connected to points _____.

    (a) 1-2
    (b) 3-4
    (c) 1-3
    (d) 1-4

13. In **Figure 4–9**, the normally open auxiliary contacts M1 are connected to points _____.

    (a) 1-2
    (b) 2-3
    (c) 1-3
    (d) 1-4

Notes

UNIT 5 — Magnetic Control

Unit 5—Introduction

Unit 4 covered the use of manual devices (snap switches) and simple automatic devices (float switches) to control small single-phase motors using 2-wire control circuits. This unit builds on that knowledge by introducing the concept of magnetic remote-control devices, used with both motors and other types of loads such as lighting. It covers different types of control circuits and different types of magnetic control devices.

5.1 Electromagnetic Control

The principle of electromagnetism is used a great deal in control circuits. Often the load equipment, such as a motor, is in a different location than the controls and operates at a different voltage. Devices using coils that operate at lower voltages are often used to facilitate these remote-control functions. They include contactors, magnetic starters (contactors with overload relays), solenoids, and magnetic relays.

Many of these devices depend on the use of coils (also called solenoid coils). As the name implies, a coil is a coil of wire that produces a magnetic field when electricity passes through it. When installed as a component in a motor starter, the energized coil magnetically pulls in a plunger with movable contacts that make contact with matching contacts from the power-supply circuit coming into the starter. **Figures 5–1 and 5–2**

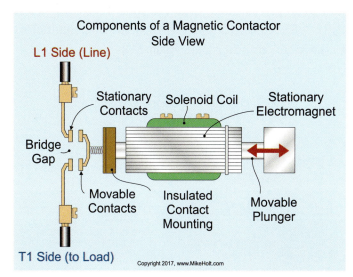

Figure 5–1

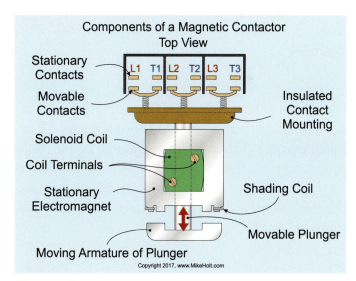

Figure 5–2

Unit 5 Magnetic Control

The plunger is normally equipped with springs that push it out when the coil is de-energized, thereby breaking the gap between the power and the load. Some coils are designed to use an up motion to close contacts, which allows gravity to assist in opening the contacts with a down motion. See **Figure 5–2**.

The terms "L1," "L2," and "L3" represent the line or power-supply (branch circuit) conductors. The terms "T1," "T2," and "T3" refer to the load-side conductors to the motor or other load. **Figure 5–3**

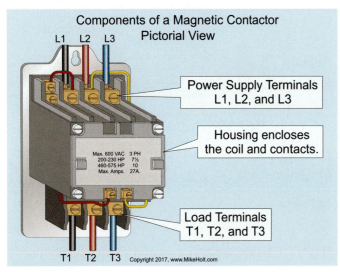

Figure 5–3

Many motors have connection instructions or diagrams marked directly on the motor or within the wiring terminal housing. The leads for connecting power to the motor are often marked T1, T2, and T3. Some motors have leads marked T1 through T9 for different connection configurations. We cover this in greater detail later in this textbook.

5.2 Power Sources for the Coil and Control Circuit

There are three basic ways to provide power to a coil and other parts of a control circuit.

1. Common Control Wiring. The power to the control circuit is taken from L1 and L2 of the contactor (magnetic starter), **Figure 5–4**. This can be done with both single-phase and three-phase contactors. The contactor coil must have the same voltage rating as the contactor, typically 240V. One advantage to the common control wiring method is that it saves cost and enclosure space. However, it shouldn't be used for 480V motor circuits because operating the pilot devices of the control circuit at 480V increases the hazard to equipment operators and maintenance personnel.

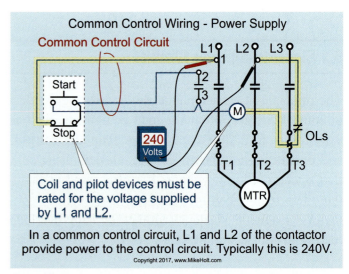

Figure 5–4

Author's Comment: There are some limited cases where 480V controls are used. Extreme caution must be exercised for these applications.

Magnetic Control — Unit 5

CAUTION: *Always use a voltmeter to confirm control voltages, never make assumptions about voltage without testing.*

480V motors typically have 120V control circuits supplied from a transformer or use a separate control wiring circuit (see No. 2 and 3 below). It's common to use 24V controls for HVAC and energy management systems.

2. Transformer Control Wiring. A control transformer is used to reduce the voltage from L1 and L2 of the contactor to lower voltage levels for the control wiring (typically 480V to 120V). This permits pilot devices and coils to be rated for a lower voltage than the power conductors, and the lower voltage is safer for equipment operators and maintenance personnel. **Figure 5–5**

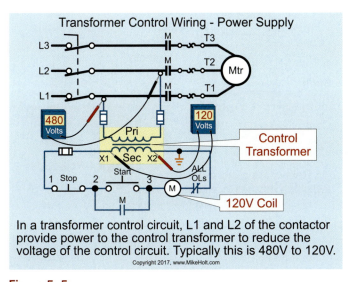

Figure 5–5

A control transformer can also be powered by a separate control circuit (see No. 3 below) instead of being powered by L1 and L2 of the contactor. In this case, it's a Class 1 circuit and must be installed according to the requirements of Article 725 of the *NEC*.

3. Separate Control Wiring. The power source for the control circuit is separate from the power circuit wiring. This is considered a Class 1 control circuit and must be installed according to the requirements of Article 725 of the *NEC*. The *Code* states that a Class 1 circuit can be rated up to 600V, but 120V is typical for motor control circuits. **Figure 5–6**

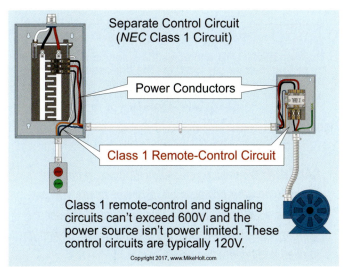

Figure 5–6

CAUTION: *Extra care should be taken where a separate power supply is used for control circuits. Turning off the power to the motor leaves the control circuit energized. If an additional power source is used, it must be clearly indicated on the motor control schematic.*

5.3 Coil Applications

Solenoids

Figure 5–7 shows a control circuit with a solenoid and a NO momentary-contact PB. When the PB is pushed, the solenoid coil is energized and pulls in the plunger. When the PB is released, the solenoid de-energizes and a spring on the plunger pushes it back out. Among other applications, solenoids are used for electric locks.

Unit 5 | Magnetic Control

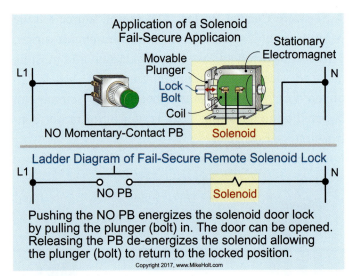

Figure 5–7

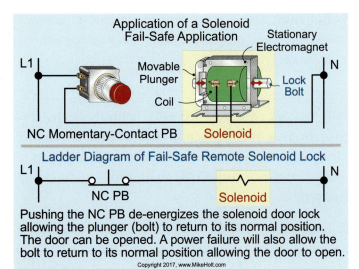

Figure 5–8

CAUTION: When using solenoids for locks, if the door is locked when the power is off, a power failure will prevent the door from opening. This is called a fail-secure system. Fail-safe systems are locked when power is applied and open when power is lost.

Author's Comment: **Figure 5–8** shows a fail-safe installation. A fail-safe installation will use a NC pushbutton and the solenoid will stay energized unless the NC pushbutton is pressed or the power to the circuit is interrupted. The lock bolt in the fail-safe solenoid lock uses the other end of the movable plunger from the application shown in the previous example.

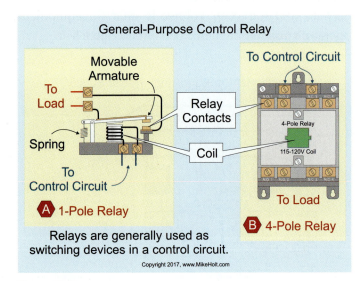

Figure 5–9

Relays

A magnetic relay, also called an "electromechanical relay," is basically a switch that uses a coil to operate one or more sets of contacts, **Figure 5–9**. The main difference is that relays aren't designed to carry the same high currents that contactors and motor starters can carry.

Relays are typically rated 15A or less, but there are some rated 20A and 30A. Higher ampere-rated devices that operate using the same principles as relays are called contactors, which have ratings ranging from about 20A up to 1,200A.

Relays come with many different configurations and ratings and are used for many different functions in control and signaling circuits.

Magnetic Control Unit 5

Relays are used for sequencing operation controls, master controls, and interlocking parts of equipment and control circuits in electrical isolation controls, in addition to many other functions. They're used in low-voltage wiring for turning on lights and other equipment. Relays can also have timed functions such as time-delay open and time-delay close.

Contactors

Contactors are relay-type switches used to open and close power circuits, and are usually rated from about 20A up to 1,200A. They don't provide overload protection. They can be manually or magnetically controlled. Contactors are generally used to control power circuits such as motors, lighting and lighting panels, and transformers. **Figure 5–10**

In **Figure 5–10B**, the terminals in the middle and front of the contactor are the coil-connection terminals. Some contactors come with prewired jumpers to the coil from the L1 and L2 power lines. When wired this way, power is provided to the contactor by turning on a circuit breaker or closing a disconnect switch. The coil automatically energizes and closes the power contacts, energizing the load. One or both of these jumpers are removed when adding control devices. In this case, the coil operates at the line voltage of L1 and L2. When this arrangement is used in a 480V system, a transformer is usually used in order to provide 120V control voltage. This allows all the pilot lights, switches, and pushbuttons that are used by equipment operators, to be a lower and safer voltage.

Some magnetic contactors have a jumper to an extra power terminal, **Figure 5–10B**. This terminal can be used to provide power to a common control circuit.

The wiring diagrams in **Figures 5–11A and 5–11B** show that the power to the coil or control circuit (or control transformer) is always taken from L1 and L2, even when the contactor is three-phase. (This statement doesn't apply when a separate control circuit is used to power the coil.)

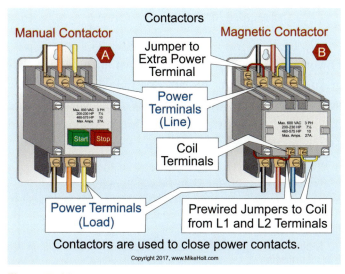

Figure 5–10

Figure 5–10A shows a manual contactor with a built-in start-stop or on-off switch.

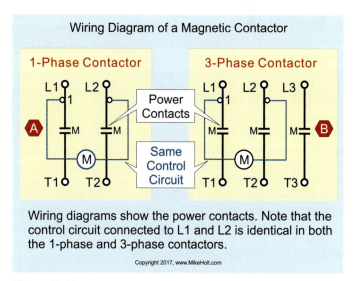

Figure 5–11

Unit 5 | Magnetic Control

Look at the button-like projections (plunger tabs) on the coil access plate in order to tell whether or not a coil is energized. When the buttons are in, the coil is energized. When the buttons are out, the coil is de-energized. Don't confuse these projections with reset buttons. **Figure 5–12**

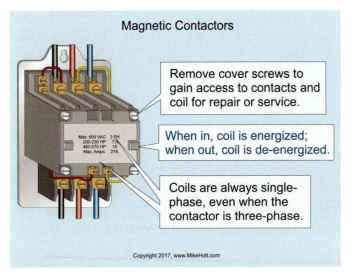

Figure 5–12

CAUTION: *Manually pushing in the plunger tabs energizes the load side of the contactor. In some cases, pushing these tabs may cause damage to the equipment.*

Contactor Power Contacts

When there's no power to the coil, the NO main power contacts are open. When power is applied, the coil energizes, and closes the NO main power contacts, which then energize the load terminals of the contactor. When the circuit to the coil opens, the reverse operation takes place. The coil de-energizes and the main power contacts open to de-energize the load terminals.

Author's Comments:

- The power contacts inside the contactor are sometimes damaged by arcing, which occurs because the contacts are breaking heavy load currents. Arcing causes the contact surface to be blackened (oxidized), but this oxidation is conductive and makes a good conductor of electricity. Contacts will also pit from the arcing and eventually wear out. In some cases the contacts can be replaced, while other types may require the entire contactor to be replaced when the contacts wear out. Under some circumstances, the contacts may actually weld together due to excessive current caused by a short circuit or ground fault. If the damage isn't too bad, the contacts may be pried apart and dressed with a file or similarly cleaned up for re-use. Check with the equipment manufacturer for their recommendations.

- When the voltage to the coil drops to a level where it can't maintain the contacts in a closed position, the contacts close and release very rapidly. This makes a loud noise called "chatter."

Power contacts aren't always shown in a ladder diagram, **Figure 5–13A**. As an electrician, you must be aware that they're there and how they work. On the other hand, the power contacts are frequently shown on wiring diagrams. **Figure 5–13B**

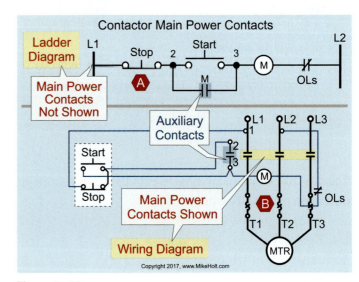

Figure 5–13

58 | Mike Holt Enterprises | *Understanding Basic Motor Controls*

Magnetic Control Unit 5

5.4 Remote Control—Introduction

Remote-Control Circuit. A remote-control circuit is any electric circuit that controls any other circuit through a relay or equivalent device.

Figure 5–14A is a pictorial diagram of a pushbutton (PB) controlling the coil of a magnetic contactor. Pressing the NO PB allows current to flow from L1 to the coil. The jumper from L2 is already a complete path to the other side of the coil, so it's energized when the PB is pushed and held in. The energized coil closes the power or line contacts to the load side of the contacts. Releasing the momentary-contact PB stops the current flow, de-energizing the coil which interrupts power to the load by opening the main power contacts L1-T1, L2-T2, and L3-T3 within the contactor.

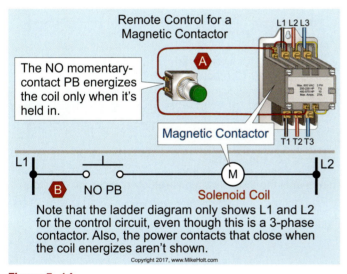

Figure 5–14

The control schematic shown in **Figure 5–14B** is a ladder representation of the pictorial drawing. Note that the power contacts between L1-T1, L2-T2, and L3-T3 aren't shown. Remember that when a contactor is shown as part of the control circuit, the M refers to the coil, not the load.

In a wiring diagram such as the one in **Figure 5–15**, the power contacts are typically shown. **Figure 5–15** also shows that the control circuit for the single-phase contactor is identical to the control circuit for the three-phase contactor.

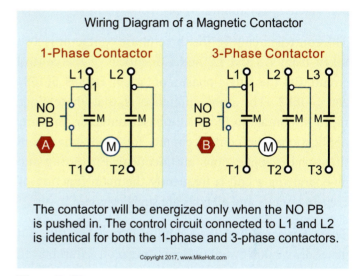

Figure 5–15

Figure 5–16 is showing the sequence of operation for the control circuit for both the single-phase and three-phase contactors in **Figure 5–15**.

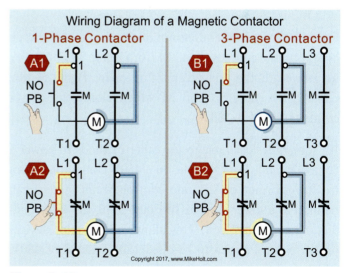

Figure 5–16

Understanding Basic Motor Controls | Mike Holt Enterprises

Figure 5–16A1 shows there's already power to one side of the coil from L2, and power to one side of the NO PB from L1. When the NO PB is pressed, **Figure 5–16A2**, the path from L1 to the coil is complete, both M contacts of the single-phase contactor close and energize terminals T1 and T2. As soon as the PB is released, the coil de-energizes and the M contacts open.

The control circuit for the three-phase contactor is also taken from L1 and L2 and is identical to the control circuit for the single-phase contactor, **Figures 5–16B1 and 5–16B2**. The only difference is that there's one more M contact in the three-phase contactor. In many applications, the control circuits for single-phase and three-phase applications are identical. Energizing and de-energizing a coil is frequently the main function of control circuits and all coils are single-phase.

There are some uses for a control circuit like this, but generally we don't want to keep a finger on a start button to maintain power to the load. In most cases, the desired function is to "turn it on" when it's needed and "turn it off" when finished. This 2-wire control circuit can be utilized in different ways by replacing the PB with a maintained-contact switch. Examples are a time clock, float switch, or toggle switch, **Figure 5–17**. Because this control circuit receives its power directly from the contactor, it's a common control circuit.

Figure 5–18 is a ladder diagram of the single-pole switch operating the contactor coil M from **Figure 5–17**. There's no power to the coil when S1 is open, **Figure 5–18A**. Closing S1 energizes coil M which closes the power contacts. **Figure 5–18B**

It's sometimes desirable to use other methods to power a control circuit. For example, on a 480V contactor, a control transformer or separate control circuit system can be used at a lower voltage. In **Figure 5–19**, the 480V contactor has a 120V coil. This allows all the pilot devices on the control circuit to be rated 120V instead of 480V, which is safer for personnel operating and maintaining the system and may be less expensive.

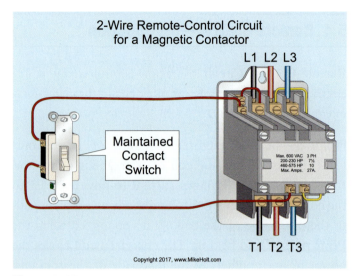

Figure 5–17

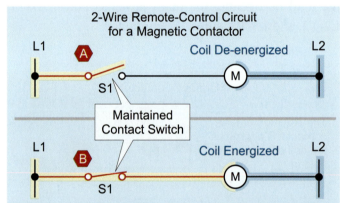

Closing the 1-pole toggle switch will energize the contactor coil. Contactor power contacts L1-T1, L2-T2, and L3-T3 will close until the toggle switch is returned to the off position.

Figure 5–18

A separate control circuit of this type can be a Class 1 remote-control circuit as covered in Article 725, Part II of the *NEC*. The common control circuit is tapped from the contactor and is covered by Article 430, Part VI of the *NEC*. **Figure 5–20**

Magnetic Control — Unit 5

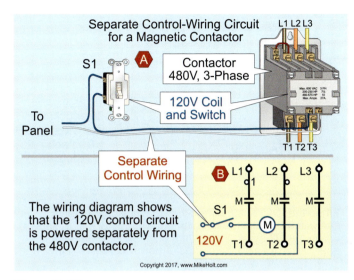

Figure 5–19

5.5 Lighting Contactor

A contactor used to control lighting circuits or a lighting panel is called a lighting contactor. **Figure 5–21** shows a typical lighting contactor with six normally open (NO) sets of contacts controlled by one coil.

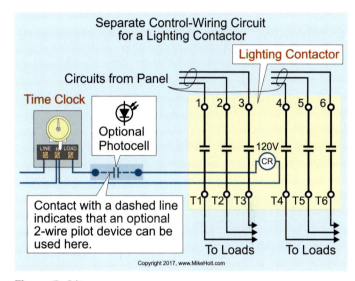

Figure 5–21

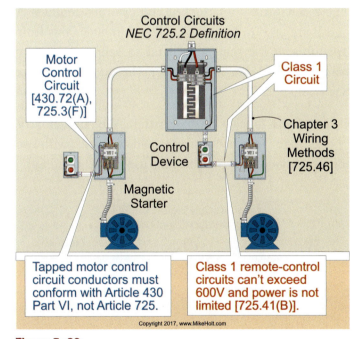

Figure 5–20

The control circuit consists of the coil, a time clock, and two conductors. When the time clock operates, the coil energizes and the six sets of contacts close by the same action described in the previous examples. The only difference is that there are six sets of power contacts instead of two or three sets.

This lighting contactor has six separate 120V or 277V circuits on the line side (top) of the contactor. The terminals on the bottom are the connecting points for the conductors running out to the assigned lighting loads. The neutral conductors pass through the enclosure, unbroken by the contactor. The six sets of power contacts can also supply two three-phase circuits or three 2-pole, single-phase circuits. The load conductors (T1 through T6) aren't energized until the time clock (TC) energizes the coil.

Unit 5 | Magnetic Control

There are many types of lighting contactors available with different ampere ratings and different numbers of contacts.

The source of electric power to the time clock and the coil isn't shown in **Figure 5–21**. This can come from a separate external 120V or higher-voltage circuit, or the time clock can be supplied from one of the circuits being controlled by the contactor. It's essential to provide the correct voltage to the time clock operating circuit and to the lighting contactor coil.

Author's Comment: A dashed line with a set of contacts shows where an optional 2-wire pilot device can be added to the control circuit, **Figure 5–21**. In this example, the location of the optional device is after the time clock, to ensure that the clock mechanism continues to run. If the optional device is located before the time clock, the clock motor won't run when the contacts of the optional device are open.

There are two basic types of control circuits for lighting contactors:

Electrically Held. This type of control circuit was discussed in this unit. When the coil is energized, the power contacts close; when the coil is de-energized, the power contacts open.

Mechanically Held. The mechanically held contactor shown in **Figure 5–22** has two coils and maintained-contact power contacts (not shown), that operate in the same way that a toggle switch does, it's On in one position, and Off in the other position. It's common to use a mechanical latch that falls into place to keep the contactor in the On position once energized. The unlatch coil simply releases the latching mechanism allowing the spring loaded contactor to return to the Off position.

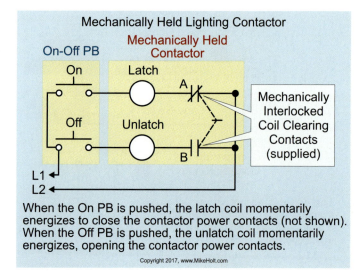

Figure 5–22

The mechanically interlocked coil clearing contacts A and B are used to keep the latch and unlatch coils from operating at the same time, and to keep power from being applied to a coil once it's performed its function. See **Figure 5–22**.

Figures 5–23 through 5–26 illustrate the sequence of operation for this mechanically held contactor with two momentary-contact pushbuttons used for On and Off.

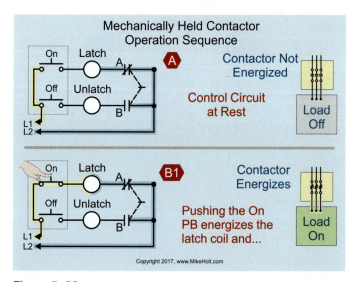

Figure 5–23

Magnetic Control — Unit 5

Load On. When the momentary-contact On button is pushed, the latch coil temporarily energizes and pulls the power contacts closed, **Figure 5–23B1**. When the power contacts close, the mechanical interlock contacts A open and B close, **Figure 5–24B2**. This causes the latch coil to de-energize. The result is that the load remains energized, with both the latch and unlatch coils de-energized. **Figure 5–24C**

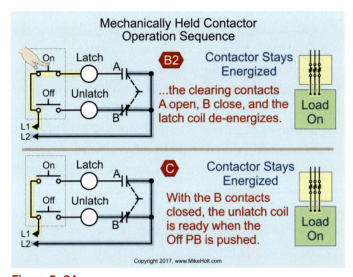

Figure 5–24

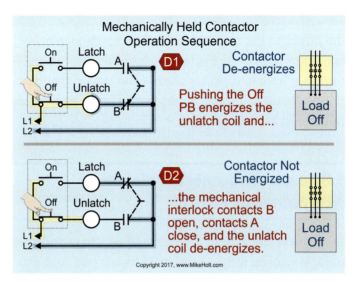

Figure 5–25

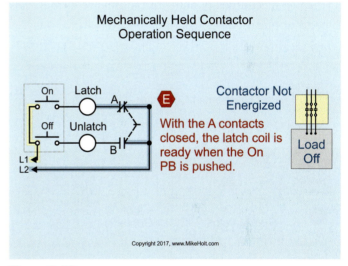

Figure 5–26

Load Off. When the momentary-contact Off button is pushed, the unlatch coil temporarily energizes and pulls the power contacts open, or releases the mechanical latch holding the spring-loaded contactor in the On position, which de-energizes the load, **Figure 5–25D1**. When the power contacts open, the mechanical interlock contacts B open and A close. This causes the unlatch coil to de-energize, and the panel remains de-energized, **Figure 5–25D2**. With the mechanical interlock contacts A closed, the latch coil is ready when the On pushbutton is pushed again. **Figure 5–26E**

Both the latch (open) and unlatch (close) coils are only energized long enough to open or close the power contacts. The rest of the time these coils are off. This saves power consumption on the control circuit and the control equipment lasts longer.

This description illustrates an operational difference between electrically and mechanically held contactors. In an electrically held contactor, the power contacts open upon loss of power to the electromagnet, and then close again when power is restored. This is sometimes referred to as "fail-off."

Unit 5 | Magnetic Control

This isn't true for a mechanically held contactor. When the power to the control circuit for a mechanically held contactor is lost, the contacts remain in whatever position they were in (open or closed) and stay in that position even when power is restored. This is sometimes referred to as "fail-last."

5.6 Feeder Disconnect Contactor with Automatic Control

In cases where multiple large lighting contactors are used, it may be more economical to use one contactor whose load side supplies a distribution panel that feeds the individual lighting circuits as shown in **Figure 5–27**. Typically, mechanically held contactors are used in this type of application.

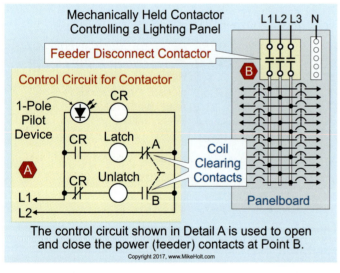

Figure 5–27

The latch and unlatch coils and the mechanical interlock A-B shown in **Figure 5–27A** are physically located with the power contacts shown in **Figure 5–27B**. The diagram separates these to make it easier to see how the control circuit functions. The single-pole pilot device in series with the control relay (CR) can be a photocell or timer to add an automatic On and Off to the control circuit.

Author's Comment: Programmable logic controller (PLC) control systems are also commonly used for energy management systems, in which case the photocell feeds the On-Off command to a PLC logic input device instead of directly to the control relay.

Lighting Panel On. When the pilot device (photocell) contacts close, the CR coil energizes, **Figure 5–28B**, the NO CR contacts close and temporarily energize the latch coil, which closes the feeder contacts, energizing the panel. Additionally, the coil-clearing contacts' mechanical interlock opens the clearing contacts A, and closes the clearing contacts B allowing L2 power to one side of the unlatch coil, **Figure 5–29C**. This puts the unlatch coil in a position to receive power from L1. Note that when the clearing contacts A open, the latch coil is also de-energized.

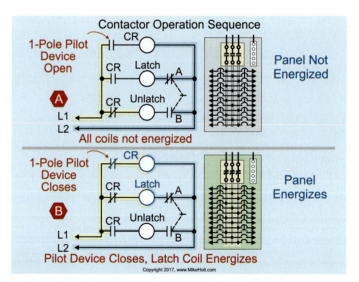

Figure 5–28

Author's Comment: When the pilot device (photocell) closes and energizes the CR coil (which is electrically held), the NC CR contacts in series with the unlatch coil open. This set of contacts stays open until the CR coil de-energizes.

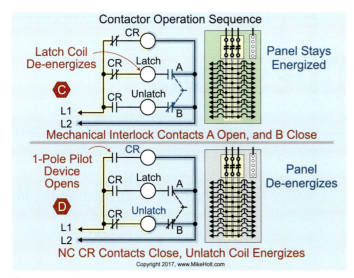

Figure 5–29

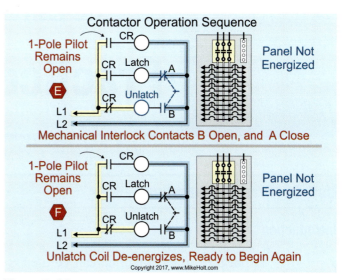

Figure 5–30

Lighting Panel Off. When the pilot device (photocell) contacts open, the CR coil de-energizes, and the NC CR contacts in series with the unlatch coil close, Figure 5–29D. Remember that the mechanical interlock closed the B contacts on the L2 side of the unlatch coil when the latch coil energized, Figure 5–29C, and the unlatch coil temporarily energizes and opens the power contacts controlling the feeder to the panelboard.

Also, the mechanical interlock closes the A contacts on the L2 side of the latch coil, Figure 5–30E. Now the contactor is set so it will be ready to energize the panel again when the pilot device (photocell) closes once more. Figures 5–30F and 5–28A

Mechanically held relays and contactors have many different applications. They're frequently combined with other pilot devices and control devices.

Unit 5—Conclusion

This unit introduced the subject of magnetic motor control, which is widely used for the remote control of both single-phase and three-phase motors. It also touched on mechanically held contactors. It covered important concepts including the following:

- Circuit types classified by power source—common control circuits, transformer control wiring, and separate control wiring.

- Control devices—solenoids, relays, and contactors (both mechanically held and electrically held).

- Remote-control circuits.

- Using 120V control circuits and magnetic devices to control 480V loads.

Unit 5—Practice Questions

Introduction

1. _____ are devices using coils that can be used to facilitate remote-control functions.

   (a) Contactors
   (b) Magnetic starters
   (c) Solenoids
   (d) all of these

5.2 Power Sources for the Coil and Control Circuit

2. The terms "T1," "T2," and "T3" refer to the terminals on the _____.

   (a) line side of a motor starter
   (b) load side of a motor starter
   (c) connection points for a control circuit
   (d) connection points for a stop-start pushbutton station

3. With common control wiring, the power source for the control circuit is separate from the power circuit wiring.

   (a) True
   (b) False

4. A common control circuit shouldn't be used when the branch circuit for the motor is 480V unless extreme caution is exercised.

   (a) True
   (b) False

5. A control transformer typically reduces the voltage from L1 and L2 for the control circuit, such as reducing a 480V branch circuit for the motor to 120V for the control circuit.

   (a) True
   (b) False

6. A separate control circuit is _____.

   (a) not taken from the branch circuit feeding the motor
   (b) typically a Class 1 control circuit
   (c) normally taken from L1 and L2
   (d) a and b

5.3 Coil Applications

7. Contactors don't provide overload protection.

   (a) True
   (b) False

5.4 Remote Control—Introduction

8. A remote-control circuit is any electric circuit that controls any other circuit through a relay or equivalent device.

   (a) True
   (b) False

Practice Questions — Unit 5

5.5 Lighting Contactor

9. In a(n) _____ contactor, when the coil is energized, the power contacts close. When the coil is de-energized, the power contacts open.

    (a) manually held
    (b) electrically held
    (c) load on
    (d) load off

10. A _____ contactor has two coils and maintained-contact power contacts, and is similar to a simple toggle switch in that it's On in one position, and Off in the other position.

    (a) mechanically held
    (b) electrically held
    (c) load on
    (d) load off

Practice Questions—General

Note: The following questions are based on any part of this textbook up through this unit.

11. In **Figure 5–31**, a 480V/120V control transformer is being used. The control relay _____.

    (a) is connected to the 120V control circuit
    (b) has a set of contacts that activates a 480V coil
    (c) coil and the set of CR contacts are one device
    (d) all of these

12. In **Figure 5–31**, when the start PB is pushed, the _____.

    (a) M coil energizes the CR relay
    (b) CR energizes the NO CR contacts and de-energizes the M coil
    (c) CR closes the NO CR contacts and energizes the M coil
    (d) motor will stop

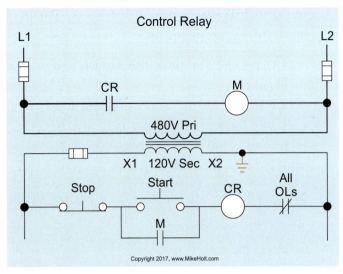

Figure 5–31

13. In **Figure 5–32**, the main power contacts are _____.

    (a) not shown in the ladder diagram A
    (b) shown in the wiring/connection diagram B
    (c) not shown in either diagram
    (d) a and b

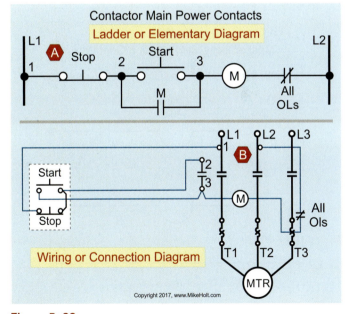

Figure 5–32

Unit 5 | Practice Questions

14. In **Figure 5–32**, the power for the control circuit is taken from _____.

    (a) L1 and L2 for both the ladder and wiring diagrams
    (b) L1 and L2 for the ladder diagram and L1 and L3 for the wiring diagram
    (c) L1 and L3 for both diagrams
    (d) L2 and L3 for both diagrams

15. In **Figure 5–32**, when the start PB is pushed, the M coil _____.

    (a) closes the power contacts
    (b) closes the auxiliary contacts 2-3
    (c) energizes
    (d) all of these

16. In **Figure 5–33**, the mechanically held contactor has _____.

    (a) mechanically interlocked coil clearing contacts
    (b) a latch coil
    (c) an unlatch coil
    (d) all of these

17. In **Figure 5–33**, when the On PB is pushed the _____.

    (a) latch coil stays energized until the Off PB is pushed
    (b) unlatch coil stays energized until the Off PB is pushed
    (c) latch coil momentarily energizes to close the contactor power contacts
    (d) unlatch coil momentarily energizes to close the contactor power contacts

18. In **Figure 5–33**, if the power contacts are closed when the Off PB is pushed, the _____.

    (a) latch coil stays energized until the Off PB is pushed
    (b) unlatch coil stays energized until the On PB is pushed
    (c) unlatch coil momentarily energizes, opening the contactor power contacts
    (d) latch coil is energized closing the power contacts

19. In **Figure 5–33**, after the On PB is pushed and released _____.

    (a) the mechanically held contacts A will be open
    (b) the mechanically held contacts B will be closed
    (c) both coils will be de-energized
    (d) all of these

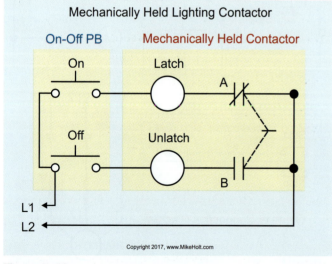

Figure 5–33

UNIT 6

Magnetic Motor Starters

Unit 6—Introduction

The previous unit covered the basics of magnetic motor control and mechanically held contactors. This unit extends that knowledge to explain the construction and operation of magnetic motor starters. This important type of equipment is used to control larger single-phase and three-phase motors in a wide range of commercial and industrial applications.

6.1 Magnetic Motor Starters

A magnetic motor starter is essentially a magnetic contactor with an overload relay assembly added. A solenoid coil energizes and closes a set of contacts, completing a circuit, which energizes the load. The fundamental principle of motor control is switching this coil on and off in accordance with the logic of the control circuit. Additional control wiring often makes use of one or more auxiliary contacts which are operated by the same coil. Figure 6–1

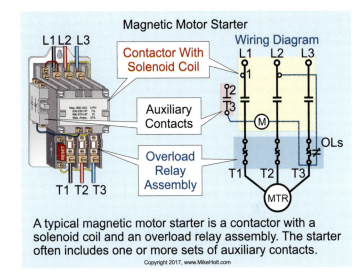

Figure 6–1

The overload (OL) protection is frequently part of the motor control circuit. Short-circuit and ground-fault protection is typically provided by a circuit breaker or a set of fuses. It's very important that you understand a few *NEC* definitions to understand how this works.

> **Author's Comment:** This subject is covered in greater detail in Annex B.

Overload vs. Overcurrent Protection. The *NEC* definition of "Overcurrent" is any current in excess of the rated current of equipment or the ampacity of a conductor. Overcurrent may result from (1) an overload, (2) a short circuit, or (3) a ground fault, Figure 6–2.

Overload Relay-Motor Running Protection

Overcurrent protection for motors is frequently divided into two categories. One category is overload protection (motor running protection). The other category is short-circuit and ground-fault protection.

Unit 6 | Magnetic Motor Starters

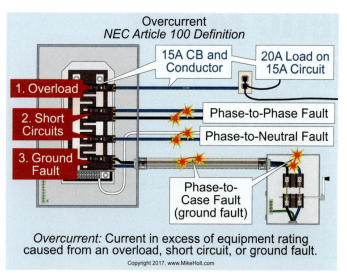

Figure 6–2

Short circuits and ground faults result from faults in the wiring which can carry large amounts of current. Overloads aren't fault conditions, but just the result of excessive current flowing in the circuit. The *NEC* defines an "overload" as the operation of equipment in excess of normal full-load current ratings. If the condition persists for a sufficient amount of time, an overload can cause damage or dangerous overheating of the apparatus.

Overload protection devices (OLs) are intended to protect motors, motor control apparatus, and motor branch-circuit conductors against excessive heating due to motor overloads and failure to start. It's possible for a motor to become so hot it will burn out or start a fire. Some of the causes of overload are:

- Low voltage to the motor.
- A locked rotor.
- The motor is too small for the application.
- Bad bearings.
- Single-phasing, meaning one conductor of a three-phase circuit fails, causing it to run on two phases.

Overload devices must have enough time delay built in to stay closed during the high starting current of the motor, **Figure 6–3**. An overload protection device for a motor is a current-sensing device that opens the control circuit to the magnetic motor starter coil. The overload device should be able to carry small overloads that aren't detrimental to the motor for short periods of time, but it should open if the overload persists. For this reason, overload devices have many different ratings and are normally sized between 115 and 125 percent of the normal running current of the motor. However, in some cases higher percentages are permitted (see Article 430, Part III of the *NEC*). **Figure 6–4**

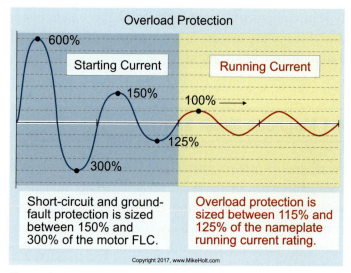

Figure 6–3

Author's Comment: There are cases where the short-circuit and ground-fault protection will exceed 300 percent such as with instantaneous trip breakers.

Overload protection for motors doesn't provide ground-fault or short-circuit protection. Overcurrent protection for motors is usually provided with two types of protection devices. Fuses or circuit breakers provide the ground-fault and short-circuit protection. **Figure 6–5**

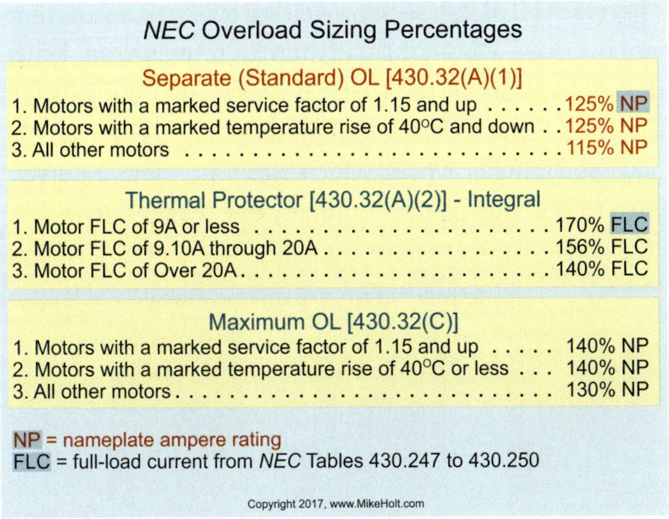

Magnetic Motor Starters — Unit 6

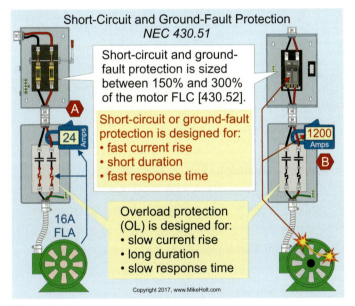

Figure 6–4

Figure 6–5

On the other hand, short-circuit current and ground-fault current is many times higher than running current. These conditions happen very quickly and deliver a high amount of destructive energy. It's essential that the short-circuit and ground-fault protection device acts as quickly as possible to open the circuit and minimize the damage caused by high-current faults. **Figure 6–5B**

Thermal Overloads

A common type of overload device is a eutectic alloy thermal overload. This type of overload device is sometimes called a heater. This overload device consists of a tube that contains a eutectic alloy (solder), **Figure 6–6**. The tube contains a pin with a ratchet wheel on the end of it. Normal current runs through the heating element. When normal load current is running through the heating element, the pin and ratchet wheel are "frozen" and can't turn. If an overload condition develops, the current through the heating element increases to the point where the solder in the tube melts and allows the pin and ratchet wheel to turn freely. When the melting alloy cools, it freezes the pin and ratchet again.

Overload current is just higher than normal running current. It rises slowly and has a long duration, **Figure 6–5A**. This is what overload protection is designed for.

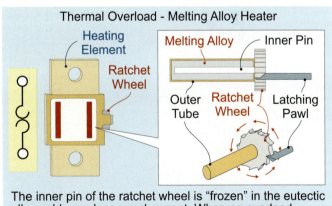

Figure 6–6

Understanding Basic Motor Controls | Mike Holt Enterprises | 71

Unit 6 | Magnetic Motor Starters

Thermal OL Relay. The melting alloy thermal overload from **Figure 6–6** combined with a set of contacts are the basic components of a thermal overload relay unit, **Figure 6–7**. Current from the motor runs through the thermal OLs. The frozen pin and ratchet wheel locks the contacts closed, **Figure 6–7A**. This closed set of contacts maintains a current path to one side of the coil in the magnetic starter. When the motor is off, or no overload condition exists, the melting alloy remains solid and the contacts stay closed. If an overload condition develops, the current through the thermal overload increases which melts the solder, allows the pin and ratchet wheel to turn, then the pawl latch releases and the loaded spring behind the contacts pushes the contacts open, **Figure 6–7B**. This interrupts power to the contactor coil, opening the main power contacts, and stops the motor.

Thermal OL Relay Reset. Melting alloy types of thermal overload relays normally have a reset button. When the solder alloy in the thermal overload cools, pushing the reset button closes the contacts and re-latches the pawl and ratchet wheel, which again provides a current path to one side of the contactor coil. **Figure 6–8**

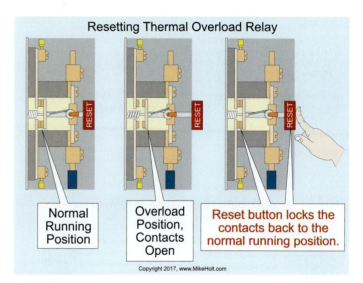

Figure 6–8

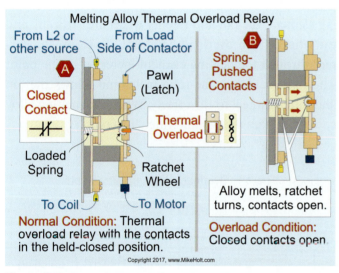

Figure 6–7

Author's Comment: A NC contact symbol is used in motor control schematics to represent the motor overload contacts of the overload relay device. Technically, these contacts are being held closed and shouldn't be confused with how auxiliary contacts or power contacts in a motor starter operate.

Author's Comment: Figure 6–9 shows the thermal overload relay assembly connected to the magnetic contactor. In order to read motor schematics, it's important to remember that there are two parts to the overload relay device. The actual OL device, or heater, carries the branch-circuit power when the contactor is energized, **Figure 6–9A**. The closed OL relay contacts have the control circuit power running through them, **Figure 6–9B**. The reset button isn't usually shown in motor schematics.

CAUTION: *Extreme care should be taken if the contactor has been de-energized because of an overload trip. Check the motor and all connections for damage prior to pushing the reset button.*

Magnetic Motor Starters — Unit 6

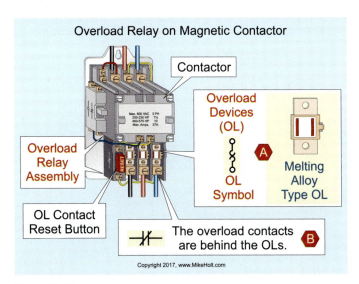

Figure 6–9

In some small motors, overload devices are built into the motor. Also, there are limited applications where time-delay or dual-element fuses can provide overload protection for the motor and motor branch circuit, as well as short-circuit and ground-fault protection (see 430.55 of the *NEC*). A disadvantage of using fuses for overload protection is that they aren't reusable.

OL Relay Symbols in Schematics. Remember that there's branch-circuit current running through the actual overload while the control circuit current is running through the closed contact portion of the OL relay. See **Figure 6–7**. Wiring diagrams normally show all of the overload units but only one set of closed contacts. **Figure 6–10**

Number of Thermal OL Units. Table 430.37 of the *NEC* typically requires one overload relay unit for every ungrounded (hot) conductor of the circuit supplying the motor. This means three overload units for a three-phase starter, two overload units for a 208V or 240V, single-phase starter, and one overload unit for a 120V, single-phase starter.

Using two overloads in a three-phase motor circuit isn't permitted. The loss of one line of a three-phase circuit causes high currents on the other two lines and causes serious unbalanced load problems. A three-phase motor can keep running on two lines, but it won't usually restart.

Author's Comment: Although no longer permitted, at one time it was common to find two overloads instead of three overloads for a three-phase motor installation. This OL protection method can still be found on some older installations.

Alternate OL Protection Technique. Overload relay units aren't always required when other approved means of overload protection are provided (see Table 430.37 Ex of the *NEC*).

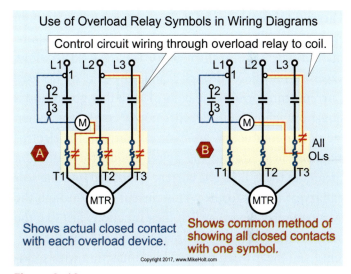

Figure 6–10

Ladder diagrams usually show just the control circuit portion of the OL relay as one set of closed contacts marked "OL" or sometimes "All OLs," **Figure 6–11**. Since the OL relay units are all wired in series with each other, if any single OL opens, the control circuit will de-energize.

Unit 6 | Magnetic Motor Starters

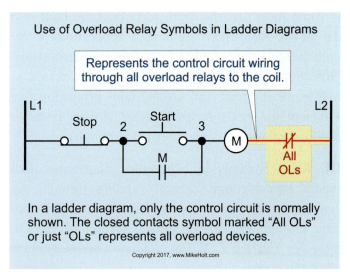

Figure 6–11

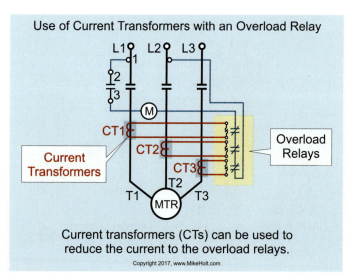

Figure 6–12

Thermal OL Relay with CT. For large motors with high currents, it's impractical to use large thermal OL units. Instead, current transformers (CTs) are used to allow lower current flow through standard OL relay devices. Current transformers are coils of wire that go around a single branch-circuit or feeder power conductor. When the power conductors are carrying current, the electromagnetic field around the power conductor induces a current in the CT, just as current is induced into the secondary of a transformer. This current runs through the overload relay device, which then functions just like the overload relay device previously discussed, or the current from the CT can be used in conjunction with solid-state circuitry to open the control circuit. **Figure 6–12**

Author's Comment: CTs can be applied to other aspects of control wiring. They're sometimes used for monitoring and metering purposes.

Troubleshooting an Overload Condition. The cause of any overload must be determined and any necessary corrections made. Repeated overheating of the motor will cause damage to the winding insulation and shorten the life of the motor. In a new installation, repeated overload trips may indicate that the next size up overload unit is necessary. See the example of an OL Selection Chart, which can sometimes be found on the inside cover of the starter enclosure. **Figure 6–13**

Motor FLA (Nameplate Full-Load Current)			Thermal Unit Number
1 TU	2 TU	3 TU	
0.29 - 0.31	0.29 - 0.31	0.28 - 0.30	B 0.44
0.32 - 0.34	0.32 - 0.34	0.31 - 0.34	B 0.51
0.35 - 0.38	0.35 - 0.38	0.35 - 0.37	B 0.57
0.39 - 0.45	0.39 - 0.45	0.38 - 0.44	B 0.63
0.46 - 0.54	0.46 - 0.54	0.45 - 0.53	B 0.71
0.55 - 0.61	0.55 - 0.61	0.54 - 0.59	B 0.81
0.62 - 0.66	0.62 - 0.66	0.60 - 0.64	B 0.92
0.67 - 0.73	0.67 - 0.73	0.65 - 0.72	B 1.03
0.74 - 0.81	0.74 - 0.81	0.73 - 0.80	B 1.16
0.82 - 0.94	0.82 - 0.94	0.81 - 0.90	B 1.30
0.95 - 1.05	0.95 - 1.05	0.91 - 1.03	B 1.45
1.06 - 1.22	1.06 - 1.22	1.04 - 1.14	B 1.67
1.23 - 1.34	1.23 - 1.34	1.15 - 1.29	B 1.88
1.35 - 1.51	1.35 - 1.51	1.28 - 1.43	B 2.10

Figure 6–13

Magnetic Motor Starters — Unit 6

Author's Comments:

- Motor starters and motor control equipment are installed in many types of environments. The *NEC* requires that all electrical equipment be suitable for the environment in which they're installed [110.3 and 110.11]. For determining the type of enclosure(s) needed for different environments, an excellent source for information can be found at www.nema.org. Look for NEMA Enclosure Types.

- Remember that numbers in brackets such as those above are cross-references to specific sections of the *National Electrical Code*.

6.2 Other Overload Protection Methods

Bimetal Overload Relay. This is another type of commonly used thermal overload device. The heater element of the relay is made of dissimilar metals that, when heated, expand at different rates. The difference in this rate of expansion causes the bimetal strip to warp and bend as the temperature is increased. This movement activates a trip bar, which opens the set of NC contacts and opens the control circuit to the contactor coil.

A bimetal overload relay can be adjusted to automatically reset after tripping once the relay cools down. This method is used where manually pushing the reset button is undesirable or difficult. Automatic resetting shouldn't be used where automatic restarts will create a hazard to persons or a mechanical process. Care should be used on 2-wire circuits because automatically resetting the overload relay can cause unexpected restarts of the equipment, which can be dangerous to personnel. When used on a 3-wire control circuit, the automatic reset won't cause automatic restarts of the equipment.

Solid-State Overload Relay. Solid-state relays don't work on the principle of heat, so they operate at cooler temperatures than thermal overload devices. A solid-state relay uses current transformers to monitor current in each line to the motor. When the current reaches a predetermined level, it trips the overload relay, which interrupts the control circuit power to the contactor coil. An advantage of solid-state relays is that they can have several different current-trip settings, and other protection features can be built in.

Overload Relay Class Designations

Overload relays have 10-second, 20-second, or 30-second ratings. These ratings are the maximum seconds an OL takes to trip at 600 percent of its current rating. For example, a Class 20 overload relay trips in 20 seconds or less if the current is 600 percent of its rating. Different classes of overload relays include:

- **Class 10 Overload Relay.** Typically used with hermetic motors, and motors with short locked-rotor time capacity.

- **Class 20 Overload Relay.** A general-use type relay.

- **Class 30 Overload Relay.** Used for motors with large loads where extra accelerating time is required.

6.3 Auxiliary Contacts

In addition to a contactor and an overload relay assembly, most magnetic motor starters contain one or more sets of auxiliary contacts as standard equipment. It's common for an auxiliary contact device to have one set of NO contacts and one set of NC contacts. Many magnetic motor starters are designed to accept an additional set of auxiliary contacts that can be added as an accessory device which either snaps in, or plugs in.

Figure 6–14A shows a motor starter with an auxiliary contact assembly. This assembly has a set of NO contacts with wiring terminals 2 and 3, and a set of NC contacts with wiring terminals 4 and 5. **Figure 6–14B** shows the same arrangement as represented in a wiring diagram.

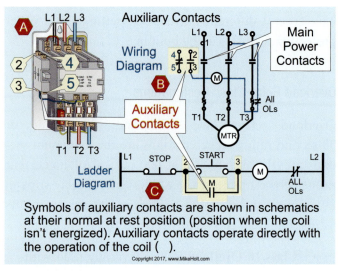

Figure 6–14

Figure 6–14C shows a typical 3-wire control circuit in a ladder diagram that uses the NO contacts of the auxiliary contact assembly. NC auxiliary contacts 4 and 5 aren't used for this control circuit. The set of NO contacts marked M under the start PB is the set of auxiliary contacts. In this case, the numbers 2 and 3 indicate where the control wires for the start PB are connected, rather than the actual terminals 2 and 3 of the NO auxiliary contacts. Notice that the M on the contacts corresponds with the M in the coil symbol, indicating that this particular set of contacts is operated directly by the coil with the same letter identification.

Auxiliary contacts are used for various purposes. NO auxiliary contacts are very commonly used as "seal-in" contacts. Seal-in contacts primarily function to eliminate the necessity of manually holding the start pushbutton once the coil has been energized. When a NO auxiliary contact is connected in parallel with a NO momentary-contact PB, it acts like a holding circuit and maintains power to the coil to keep the load-side equipment energized by the power contacts.

Author's Comment: The seal-in function is covered in more detail in Unit 7, where 3-wire control circuits are introduced.

6.4 Motor Starter Add-On Accessory Devices

Other optional devices that can be added to most motor starters are:

- **Fuse Holders.** Either one or two fuse holders are available to provide protection for control circuits or control circuit transformers.
- **Pneumatic Timer.** Provides on-delay or off-delay for the contactor or motor.
- **Additional Lug Kit.** Adds more terminals for control or power wiring.
- **Additional Power Pole.** Provides an extra set of power contacts.

Unit 6—Conclusion

This unit explained the operation and use of magnetic motor starters. It discussed motor overload protection devices in detail, and also covered auxiliary contacts and motor starter add-on accessories. Now that we've covered basic types of manual and automatic motor control devices, we'll describe basic control circuits in the next unit.

Unit 6 Practice Questions

Unit 6—Practice Questions

6.1 Magnetic Motor Starters

1. It's possible for a motor to become so hot that it will burn out or start a fire. A common cause of overload is _____.

    (a) low voltage to the motor
    (b) a locked rotor
    (c) single-phasing (one line of a three-phase circuit fails)
    (d) all of these

2. Overcurrent may result from _____.

    (a) overload
    (b) short circuit
    (c) ground fault
    (d) any of these

3. Overload current _____.

    (a) rises slowly and has a long duration
    (b) rises quickly and has a long duration
    (c) rises quickly and has a short duration
    (d) rises slowly and has a short duration

4. Short-circuit or ground-fault current is many times higher than running current and must open the protection device as quickly as possible to minimize the damage.

    (a) True
    (b) False

5. The *NEC* typically requires _____ overload relay unit(s) for every ungrounded conductor.

    (a) one
    (b) two
    (c) three
    (d) four

6. A very common type of overload device is a eutectic alloy thermal overload. This type of overload device is sometimes called a _____.

    (a) thermos
    (b) freezer
    (c) heater
    (d) cooler

6.2 Other Overload Protection Methods

7. Overload relays have 10-second, 20-second, or 30-second ratings. These ratings are the maximum seconds an OL takes to trip at _____ percent of its current rating.

    (a) 100
    (b) 200
    (c) 400
    (d) 600

Unit 6 | Practice Questions

8. A _____ overload relay is typically used with hermetic motors, and motors with short locked-rotor time capacity.

   (a) Class 10
   (b) Class 20
   (c) Class 30
   (d) Class 40

Practice Questions—General

Note: The following questions are based on any part of this textbook up through this unit.

9. In **Figure 6–15**, the magnetic motor starter is designated by the letter _____.

   (a) A
   (b) B
   (c) C
   (d) D

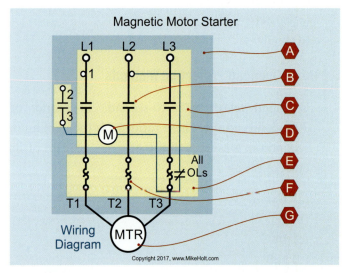

Figure 6–15

10. In **Figure 6–15**, the power contacts for the magnetic motor starter are designated by the letter _____.

    (a) A
    (b) B
    (c) C
    (d) D

11. In **Figure 6–15**, the coil for the magnetic motor starter is designated by the letter _____.

    (a) C
    (b) D
    (c) E
    (d) F

12. In **Figure 6–15**, the overload relay assembly for the magnetic motor starter is designated by the letter _____.

    (a) C
    (b) D
    (c) E
    (d) F

13. In **Figure 6–15**, the motor that's supplied by the magnetic motor starter is designated by the letter _____.

    (a) D
    (b) E
    (c) F
    (d) G

14. In **Figure 6–15**, the thermal overload (heater) is designated by the letter _____.

    (a) C
    (b) D
    (c) E
    (d) F

15. In **Figure 6–16**, the ladder diagram is indicating that there is(are) _____ set(s) of auxiliary contacts.

    (a) one
    (b) two
    (c) three
    (d) four

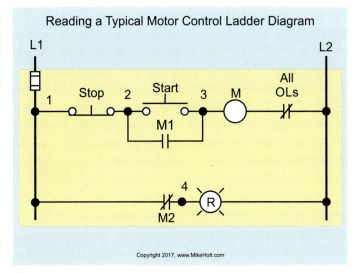

Figure 6–16

16. In **Figure 6–16**, the overload contacts are connected between _____.

    (a) L1 and the stop PB
    (b) L2 and point 4
    (c) L2 and the coil
    (d) L2 and the pilot light

17. In **Figure 6–16**, if the motor is off, when the start PB is pressed the _____.

    (a) OL contacts will open
    (b) OL contacts will remain closed
    (c) M1 auxiliary contacts will open
    (d) M2 auxiliary contacts will close

18. In **Figure 6–16**, the M2 auxiliary contacts are connected to points _____.

    (a) 2-3
    (b) 4-5
    (c) L1-4
    (d) L2-3

19. In **Figure 6–16**, if the OL contacts are open, the M coil _____ when the start PB is pressed.

    (a) can't be energized
    (b) can be energized
    (c) will burn out
    (d) will short circuit

Notes

UNIT 7 — Basic Control Circuits

Unit 7–Introduction

Units 4 through 6 covered motor control schematics, the basics of magnetic control, and motor control devices. This unit builds on that foundation of knowledge to discuss control circuits in more detail. Knowing when and how to use different types of control circuits is at the heart of understanding motor controls and working on them. This unit also goes into more detail about the important subject of pilot devices such as start-stop pushbuttons. These allow motor control units to be remotely controlled from one or more locations.

The basis for most control wiring is either a 2-wire control circuit or a 3-wire control circuit. As controls become more complicated, there may be several 2-wire or several 3-wire control circuits involved. There may even be a combination of both types. The circuitry from a magnetic starter using a 3-wire control circuit to the field pilot devices may also require more than three conductors to meet all circuiting needs.

7.1 2-Wire Control Circuits

2-wire control circuits are used for applications that need to be self-starting (see Unit 4). These include applications such as pumping stations, air-conditioning (HVAC) equipment and fans, and refrigeration equipment.

A 2-wire control circuit doesn't have low-voltage protection. This means that if the equipment is running when there's a power loss or brownout (voltage reduction), the equipment will automatically restart when the power is restored.

> **CAUTION:** *2-wire control circuits shouldn't be used where automatic restart after a power loss will create a safety hazard for personnel working around the restarting equipment. A power loss can be caused by a utility outage, or the equipment disconnect being turned off and back on. In locations where there are a large number of motors, automatic restart can cause an undesirable power surge when power is restored.*

Unit 4 covered some applications using 2-wire pilot devices such as toggle switches and float switches to complete a circuit to start a motor. In Unit 5, we used 2-wire pilot devices such as photocells to control a lighting contactor. This unit explains using the same concepts to energize the coil of a motor starter.

A basic 2-wire control circuit goes from a power supply, which is L1 if from the contactor (for a common control-wiring circuit) to a 2-wire control device such as a float switch, pressure switch, temperature switch, or 1-pole switch, then goes to one side of the starter coil, **Figure 7–1**. In this example, the 2-wire control is a series circuit between L1 and the coil. The control wiring on the other side of the coil is generally used for the overload protection and is connected to L2.

Unit 7 | Basic Control Circuits

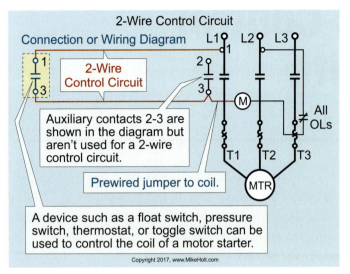

Figure 7–1

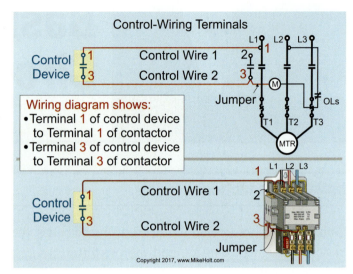

Figure 7–2

Author's Comment: The term "low-voltage release" is used with 2-wire circuits that have a maintained-contact pilot device(s) in series with the coil. See **Figure 7–1**. This type of control is used when the starter must function automatically without a human operator. Don't confuse this phrase with "low-voltage protection" which applies to 3-wire circuits and manual restart after a power failure. This concept is explained more fully later in this unit.

CAUTION: *The terminal numbers found on a schematic won't always match up with terminal numbers found on some wiring devices. Different manufacturers will use different numbering systems. Wiring must always be based on function, not on terminal numbers. As a reminder, we're matching many terminal numbers in this textbook only for the purpose of making it easier for students to learn.*

Notice the numbers 1 and 3 at the terminals of the 2-wire control device, **Figure 7–2**. The same numbers can be found on the motor starter schematic. These numbers are used to indicate where the control circuit conductors are terminated. The conductor (control wire 1) that terminates to terminal 1 of the control device connects to terminal 1 in the motor starter (next to L1). The conductor (control wire 2) from terminal 3 of the control device connects to terminal 3 of the auxiliary contacts in the motor starter. This is essentially the same as connecting it to the coil because the auxiliary contacts aren't being utilized in this control circuit. There's usually a factory-installed jumper between the coil and terminal 3 of the auxiliary contact, so field wiring is typically done to terminal 3. If the jumper isn't installed, the field wiring will terminate to the coil.

Optional Wiring

Some pilot devices have more than one set of contacts. This allows a single device to be more versatile and used for more applications. A schematic often indicates optional wiring by using dashed lines with instructions. In **Figure 7–3**, a float switch has two different sets of contacts. It's up to the installer or designer of the control circuit to determine how these will be wired. In this example, one end of wire A (solid line) is connecting the NC contacts of the float switch. The optional wiring is the dashed line from the NO contacts. The instructions under the wiring diagram state that wire A must be removed and connected as shown by the dashed line for a sump-pump application.

Basic Control Circuits — Unit 7

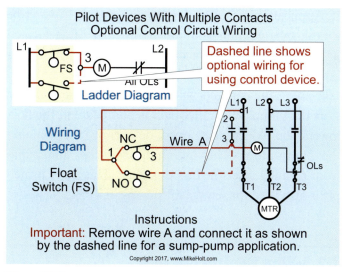

Figure 7–3

Application 1—Tank Filling Application

NC Contacts (Solid Line A). This application leaves wire A on the NC contact as shown in the diagram, **Figure 7–4**. Since the NC contacts are open when the tank is full, they'll close when the liquid level drops. This function can be used for something like automatically filling a watering tank for livestock.

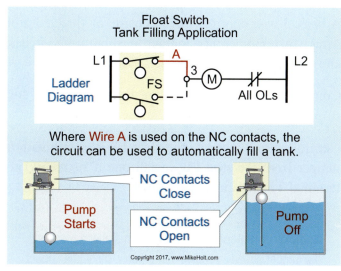

Figure 7–4

Operation Sequence for Automatic Filling. If the tank is full, the NC contacts are open and the motor is off, **Figure 7–5B**. When the liquid level drops to a certain point, the NC contacts close, the M coil energizes, the main power contacts close, and the pump runs, **Figure 7–5A**. As the liquid level rises to a certain point, the NC contacts open, the M coil de-energizes, the main power contacts open, and the pump stops. **Figure 7–5B**

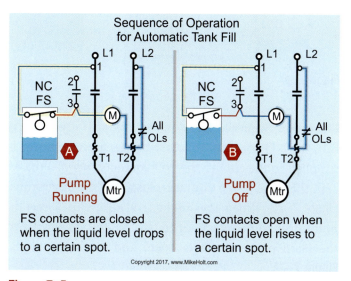

Figure 7–5

Application 2—Sump-Pump Application

NO Contacts (Dashed Line). Since the NO contacts are closed when the tank is full, they'll open when the liquid level drops. If you want to use the NO contacts of the float switch, wire A must be removed from the NC contacts and placed on the NO contacts, **Figure 7–6**. This function can be used for something like an automatic sump pump.

Unit 7 | Basic Control Circuits

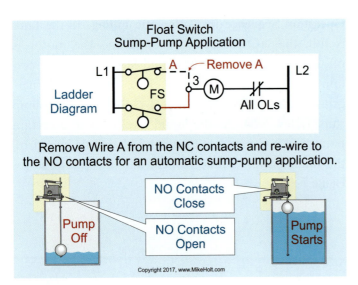

Figure 7–6

Operation Sequence for a Sump Pump. If the tank is full, the NO contacts are closed so as soon as power is supplied to the circuit, the NO contacts energize the M coil, the main power contacts close, and the pump runs, Figure 7–7B. When the liquid level drops to a certain point, the NO contacts open, the M coil de-energizes, the main power contacts open, and the pump stops. Figure 7–7A

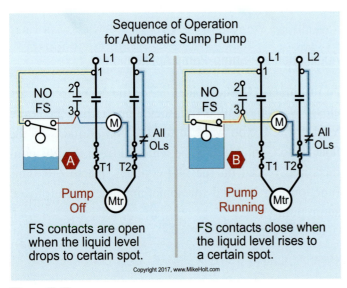

Figure 7–7

If Application 2 is used for a sump pump, it won't be a tank-type container. Sump pumps are often located in or near a small pit in the lowest part of a floor. As liquid seeps into the pit, the float will rise and at a certain point, the contacts will close, energize the coil, and start the pump. When the water is pumped out, the float lowers, the NO contacts open, de-energize the coil, and the pump stops. This automatically keeps the pump from running after the liquid is gone. This same principle is also used for sewage lift pumps.

7.2 3-Wire Control Circuits

Because 3-wire control circuits are more flexible, they're used more often than 2-wire control circuits. A 3-wire control circuit has built-in low-voltage protection. 3-wire circuits should always be used where the automatic restart of equipment after a power loss will be a danger to personnel or to the machine process.

Basic 3-Wire Control Circuit Wiring

A basic 3-wire control circuit consists of three control wires, two momentary-contact pushbutton switches, and one set of auxiliary contacts. **Figure 7–8**

Control wire 1 connects to the line side of the NC stop PB.

Control wire 2 connects the start PB (the side with a jumper from the stop PB; install one if necessary) to terminal 2 of the auxiliary contact.

Author's Comment: Some pushbutton stations come with the jumper already installed, but in most cases the jumper must be added by the installer.

Basic Control Circuits Unit 7

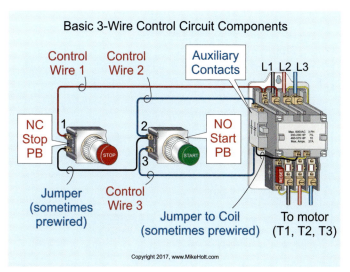

Figure 7–8

Author's Comments:

- Remember, the letter M in the circle symbol in Figure 7–9 is the coil, not the motor. The contacts marked M are the auxiliary contacts, not the motor branch-circuit power contacts.

- Notice that the start PB, stop PB, coil, and overloads are all in series with each other and this entire circuit is in parallel with the power source (motor starter L1 and L2 in this case). The entire 3-wire circuit is connected between one side of the coil and one line of the power source (L1 in this case), while the overloads are connected between the other side of the coil and the other line of the power source (L2 in this case). These points will be more important later when the 3-wire control circuit(s) become more complicated. When learning about motor controls, it's important to keep things in perspective by remembering the basics.

Control wire 3 connects the other side of the start PB (the side without a jumper) to terminal 3 of the auxiliary contact.

A NC stop PB is wired in series with the coil of the contactor and a NO start PB is wired in series with the coil, but also connected in parallel with the auxiliary contact. Figure 7–9

Sequence of Operation

A sequence of operation is a detailed list of the steps it takes to perform a task. Each action of the sequence is based directly on a previous event. For example, you're sitting in a chair and you want the light over your head turned on. To describe this process, you can simply say, "I get up and turn on the light." But if you describe it as a sequence of operation, it will be something like, "I stand up, take one step with my left leg, take one step with my right leg, raise my right arm, use my right index finger to move the switch handle to the On position, and the light comes on."

To apply this concept to the basic 3-wire control circuit, start with whatever action you're trying to accomplish. The goal is to energize and de-energize the coil. The coil must have power to operate. The overload side of the coil is already taken care of in the example with L2 through the overload relay contacts, so that one side of the coil is hot all the time, Figure 7–10A1. The OL contacts aren't opened or closed by the coil.

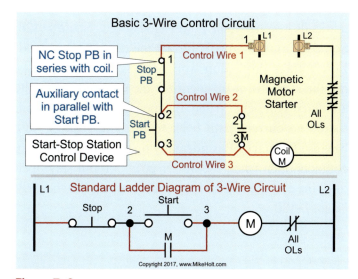

Figure 7–9

Understanding Basic Motor Controls | Mike Holt Enterprises   85

Unit 7 | Basic Control Circuits

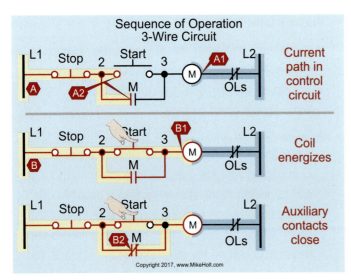

Figure 7–10

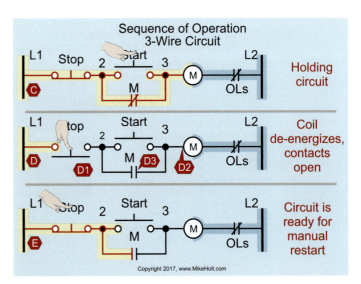

Figure 7–11

Operation from Rest (Motor not Running). In this example, there's a continuous current path from L1 of the power source, through the NC stop PB to the line side of the NO start PB, and to terminal 2 of the auxiliary contact, **Figure 7–10A2**. When the start PB is pushed, a current path is provided through the start PB to the coil, **Figure 7–10B1**, which starts the motor (the power contacts aren't shown).

The coil closes the auxiliary contacts, **Figure 7–10B2**. This closed set of contacts is the "holding circuit" or "sealing circuit." When the start PB is released as shown in **Figure 7–11C**, the auxiliary contacts stay closed and maintain a continuous current path to the coil, even though there's no longer a path through the start PB. This held-closed set of auxiliary contacts is electrically holding (or connecting) the circuit to the coil.

> **Author's Comment:** Remember that auxiliary contacts 2-3 are physically closed by the coil when it's energized. These contacts will remain closed as long as power is maintained to the coil.

Operation for Stop (Motor is Running). When the stop PB is pushed, the path to the coil is interrupted, **Figure 7–11D1**. This causes the coil to lose power, **Figure 7–11D2**. When the coil de-energizes, the auxiliary contacts open (drop out), **Figure 7–11D3**, and the motor stops. When the stop PB is released, **Figure 7–11E**, the circuit is ready to be started again.

Low-Voltage Protection. This means that if power goes off to the control circuit, the equipment won't automatically restart when power is restored, **Figure 7–12B**. Someone must manually restart the equipment instead. Low-voltage protection works the same way as pushing the stop PB; it de-energizes the coil and opens the auxiliary contacts. When the power comes back on, there's no current path back to the coil, **Figure 7–13C**, because the start PB is normally open and the auxiliary contacts open when the power goes out and stay open until the coil is energized again by pressing the start PB. **Figure 7–13D**

86 | Mike Holt Enterprises | *Understanding Basic Motor Controls*

Basic Control Circuits — Unit 7

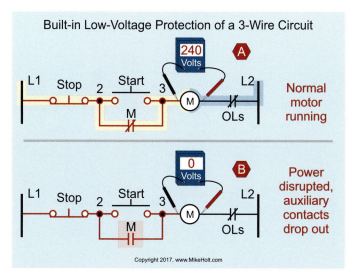

Figure 7–12

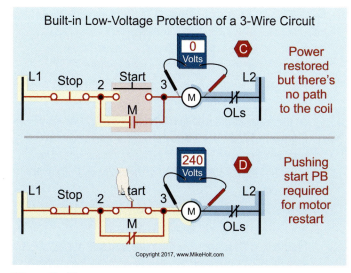

Figure 7–13

Low-voltage protection only applies to magnetic controls. It's an inherent function of 3-wire control circuits because of the use of auxiliary contacts, which are used as holding contacts (also called "sealing contacts," an "electric holding circuit," "memory contacts," or a "maintaining circuit"). This set of holding contacts is electrically held, which means they can only be closed when there's power producing the electromagnetic field which holds them closed.

Safety Function. This is what makes 3-wire control circuits safer than 2-wire control circuits. They work the same way as if a circuit breaker is turned off or tripped, or a disconnect opens. Someone operating or doing maintenance on the equipment won't be caught by surprise when the circuit breaker is reset or the equipment disconnect closes. For example, if a person is working on a lathe controlled by this type of 3-wire circuit, when the power goes out, the lathe stops. The lathe won't automatically restart when the power is restored and the worker won't be injured. The PB must be manually pushed again in order for the motor to restart.

7.3 3-Wire Circuit in a Wiring (Connection) Diagram

It's very common to find the same standard 3-wire control circuit that we just covered in **Figure 7–12** in wiring (connection) diagrams, like the one shown in **Figure 7–14**. The wiring diagram provides more of an actual picture of the components and the physical relationship between those components than do ladder diagrams, which provide more functional-type information.

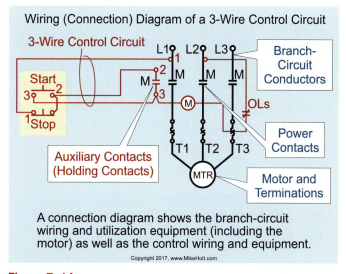

Figure 7–14

Understanding Basic Motor Controls | Mike Holt Enterprises   87

Unit 7 | Basic Control Circuits

One of the main differences between wiring diagrams and ladder diagrams is that a wiring diagram shows the branch-circuit contacts and equipment (including the motor) as well as the control circuit contacts and equipment. It's also very common to see both ladder and connection diagrams on the same schematic, **Figure 7–15**. In this figure, the 3-wire circuit is called a "common control circuit" because its power is being taken directly from L1 and L2 of the motor-starter contactor. This is also called a "tapped motor-control circuit."

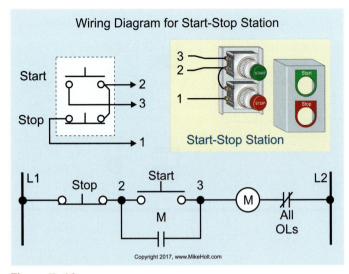

Figure 7–16

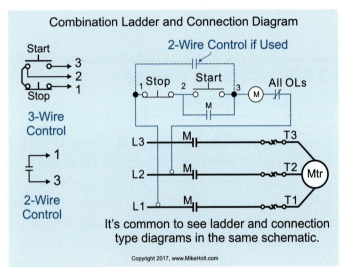

Figure 7–15

A common wiring diagram for connecting a start-stop pushbutton station to a motor starter combines a ladder diagram and a start-stop pushbutton station labeled with numbers to show where the control conductors are connected in the motor-starter enclosure or control wire cabinet. The arrowed lines indicate connections made by the installer. **Figure 7–16**

Author's Comment: The arrowed lines with terminal numbers in **Figure 7–16** aren't always shown with arrows. Plain lines with terminal numbers are also used.

Exercise: This exercise is designed to teach you how to read wiring diagrams. It will also help you learn how to trace out a control circuit and locate termination points. You need two pencils or pens to do this exercise. Start this exercise on **Figure 7–17**.

1. Place pencil one (P1) on the line side of the NC stop PB of the PB station, **Figure 7–17A1**. Place pencil two (P2) on the ladder diagram on the line side of the NC stop PB, **Figure 7–17A2**. This shows the point where the control wire with a number 1 connects between the line side of the stop PB in the PB station and L1 at the motor control starter enclosure.

2. Move P1 to the load side of the NC stop PB (PB station), which is the line side of the jumper to the start PB, **Figure 7–17B1**, and move P2 to the load side of the NC stop PB. P2 should be on the line side of the jumper to the start PB.

3. Move P1 across the jumper to the line side of the NO start PB (PB station), **Figure 7–18C1**, and move P2 across to the line side of the NO start PB, **Figure 7–18C2**. This shows that control wire 2 in the PB station connects to terminal 2 of the ladder diagram. Note that terminal 2 in the ladder diagram is connected to the auxiliary contact symbol M.

4. Move P1 across to the load side of the NO start PB, **Figure 7–18D1**, and move P2 across to the load side of the NO start PB, **Figure 7–18D2**. This has a control wire labeled with a number 3. It shows that the load side of the NO start PB is connected somewhere between terminal 3 of the auxiliary contacts and the L1 side of the coil.

Basic Control Circuits — Unit 7

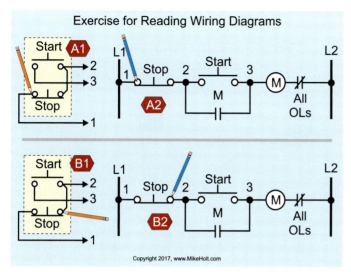

Figure 7–17

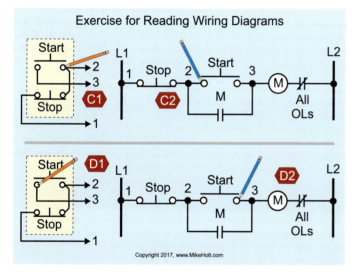

Figure 7–18

7.4 Multiple Start-Stop Pushbutton Stations

Additional start-stop stations can be added to a 3-wire control circuit. The additional stop pushbuttons are wired in series with each other and must be placed in the control circuit between the power supply (such as L1) and the line side of the start pushbutton(s) (the terminal 2 side of the auxiliary contact).

Any number of stations can be added, and pushing any one of the stop pushbuttons will de-energize the coil, Figure 7–19A. The additional start pushbuttons are wired in parallel with the other start pushbuttons. Figure 7–19B.

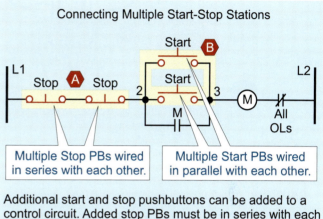

Figure 7–19

To get a better idea of how multiple start-stop stations might be laid out on a job, use a riser-type diagram, Figure 7–20. You won't normally find a riser diagram with the control equipment, but they're sometimes found on job blueprints. The lines between boxes represent the raceway and the slashes on that line represent the number of conductors. This type of riser diagram often has raceway and conductor sizes noted on it.

Figure 7–20B shows the control wire terminations and splices needed to wire this control circuit. When wiring multiple start-stop PB stations, the jumper between the load side of the stop PB and terminal 2 of the start PB must be removed from all added PB stations except the last one in the circuit.

Understanding Basic Motor Controls | Mike Holt Enterprises — 89

Unit 7 | Basic Control Circuits

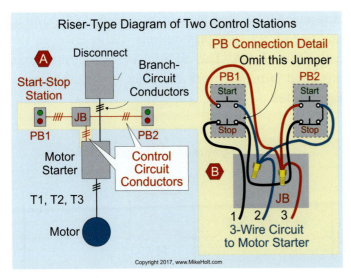

Figure 7–20

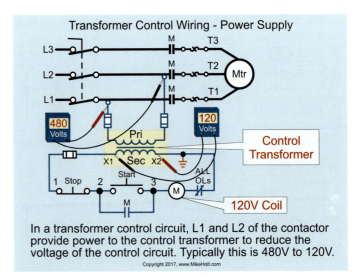

Figure 7–21

CAUTION: *Careful consideration should be given to multiple start-stop stations for a motor or equipment. Additional safety features may need to be added to the control circuit to reduce or avoid hazardous starting of equipment. For example, when setting up or doing maintenance on a machine, it can be hazardous to a person whose hand is in the machine if someone else pushes a start button at a different location. To avoid this hazard, the control circuit can be wired to lock out all of the multiple start-stop stations except the one directly at the machine being set up or serviced.*

3-Wire Control Circuit Supplied by a Control Transformer

Control transformers are frequently used in motor controls. They reduce the supply voltage (usually 480V) to control circuit voltage (usually 120V), which provides greater safety to personnel, **Figure 7–21**. Some control transformers have built-in fuseholders on the primary and/or secondary side of the transformer.

When wiring a step-down transformer, the higher voltage terminals have a letter "H" with the terminal numbers. The lower voltage terminals have the letter "X" with the terminal numbers. **Figure 7–22**

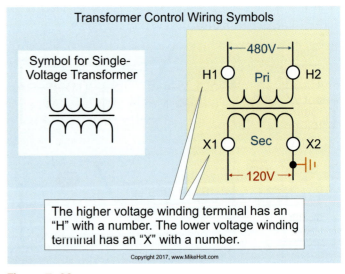

Figure 7–22

Many control transformers have several different connection configurations that allow them to be connected to a variety of primary voltages. Control transformers with a multiple voltage configuration are called "multi-tap transformers," and a transformer with two voltages is commonly called a "dual-voltage transformer." **Figure 7–23**

Basic Control Circuits — Unit 7

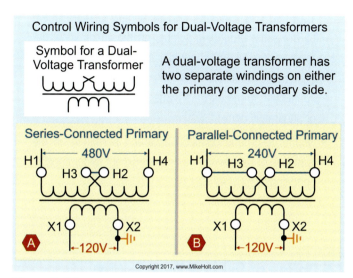

Figure 7–23

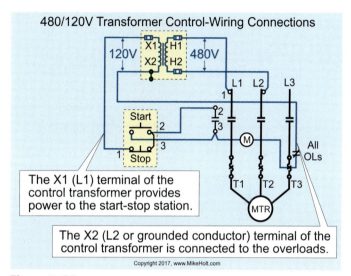

Figure 7–24

Figure 7–24 shows an example of how a 480V motor starter with a 480/120V control transformer is connected to the 120V control circuit. A stop-start PB station is wired on the L1 (X1) side and the OLs are wired on the L2 (X2) side.

A dual-voltage transformer has two separate windings on either the primary or secondary. For example, a control transformer has a primary rated for either 480V or 240V with the secondary being 120V. If the supply conductors are 480V, the two primary windings are connected in series, **Figure 7–23A**. If the supply conductors are 240V, the two primary windings are connected in parallel. **Figure 7–23B**

Author's Comment: Transformers can be used for many applications besides motor control, and sometimes it's desirable to step the voltage up, sometimes it's desirable to step the voltage down. The term "primary" always applies to the supply side of the transformer, which isn't always the high-voltage side, and the term "secondary" always applies to the load side of the transformer. The terminals with the letter H are always the higher-voltage side and the terminals with the letter X are always the lower voltage side. When dealing with control transformers, they're almost always a step-down transformer with the primary voltage higher than the secondary, so we'll refer to them as step-down transformers for this discussion. Just be aware that in a step-up transformer, the primary will be the X terminals and the secondary the H terminals.

Arrangement of a 3-Wire Control Circuit with a Neutral Conductor

Where one side of the motor control circuit is grounded, the circuit and its components must be arranged so that an accidental ground fault in the control circuit remote from the motor controller won't start the motor, or bypass manually operated shutdown devices or automatic safety shutdown devices [430.74].

CAUTION: *Wiring a start-stop station in the neutral conductor can cause accidental starting of the motor if a ground fault occurs on the load side of a start PB wired in the neutral conductor.* **Figure 7–25**

Unit 7 | Basic Control Circuits

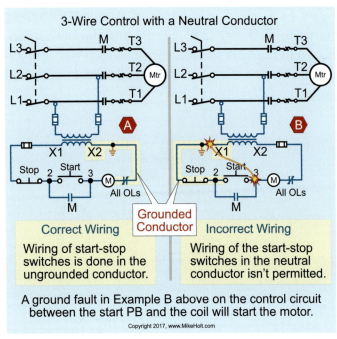

Figure 7–25

The ground fault, shown in **Figure 7–25B**, makes a connection between the neutral conductor and the metal enclosure or metal raceway (equipment grounding conductor). The metal path provided by the metal enclosure or raceway becomes a "parallel conductor" from the power source and provides a bypass around the start PB.

Author's Comments:

- The grounding symbol used on the neutral conductor in the schematics represents a connection between the secondary terminal X2 and the case of the transformer, or the case of the equipment in which the transformer is installed. It's not an actual grounding electrode installed at the transformer [250.20(B)]. Remember that metal equipment enclosures, metal raceways, and other non-current-carrying metal parts are usually connected to the equipment grounding conductor, which is connected to the earth at the electrical service or separately derived system. Similarly, a separate 120V control circuit (Class 1 circuit) has a neutral conductor and is represented by the same grounding symbol on the schematics, but there isn't a neutral conductor connection to the metal equipment enclosure. The actual grounding electrode connection to the earth is made at the electrical service or separately derived system.

- Neutral-to-ground connections aren't permitted on the load side of the service equipment except under specific conditions [250.142(B)].

7.5 Option of Using a 2- or 3-Wire Circuit in One Diagram

It's common to have a line or connection diagram that shows connection points for both a 2-wire control circuit and a 3-wire control circuit. In the **Figure 7–26** ladder diagram, the 2-wire circuit is represented by the dashed lines and identifying text, "2-Wire Control if Used." If a 3-wire circuit is used, it's connected to points 1, 2, and 3. If the 2-wire circuit is used, it's connected to points 1 and 3.

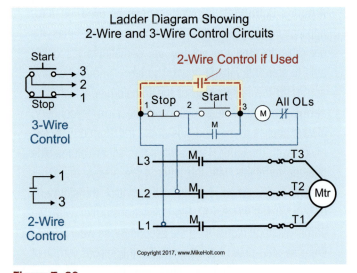

Figure 7–26

92 | Mike Holt Enterprises | *Understanding Basic Motor Controls*

Basic Control Circuits — Unit 7

Figure 7–27 shows the same motor control circuit on a wiring diagram. It doesn't show the dashed line representation of the 2-wire circuit, but it does show the same connection points for both circuits. The actual motor connections are also shown in this example.

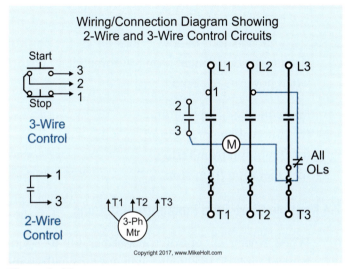

Figure 7–27

For most applications, a 2-wire and 3-wire control circuit shouldn't be used in the same control circuit unless there's an intervening device (such as a selector switch) that keeps the 2-wire and 3-wire circuits from being able to function at the same time.

CAUTION: *Careful consideration must be given to having both a 2-wire and 3-wire circuit functional in one control circuit. When the contacts of the 2-wire device in the 2-wire circuit are closed, and a power failure occurs, automatic restart of the motor can occur when power is restored. If a 2-wire device on the 2-wire circuit is connected to points 1 and 3 as was shown in* **Figure 7–26**, *the motor will start when the contacts of the 2-wire device close. Under this condition, the stop PB of the 3-wire circuit won't work. When the contacts of the 2-wire circuit are open, the start and stop PB of the 3-wire circuit will function normally.*

Unit 7—Conclusion

This unit explained basic control circuits, particularly the differences between 2-wire and 3-wire control schemes. It also covered related subjects such as:

- Holding circuits (also called "sealing circuits").
- Low-voltage protection with 3-wire control circuits, and how this improves safety.
- Reading motor control wiring (connection) diagrams.
- Pilot devices such as start-stop pushbuttons.

This unit made the important point that 3-wire control circuits are safer than 2-wire control circuits for magnetic motor control applications. This is because, if power goes out and the motorized equipment stops the equipment won't automatically restart when power is restored, as can happen with a 2-wire control circuit. The next unit also talks about an important safety subject—*NEC* overcurrent protection rules for control circuits.

Unit 7—Practice Questions

7.1 2-Wire Control Circuits

1. A 2-wire control circuit doesn't have low-voltage protection.

   (a) True
   (b) False

2. A basic 2-wire control circuit goes from a power supply, which is L1 if from the contactor (common control wiring), to a 2-wire control device such as a _____.

   (a) float switch
   (b) pressure switch
   (c) temperature switch
   (d) any of these

7.2 3-Wire Control Circuits

3. A 3-wire control circuit has built-in low-voltage protection.

   (a) True
   (b) False

4. In a basic 3-wire control circuit, the stop PB is in series with the coil, and the start PB is in parallel with the NO auxiliary contacts.

   (a) True
   (b) False

5. _____ means that if power goes off to the control circuit, the equipment won't automatically restart when power is restored.

   (a) Sequence of operation
   (b) Low-voltage protection
   (c) Operation from rest
   (d) Operation from stop

7.4 Multiple Start-Stop Pushbutton Stations

6. When wiring a control transformer for a 3-wire control circuit, the higher-voltage terminals typically have a letter _____ with the terminal numbers.

   (a) A
   (b) M
   (c) H
   (d) X

7. Where a dual-voltage control transformer is used, and the control circuit is 120V on the secondary, the _____.

   (a) dual primary windings are connected in series if 480V
   (b) dual primary windings are connected in parallel if 240V
   (c) dual primary windings are connected in parallel if 480V
   (d) a and b

Practice Questions—General

Note: The following questions are based on any part of this textbook up through this unit.

8. In **Figure 7–28**, which of the following statements is true?

    (a) The 3-wire control circuit is connected to points 1 and 3.
    (b) The 2-wire control circuit is connected to points 1 and 3.
    (c) The auxiliary contacts are used to activate the 2-wire control device.
    (d) A 2-wire control circuit can't be used to control a three-phase motor.

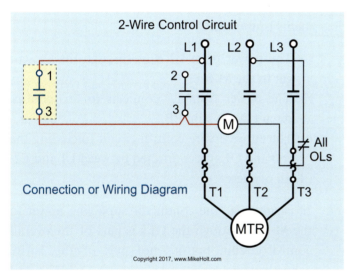

Figure 7–28

9. In **Figure 7–28**, the 2-wire control device is connected in series with the M coil.

    (a) True
    (b) False

10. In **Figure 7–28**, if the 2-wire control device is a toggle switch in the On position, and the power goes out, _____.

    (a) the toggle switch will automatically switch to the Off position
    (b) the motor will restart when the power is restored
    (c) the motor won't automatically restart when the power is restored
    (d) auxiliary contacts 2-3 will close

11. Based on **Figure 7–29**, which of the following statements is true?

    (a) As the liquid rises, the NC contacts will open.
    (b) As the liquid rises, the NC contacts will close.
    (c) Wire A indicates a sump-pump type application.
    (d) Wire A causes the auxiliary contacts to close.

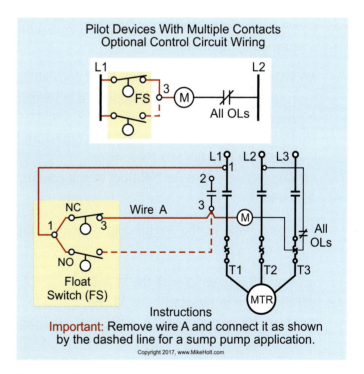

Figure 7–29

Unit 7 | Practice Questions

12. Based on **Figure 7–29**, which of the following statements is(are) true?

    (a) Coil M won't function since all the contacts have been bypassed.
    (b) Coil M will function directly from the float switch.
    (c) Coil M is in parallel with the overload contacts.
    (d) all of these

13. Based on **Figure 7–29**, which of the following statements is(are) true?

    (a) The NC float switch contacts are open when the tank is full.
    (b) The NC float switch contacts are closed when the water level drops.
    (c) The NC float switch contacts control the M coil of the magnetic motor starter.
    (d) all of these

14. Based on **Figure 7–29**, which of the following statements is(are) true about wiring the float switch for a sump-pump application?

    (a) Wire A must be connected to the M coil, which is point 3 of the auxiliary contact if a jumper is installed.
    (b) Remove wire A from the NC FS contact and reconnect it to the NO FS contact.
    (c) Connect wire A to the NC float switch contact.
    (d) a and b

15. In **Figure 7–30**, in the 3-wire control circuit, the _____.

    (a) stop PB is in series with the M coil
    (b) start PB is in series with the M coil
    (c) start PB is in parallel with the auxiliary contacts 2-3
    (d) all of these

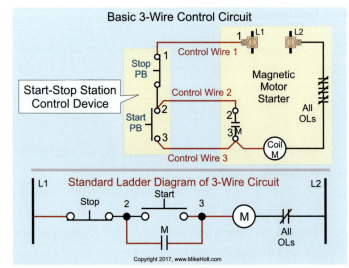

Figure 7–30

16. Based on **Figure 7–30**, which of the following statements is(are) true?

    (a) The power from L2 runs through the OLs to get to the M coil.
    (b) The power from L1 connects to this control circuit at the stop PB.
    (c) The entire 3-wire control circuit (including the coil and OLs) is connected between L1 and L2.
    (d) all of these

17. In **Figure 7–30**, the conductor supplying power to the M coil through the OLs is part of the overall control circuit, but it's not part of the 3-wire control circuit.

    (a) True
    (b) False

18. In **Figure 7–30**, if the motor isn't running, which of the following statements is true?

    (a) Pressing the start NO PB de-energizes the M coil.
    (b) After the coil energizes, the NO auxiliary contacts open.
    (c) After the coil energizes, the NO auxiliary contacts will stay closed after the start PB is released.
    (d) Pressing the stop PB energizes the M coil.

19. In **Figure 7–30**, if the motor is running, which of the following statements is true?

    (a) Pressing the NO start PB will start the motor.
    (b) The NO auxiliary contacts are closed providing a holding circuit to keep the motor running after the start PB is released.
    (c) The motor will continue running if the NC stop PB is pressed.
    (d) The motor will only run if the NO start PB is held closed.

20. In **Figure 7–30**, if the motor is running, and the power to the magnetic motor starter is interrupted, the _____.

    (a) motor will automatically restart when power is restored
    (b) NO auxiliary contacts will remain closed
    (c) motor won't restart automatically
    (d) stop PB must be pressed to restart the motor

21. In **Figure 7–31**, the primary of the control circuit transformer is connected to _____.

    (a) the stop PB and the motor OLs
    (b) L1 and L2
    (c) L1 and L3
    (d) L2 and L3

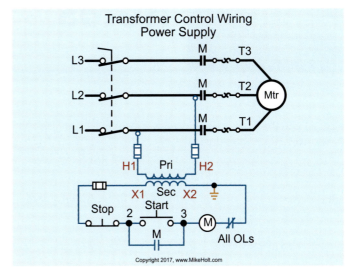

Figure 7–31

22. In **Figure 7–31**, the control transformer can be used to reduce the supply voltage to a safer level to provide greater safety to personnel.

    (a) True
    (b) False

23. In **Figure 7–31**, the 3-wire control circuit is connected to _____.

    (a) the transformer secondary terminals H1 and H2
    (b) the transformer primary terminals H1 and H2
    (c) the transformer secondary terminals L1 and L2
    (d) the transformer secondary terminals X1 and X2

24. Common voltages for a control transformer, like that shown in **Figure 7–31** are _____.

    (a) 120V primary, 480V secondary
    (b) 240V primary, 120V secondary
    (c) 480V primary, 120V secondary
    (d) b or c

Notes

Unit 8

Overcurrent Protection for Control Circuits

Unit 8—Introduction

The previous unit explained control circuit basics, particularly the important differences between 2-wire and 3-wire circuits. This unit covers a somewhat different subject; not how motor control circuits work but how they're protected against hazardous overheating in accordance with the requirements of several *National Electrical Code* rules.

8.1 Protection for Control Circuits

In many cases, the size of, number of, and location of the control circuit overcurrent protection is on the schematic, or the equipment comes with overcurrent protection already installed. The installer of the control circuits simply runs the control conductors to the pilot devices in the control enclosure.

Numerous conditions are used to determine overcurrent protection for control circuits, and many unforeseen variables can be encountered in the field. This unit describes a few basic requirements for control circuit overcurrent protection. Installers should seek additional advice from the designer, control component manufacturer, distributor, or others knowledgeable in motor control protection techniques.

In order to properly select overcurrent protection for a control circuit, it's necessary to distinguish whether the control circuit is what the *Code* refers to as a "common control circuit" or a "separate control circuit." A common control circuit is tapped from the motor branch circuit and 430.72 of the *NEC* applies. If the control circuit is from a separate source such as a panelboard, it's called a "separate control circuit" and 725.41 of the *Code* applies.

CAUTION: *In cases where opening the control circuit can create a hazard, such as the control circuit for a fire pump motor, the motor branch-circuit short-circuit and ground-fault protection device is permitted to protect the control circuit. No overload protection is required [430.72(B) Ex 1]. Article 695 of the NEC contains other special requirements for fire pumps.*

8.2 Common (Tapped) versus Separate Control Circuits

According to the *NEC*, a common (tapped) control circuit isn't considered a branch circuit. This means that either supplementary protection devices or branch-circuit protection devices are permitted to protect the control circuit [430.72(A)]. Supplementary overcurrent protection devices aren't required to be readily accessible [240.10]. They can be located inside control cabinets and motor-starter enclosures.

Unit 8 — Overcurrent Protection for Control Circuits

Overcurrent protection for a common (tapped) control circuit is based on whether the control circuit conductors stay within the motor control equipment enclosure, or extend beyond the motor control equipment enclosure. In some cases, the branch-circuit short-circuit and ground-fault protection device for the motor is permitted to protect the tapped control circuit, providing the protective device doesn't exceed the values specified in Table 430.72(B) of the *NEC*.

> **Example:** The control circuit conductor size is 14 AWG and doesn't extend beyond the motor control equipment enclosure. If the motor short-circuit ground-fault protection device is rated 100A or less, the control circuit is considered protected and no other protection is required, [Table 430.72(B), Column B], **Figure 8–1**. If the motor short-circuit ground-fault protection devices are rated more than 100A, additional protection is required for the 14 AWG control conductors [430.72(B)(1)]. In this case, protection must be afforded for the 14 AWG control conductors based on Column A of Table 430.72(B) of the NEC.

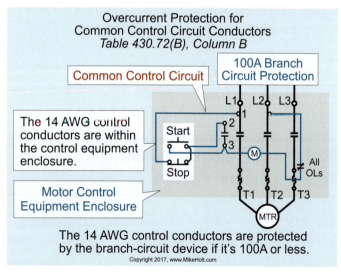

Figure 8–1

Author's Comment: Table 430.72(B), Column A, Note 1 of the *NEC* requires that conductor sizes 14 AWG and larger be protected based on the ampacity found by following the requirements of 310.15 of the *Code*. This means one should select the ampacity for the conductor from Table 310.15(B)(16) of the *NEC*, apply any derating factors that are required, and then select the protection device based on that ampacity. See Mike Holt's *Understanding the National Electrical Code, Volume 1* for more information.

On the other hand, if control conductors leave the motor control equipment enclosure and are routed to other equipment such as a start-stop station, then the motor short-circuit and ground-fault protection can't exceed the value in Column C of Table 430.72(B) of the *Code*. Using the example of 14 AWG conductors, require additional protection is required if the motor branch-circuit protective device is over 45A.

8.3 Control Conductor Sizes 16 AWG and 18 AWG

Within Motor Control Equipment Enclosure [Table 430.72(B), Column B]. The motor branch-circuit short-circuit ground-fault protection device can protect the control circuit conductors within the motor control equipment enclosure under the following conditions:

- 18 AWG control conductors are protected by the branch-circuit overcurrent protection device if the device is rated 25A or less.

- 16 AWG control conductors are protected by the branch-circuit overcurrent protection device if the device is rated 40A or less.

Overcurrent Protection for Control Circuits — Unit 8

Beyond Motor Control Equipment Enclosure [Table 430.72(B), Column C]. All 18 AWG and 16 AWG control conductors require supplemental overcurrent protection if they leave the motor control equipment enclosure. The maximum protection device size is 7A for 18 AWG and 10A for 16 AWG. **Figure 8–2**

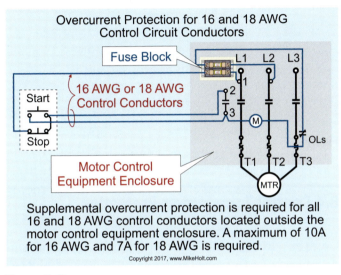

Figure 8–2

Author's Comment: It was once standard practice to allow the motor branch-circuit short-circuit and ground-fault protection device rated up to 20A to also protect control circuit conductors to a remote device (beyond the motor control equipment enclosure). This practice is no longer permitted.

Examples of Overcurrent Protection in 3-Wire Circuits

Fuse blocks can be added as an accessory device to some motor starters, or a fuse block can be added to the enclosure where the control circuit is tapped. 240V control circuits have two ungrounded conductors so two fuses are normally used, as shown in **Figure 8–3A**, but there are times when only one fuse is used for a 240V control circuit. A 120V control circuit has only one fuse in the ungrounded conductor. **Figure 8–3B**

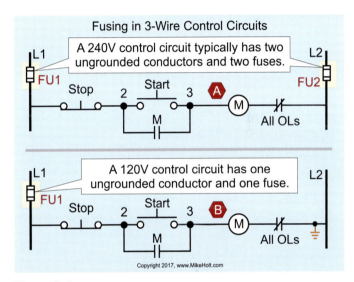

Figure 8–3

Author's Comment: Note in **Figure 8–3B** that the 120V control circuit uses an "L2" rather than an "N" for neutral or "W" for white. When a neutral conductor is used, a ground symbol is used with the L2 power line.

Unit 8 | Overcurrent Protection for Control Circuits

Separate Control Circuits—Overcurrent Protection

When the control circuit isn't tapped from the motor circuit conductor, they are considered a Class 1 remote control circuit and must be protected in accordance with 725.43 of the *National Electrical Code*. The overcurrent protection for 18 AWG control conductors must not exceed 7A, and overcurrent protection for 16 AWG control conductors must not exceed 10A, and control conductors 14 AWG and larger must be protected in accordance with their ampacity as listed in Table 310.15(B)(16). Figure 8–4

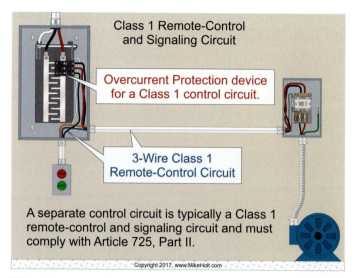

Figure 8–5

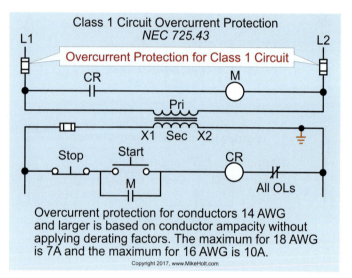

Figure 8–4

Author's Comment: Generally, conductors smaller than 14 AWG are only used by manufacturers for the internal wiring of equipment. Most field-installed control wiring is 14 AWG or larger.

A separate control circuit is typically a Class 1 non-power-limited control circuit and must comply with the requirements of Article 725, Part II of the *Code*. Figure 8–5

8.4 Control Transformer Protection

Control circuit transformers typically have a single-phase (2-wire) primary and a 2-wire secondary. Overcurrent protection is always required on the primary side of a control transformer. A single-phase, dual-voltage control transformer is still a 2-wire transformer. The size of the protection is determined by the following:

> **CAUTION:** *In cases where the opening of the control circuit will create a hazard, such as the control circuit for a fire pump motor, the motor branch-circuit short-circuit and ground-fault protection device is permitted to protect the control circuit. No other protection is required [430.72(B) Ex 1 and 430.72(C) Ex].*

Primary protection can be provided by the requirements of Table 450.3(B) of the *Code* [430.72(C)(2)]. If secondary protection is necessary, it must comply with 430.72(B) and Table 430.72(B) of the *NEC*. Overcurrent protection isn't required on the secondary side of the control transformer if:

102 | Mike Holt Enterprises | *Understanding Basic Motor Controls*

1. The size of the primary overcurrent device doesn't exceed the value determined by multiplying the appropriate maximum rating of the overcurrent device for the secondary conductor from Table 430.72(B) of the *Code* by the secondary-to-primary voltage ratio [430.72(B) Ex 2 and 725.45(D)].

Example: The control transformer is 480V-to-120V, single-phase, 2-wire. The maximum protection for a 16 AWG conductor from Table 430.72(B) of the NEC is 10A. The formula to determine the maximum primary protection size permitted is:

Protection size = Maximum Table 430.72(B) Amps x (Sec Volts/Pri Volts)

Protection size = 10A x (120V/480V)

Protection size = 2.50A, **Figure 8–6**

2. The control transformer has a primary current of 2A or less and is located in the motor control equipment enclosure, and the primary protection doesn't exceed 500 percent of the rated primary current [430.72(C)(4)].

8.5 Other Standard Control Circuit Overcurrent Protection Arrangements

- **Fusing in both primary lines and both secondary lines.** The secondary line overcurrent protection is based on Table 430.72(B), Column A of the *Code*. **Figure 8–7**

- **Fusing in both primary lines and one secondary line.** The secondary line overcurrent protection is based on Table 430.72(B), Column A of the *NEC*. **Figure 8–8**

- **Fusing in both primary lines and both secondary lines for large starters with small transformers.** This arrangement is used for coils with high VA ratings. The secondary line overcurrent protection is based on Table 430.72(B), Column A of the *Code*. **Figure 8–9**

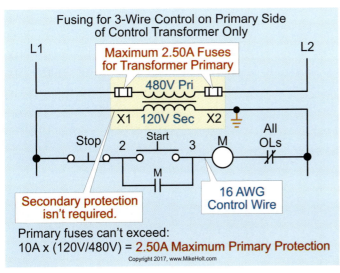

Figure 8–6

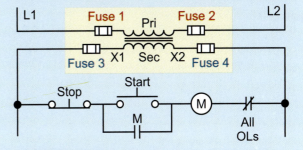

Figure 8–7

Author's Comment: Notice that this formula uses the secondary voltage divided by the primary voltage to determine a multiplier. Don't confuse this with how transformer voltages are usually stated with the primary voltage first, then the secondary voltage (480V/120V or 480V-to-120V).

Unit 8 | Overcurrent Protection for Control Circuits

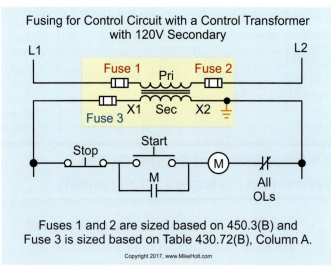

Figure 8–8

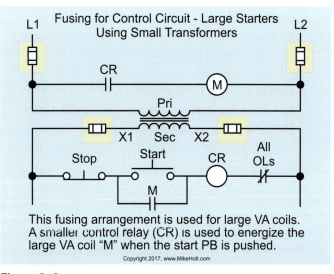

Figure 8–9

Unit 8—Conclusion

This unit explained the important subject of providing overcurrent protection for motor control circuits. Different *NEC* rules apply to common control circuits tapped from the motor power supply, and separate control circuits wired according to Article 725 of the *Code*. Subjects covered included conductor sizes, control transformers, and selecting fuses. This unit also made the important point that the *NEC* has less stringent overcurrent protection requirements in special cases where opening the control circuits can cause a hazard, such as control circuits for fire pump motors.

Unit 8—Practice Questions

Introduction

1. According to the NEC, control circuit conductors can be as small as _____ AWG.

    (a) 14
    (b) 16
    (c) 18
    (d) 20

2. In order to properly size overcurrent protection for a control circuit, it's necessary to distinguish whether the control circuit is a _____.

    (a) common (tapped) control circuit or a separate control circuit
    (b) special control circuit or a different control circuit
    (c) Class 2 or Class 3 circuit
    (d) single-phase control circuit or a three-phase branch circuit

8.2 Common (Tapped) versus Separate Control Circuits

3. According to the *NEC*, a common (tapped) control circuit is considered a branch circuit.

    (a) True
    (b) False

4. According to the *NEC*, a common (tapped) control circuit can be protected by _____.

    (a) the branch-circuit protection device supplying the motor
    (b) supplemental overcurrent protection
    (c) the OLs
    (d) a and b

8.3 Control Conductor Sizes 16 AWG and 18 AWG

5. _____ AWG control conductors located within the equipment enclosure are protected by the branch-circuit overcurrent device if it's rated 40A or less.

    (a) 14
    (b) 16
    (c) 18
    (d) 20

6. 16 AWG control conductors that extend beyond the motor control equipment enclosure must be protected with a protection device rated no more than _____.

    (a) 5A
    (b) 10A
    (c) 15A
    (d) 20A

7. Generally, conductors smaller than _____ AWG are only used by manufacturers for the internal wiring of equipment.

   (a) 14
   (b) 16
   (c) 18
   (d) 20

8. A separate control circuit is typically a _____ nonpower-limited control circuit and must comply with the requirements of Article 725, Part II of the *NEC*.

   (a) Class 1
   (b) Class 2
   (c) Class 3
   (d) Class 4

9. For a Class 1 control circuit used as a separate control circuit, control conductors 14 AWG and larger are protected at their ampacity.

   (a) True
   (b) False

8.4 Control Transformer Protection

10. Overcurrent protection is always required on the primary side of a control transformer, unless it will create a hazard such as for the control circuit for a fire pump motor.

    (a) True
    (b) False

11. In **Figure 8–10**, if the conductors on the secondary side of the control secondary are 16 AWG, and it's been determined that secondary overcurrent protection is required, the maximum overcurrent protection device will be _____.

    (a) 5A
    (b) 7A
    (c) 10A
    (d) 15A

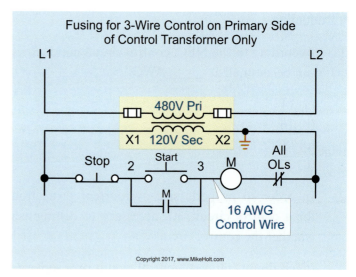

Figure 8–10

12. In **Figure 8–10**, if 16 AWG control wiring is used on the secondary side of the control transformer, secondary overcurrent protection for the 2-wire supply to the control circuit isn't required if the primary protection device doesn't exceed 10A x (120V/480V).

    (a) True
    (b) False

UNIT 9

Indicator (Pilot) Lights and Illuminated Pushbuttons

Unit 9—Introduction

Unit 8 explained overcurrent protection rules for motor control circuits. This unit returns to an operational subject and covers the uses of pilot lights (also called indicator lights) and illuminated pushbuttons. Both types of devices are used to indicate the status of a motor or associated equipment. For example, a green pilot light can mean the motor is running, while a red pilot light indicates the motor is stopped.

9.1 Pilot (Indicator) Lights

Pilot lights are also called indicator lights. Three types of lamps are commonly used in pilot lights:

- Incandescent.
- Neon—lasts longer than incandescent but provides less light.
- Light-Emitting Diode (LED)—provides the longest lamp life and is the least susceptible to damage from vibration and shock.

Pilot lights are sometimes installed so that the full voltage of the control circuit is applied to the lamp, **Figure 9–1A**. Indicator lights rated either 240V or 120V are very common in motor control circuits. However, some LED lamps and incandescent lamps aren't rated for 120V. They require a lower voltage such as 6V, 12V, or 24V.

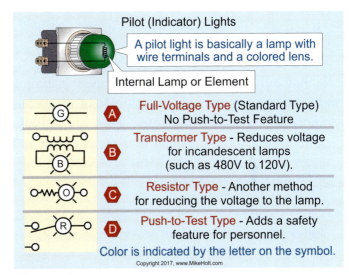

Figure 9–1

There are two common ways of supplying reduced voltage to the lamp itself:

- **Transformer Built into the Pilot (Indicator) Light.** Incandescent lamps operating at less than the rated voltage burn cooler and have extended life. **Figure 9–1B**

- **Resistor Built into the Pilot (Indicator) Light.** The voltage drop across the resistor reduces the voltage and current to the level needed for the lamp. **Figure 9–1C**

Figure 9–1D is a pilot (indicator) light that has the capacity to test the lamp to make sure it's functional. This adds an extra degree of safety for the equipment operator and maintenance personnel.

Understanding Basic Motor Controls | Mike Holt Enterprises

Unit 9 — Indicator (Pilot) Lights and Illuminated Pushbuttons

The wiring diagrams often specify a color for the pilot (indicator) light. The color to use is indicated by a letter in the pilot (indicator) light symbol. The following letters are typically used with these colors:

A = Amber
B = Blue
C = Clear
G = Green
R = Red
O = Opal (White)

Pilot (indicator) lights are frequently used in motor controls to indicate the state or condition of the circuit components as well as the motor. They can indicate the direction of rotation, status of a motor, when and if timers are functioning, the status of reduced voltage starters, and alarm conditions.

Author's Comment: There's no standard color code for the use of pilot (indicator) lights. For example, we're familiar with traffic signals that use green for "go" and red for "stop," and some apply this to motor controls and use green for "run" and red for "stop." On the other hand, some consider red as "danger" so red is used for "run" and green or another color may be used to indicate "stop."

9.2 Typical Applications for Pilot Lights in Control Circuits

Most pilot (indicator) lights operate at the full voltage of the control circuit and are connected between L1 and L2 (remember L2 can also be a neutral), **Figure 9–2**. **Figure 9–2A** shows a 120V pilot (indicator) light connected with an open switch. When the switch is closed the pilot (indicator) light receives the full voltage of the control circuit (120V) and the pilot (indicator) light comes on, **Figure 9–2B**. When the switch is released, the pilot (indicator) light goes off.

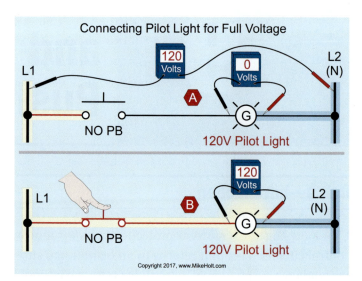

Figure 9–2

If the 120V pilot (indicator) light is incorrectly wired in series with the 120V coil shown in **Figure 9–3A**, it either won't illuminate, or perhaps a slight glow will be visible when you press the switch, because neither the coil nor the pilot (indicator) light is receiving 120V. The distribution of voltage in a series circuit depends on the relative resistances of the components wired in series.

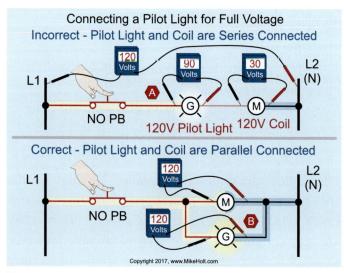

Figure 9–3

Indicator (Pilot) Lights and Illuminated Pushbuttons — Unit 9

If the coil has twice the resistance of the pilot (indicator) light, the coil will receive two-thirds of the voltage (90V) and the pilot (indicator) light will receive one-third of the voltage (30V). Probably neither one will work properly under this condition. If the 120V pilot (indicator) light is connected in parallel with the coil, as shown in **Figure 9–3B**, pressing the switch allows each device to receive 120V and both will energize and de-energize at the same time.

Pilot Light to Indicate Motor Running. When a pilot (indicator) light is used in the control circuit to indicate that the motor is running, it's typically wired in parallel with the starter coil, **Figure 9–4**. It's connected to terminal 3 of the auxiliary contact and to L2, as shown in the pictorial diagram in **Figure 9–4A**. **Figure 9–4B** shows the standard ladder-type diagram for the same control circuit. When the coil is energized, the M holding contact 2-3 maintains the circuit to the pilot (indicator) light, as it does to the coil, and the lamp stays on. **Figure 9–5**

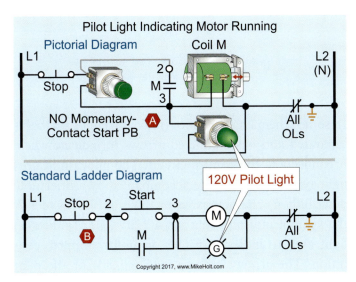

Figure 9–4

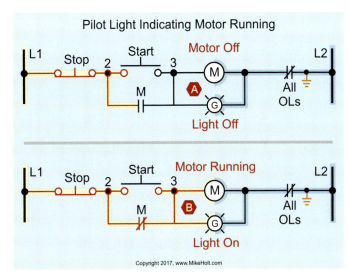

Figure 9–5

Author's Comment: Some wiring diagrams show the L2 (or neutral) side of the pilot (indicator) light connected between the overload relays and the coil. Other wiring diagrams show the pilot (indicator) light connected directly to L2 (on the other side of the overload relay). Both methods work because if an overload occurs and the NC overload relay contacts open, the coil de-energizes, dropping out auxiliary contacts 2 and 3, which in turn opens the L1 side of the pilot (indicator) light. The disadvantage to connecting the pilot (indicator) light terminal directly to L2 is that if the NC overload contacts are open, the pilot (indicator) light will still light when the start button is pressed down even though the magnetic starter coil isn't energized. This provides a false indication to the operator if he or she isn't within sight of the driven machinery.

Figure 9–6 is a typical wiring diagram of a pilot (indicator) light in a start-stop pushbutton station. The numbers at the start-stop station correspond with the terminal numbers on the line diagram. Notice that this is a 3-wire control circuit and everything operates in a typical fashion. The only modification is installing an L2 conductor to supply the other terminal of the pilot (indicator) light.

Unit 9 — Indicator (Pilot) Lights and Illuminated Pushbuttons

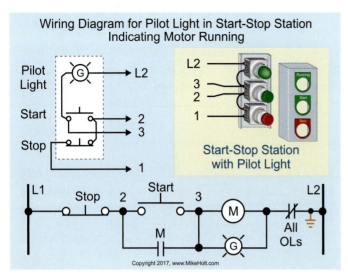

Figure 9–6

Pilot Light Indicating Motor Stopped. An additional set of auxiliary contacts can be added to the motor starter assembly. In this case we're adding a set of NC auxiliary contacts. These contacts are connected in series with the line side of the pilot (indicator) light. The other side of the pilot (indicator) light is connected to L2 (or the neutral), Figure 9–7. The pilot (indicator) light is illuminated when the coil isn't energized.

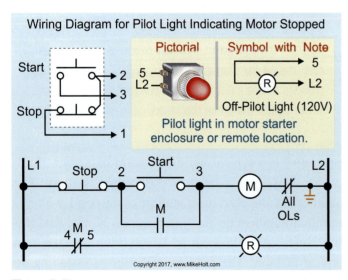

Figure 9–7

When the start PB is pushed, the NC auxiliary contacts 4-5 open, the NO auxiliary contacts 2-3 close forming the holding circuit, and the coil remains energized after the start PB is released, Figure 9–8. The pilot (indicator) light remains off because the coil is electrically holding the NC auxiliary contacts 4-5 open. When the stop PB is pushed, the coil de-energizes, the NO set of auxiliary contacts 4-5 close, and the pilot (indicator) light comes on again while the motor is off.

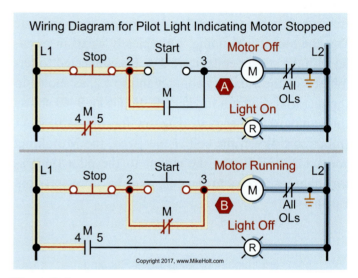

Figure 9–8

In some schematics, the pilot (indicator) light symbol is separated and has numbered arrows to indicate where it connects in the control circuit. The pilot (indicator) light symbol may also be accompanied by a brief note describing its characteristics or function. In Figure 9–7, the symbol indicates that it's a 120V pilot (indicator) light used to indicate an Off, or motor stopped, condition. The arrows indicate that one side of the pilot (indicator) light connects to point 5 and the other side connects to L2.

110 | Mike Holt Enterprises | *Understanding Basic Motor Controls*

Indicator (Pilot) Lights and Illuminated Pushbuttons — Unit 9

Author's Comment: Remember that motor control schematics seldom show the location of devices, just the electrical connections. The pilot (indicator) light can be mounted directly on the enclosure or at another location with the same wiring termination. **Figure 9–9**

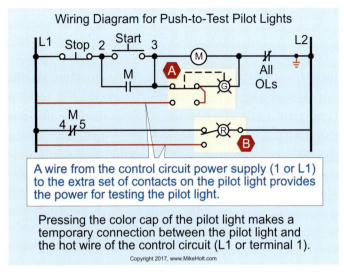

Figure 9–10

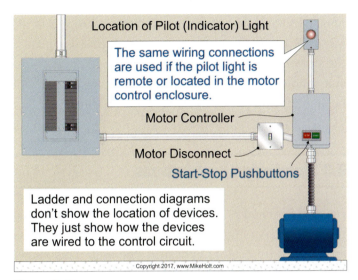

Figure 9–9

Push-to-Test. Push-to-test pilot (indicator) lights add an additional degree of safety for the operator and maintenance personnel. For example, if a pilot (indicator) light that indicates when a motor is running burns out, someone might assume that the motor is off when it isn't. **Figure 9–10** shows two push-to-test pilot (indicator) lights on the same control circuit.

Figure 9–11A shows the wiring for a green push-to-test pilot (indicator) light to indicate a motor running condition. Note that the dashed line in **Figure 9–11A** shows the mechanical interlock between the contacts and the lamp. The green pilot (indicator) light looks like two devices in the diagram but is really just one.

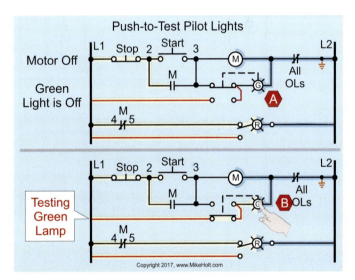

Figure 9–11

Understanding Basic Motor Controls | Mike Holt Enterprises

Unit 9 | Indicator (Pilot) Lights and Illuminated Pushbuttons

Figure 9–12B is another symbol for a red push-to-test pilot (indicator) light for a motor stopped condition. The push-to-test feature is simply an extra set of contacts (or an extra terminal) for the connection of the hot wire of the control circuit (L1 or 1). The test for both pilot (indicator) lamps is performed by pushing the color cap of the pilot (indicator) light. This opens the NC portion of the pilot (indicator) light and makes contact with the hot wire of the control circuit to provide temporary power to the lamp, which will light if it's working. Releasing the pilot (indicator) light returns it to its normal position in the control circuit.

A pilot (indicator) light is frequently used to indicate the running or non-running condition of a motor. However, the pilot (indicator) light actually only monitors the state of the coil that operates the magnetic starter that, in turn, operates the motor. For this reason, situations may occur when a remote pilot (indicator) light indicates that a motor is running when, in fact, the motor isn't running. Mechanical or electrical problems can occur at the motor or inside the motor power circuit that don't cause the starter to drop out through an overload or short-circuit condition. Likewise, a pilot (indicator) light may not be illuminated because the lamp is burned out.

9.3 Illuminated Pushbuttons

Figure 9–13 shows several symbols for an illuminated pushbutton. An illuminated PB combines a pushbutton and a pilot (indicator) light into one unit. This allows a two-unit pushbutton station to be used instead of a three-unit pushbutton station. It still takes a 3-wire control circuit plus another conductor to provide the L2 (neutral) for the other side of the pilot (indicator) light.

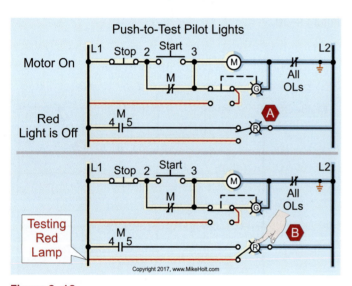

Figure 9–12

Author's Comment: Push-to-test pilot (indicator) lights must be placed in control circuits so that using the push-to-test feature doesn't interfere with other parts of the control circuit.

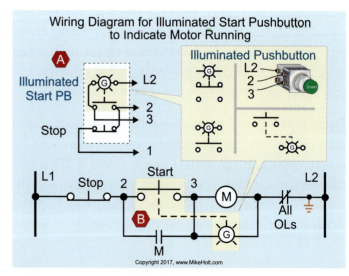

Figure 9–13

Indicator (Pilot) Lights and Illuminated Pushbuttons — Unit 9

Notice that the illuminated start PB in the wiring diagram in **Figure 9–13A** has symbols similar to a NO pushbutton. The illuminated start PB in the ladder diagram, **Figure 9–13B**, looks like the circuit we used for a separate start PB and a separate pilot (indicator) light, except there's a mechanical interlock symbol tying them together to indicate one device. **Figures 9–13A and 9–13B** represents the same device.

Pushing the illuminated start PB in **Figure 9–14** energizes the coil, closing the NO auxiliary holding contacts 2-3. This keeps terminal 3 energized, which is connected to the pilot (indicator) light in the start PB, so the pilot (indicator) light is on whenever the auxiliary holding contacts are closed. Pushing the stop PB de-energizes the coil, opening auxiliary holding contacts 2-3, and the start pilot (indicator) light goes off.

CAUTION: *Again, don't ever make a critical determination that a motor is running or not running based only on the status of a pilot (indicator) light, especially in situations that involve safety. Pilot (indicator) lights should only be used as a convenient reference, and not be relied upon to determine a safe or unsafe condition as far as the motor's operational state is concerned. This applies to separate pilot (indicator) lights as well as illuminated pushbuttons.*

Unit 9—Conclusion

This unit explained some of the uses for pilot (indicator) lights and illuminated pushbuttons in motor control circuits. It covered types and colors of lamps, typical applications of pilot lights and illuminated pushbuttons, symbols used on wiring diagrams, and a special safety application called "push-to-test." This unit made the important point that pilot (indicator) lights should be used as a convenient reference, but never relied upon to make a critical determination that a motor is either running or not running.

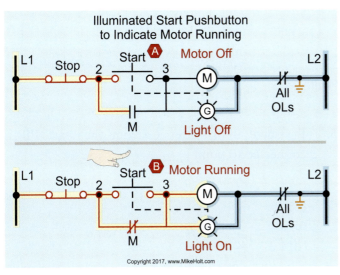

Figure 9–14

UNIT 9 Practice Questions

Unit 9—Practice Questions

9.1 Pilot (Indicator) Lights

1. _____ lamps are commonly used in pilot lights.

   (a) Incandescent
   (b) Neon
   (c) LED
   (d) any of these

2. There's no standard color code for the use of pilot (indicator) lights.

   (a) True
   (b) False

9.2 Typical Applications for Pilot Lights in Control Circuits

3. In **Figure 9–15**, letter A from the pilot light is connected to point _____.

   (a) 1
   (b) 2
   (c) 3
   (d) L2

4. In **Figure 9–15**, letter B from the start PB is connected to point _____.

   (a) 1
   (b) 2
   (c) 3
   (d) L2

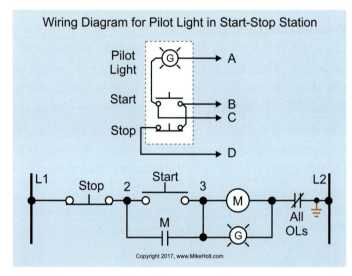

Figure 9–15

5. In **Figure 9–15**, letter C from the start PB is connected to point _____.

   (a) 1
   (b) 2
   (c) 3
   (d) L2

6. In **Figure 9–15**, letter D from the stop PB is connected to point _____.

   (a) L1
   (b) 2
   (c) 3
   (d) L2

Practice Questions — Unit 9

7. Based on **Figure 9–15**, which of the following statements is correct?

   (a) The pilot light is off when the motor is running.
   (b) The pilot light comes on when the stop PB is pressed.
   (c) The pilot light comes on when the motor is running.
   (d) The coil isn't energized when the pilot light is on.

8. In **Figure 9–15**, the G in the pilot light symbol most likely indicates _____.

   (a) go
   (b) a green light
   (c) a coil
   (d) a gray light

9. In **Figure 9–16**, letter E from the green pilot light is connected to point _____.

   (a) 1
   (b) 2
   (c) 3
   (d) L2

10. In **Figure 9–16**, letter D from the start PB is connected to point _____.

    (a) 2
    (b) 3
    (c) 4
    (d) 5

11. In **Figure 9–16**, letter C from the start PB is connected to point _____.

    (a) 1
    (b) 2
    (c) 3
    (d) 4

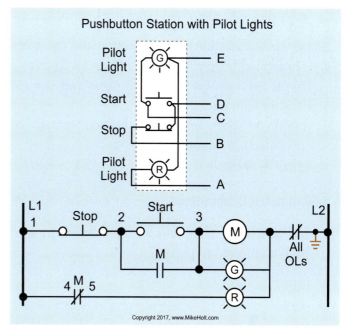

Figure 9–16

12. In **Figure 9–16**, letter B from the stop PB is connected to point _____.

    (a) 1
    (b) 2
    (c) 3
    (d) 4

13. In **Figure 9–16**, letter A from the red pilot light is connected to point _____.

    (a) 2
    (b) 3
    (c) 4
    (d) 5

14. In **Figure 9–16**, the red pilot light is on when the motor isn't running.

    (a) True
    (b) False

Understanding Basic Motor Controls | Mike Holt Enterprises

Unit 9 | Practice Questions

15. In **Figure 9–16**, when the start PB is pushed _____.

    (a) the NO auxiliary contacts close and the green pilot light comes on
    (b) the NC auxiliary contacts open and the red pilot light goes out
    (c) the M coil remains energized because M contacts 2-3 close
    (d) all of these

9.3 Illuminated Pushbuttons

16. In **Figure 9–17**, letter A from the illuminated start PB is connected to point _____.

    (a) 1
    (b) 2
    (c) 3
    (d) L2

17. In **Figure 9–17**, letter B from the illuminated start PB is connected to point _____.

    (a) 1
    (b) 2
    (c) 3
    (d) L2

18. In **Figure 9–17**, letter C from the illuminated start PB is connected to point _____.

    (a) 1
    (b) 2
    (c) 3
    (d) L2

19. In **Figure 9–17**, letter D from the stop PB is connected to point _____.

    (a) 1
    (b) 2
    (c) 3
    (d) L2

20. In **Figure 9–17**, which of the following statements is correct?

    (a) The red pilot light indicates the motor is stopped.
    (b) The green pilot light will stay on only while the NO start PB is in the NC position.
    (c) The green pilot light will remain on after the NO start PB is pressed and released.
    (d) The green pilot light will come on when the stop PB is pressed.

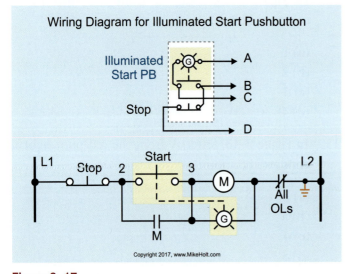

Figure 9–17

UNIT 10 — Selector Switches and Truth Tables

Unit 10—Introduction

The previous unit explained pilot (indicator) lights and illuminated pushbuttons. This unit addresses another type of control device called a "selector switch." Selector switches can have either two or three positions.

Selector switches are very common in control wiring. They're used to open and close a control circuit, or a portion of a control circuit. A selector switch is rotated by hand or key, rather than being pushed like a pushbutton switch. Selector switches usually have two or three possible maintained-contact positions. There are also selector switches that have spring-loaded momentary-contact positions or a combination of maintained-contact positions and momentary-contact positions.

10.1 Truth Tables

Graphic elements called "truth tables" or "target tables" are used to indicate the functions performed by different selector switch settings. These tables show the position of the switch contacts in relation to the switch positions. Figure 10–1

10.2 Two-Position Selector Switch

Figure 10–1A shows a two-position maintained-contact selector switch symbol. Figure 10–1B shows the associated truth table. A1 and A2 are the wire terminals for the contacts. J and K indicate positions of the switch handle.

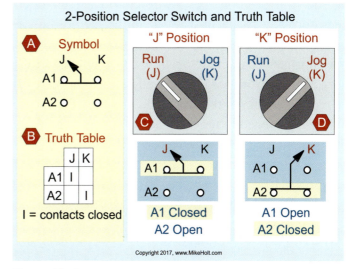

Figure 10–1

The truth table, Figure 10–1B, reads, In position J, contacts A1 are closed and contacts A2 are open, Figure 10–1C. In position K, contacts A1 are open and contacts A2 are closed, Figure 10–1D. The note under the truth table states, "I = contacts closed." Sometimes an X is used instead of an I.

Author's Comment: J and K are generic representations of functions depending on the application. For example J = Hand (manual) and K = Automatic. Another common application is J = Run and K = Jog, which is shown in Figure 10–1C.

Understanding Basic Motor Controls | Mike Holt Enterprises

Unit 10 — Selector Switches and Truth Tables

Run-Jog Application. One application for a two-position selector switch is to add a Run-Jog function to a basic 3-wire control circuit. "Jogging" (also called "Inching") is defined as the momentary operation of a motor from rest in order to make small movements of the driven machine. In this example, the A1 contacts are wired in series with control wire 2, and no wires are connected to the A2 contacts, **Figure 10–2**. While in the Run position, the 3-wire control circuit operates normally, **Figure 10–3**. While in the Jog position as shown in **Figure 10–4**, the current path to terminal 2 of the auxiliary contacts is open, which keeps the auxiliary contacts from holding the coil in when the start PB is pushed. While in the Jog mode, the start PB can be pushed or tapped to move or inch the equipment along in small increments. **Figure 10–5**

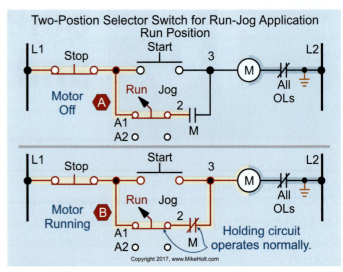

Figure 10–3

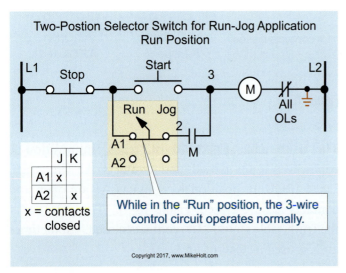

Figure 10–2

Author's Comment: Jogging (inching) can also be done without selector switches. Other common methods of jogging include selector switch pushbuttons, and the use of control relays (see Unit 18).

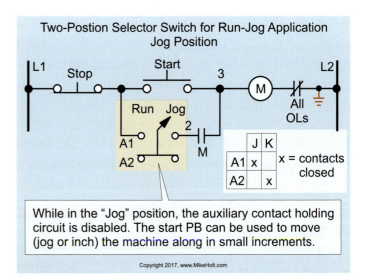

Figure 10–4

10.3 Three-Position Selector Switch

Figure 10–6A shows a three-position selector switch symbol. **Figure 10–6B** shows the associated truth table. J, K, and L indicate positions of the handle. A1 and A2 are the wire terminals for the contacts.

118 | Mike Holt Enterprises | *Understanding Basic Motor Controls*

Selector Switches and Truth Tables — Unit 10

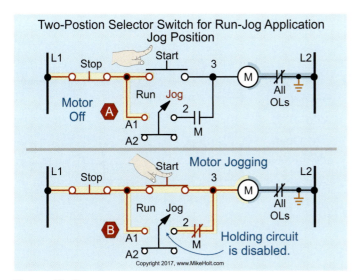

Figure 10–5

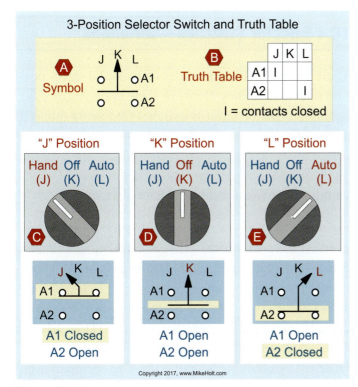

Figure 10–6

The truth table, Figure 10–6B, reads, In position J, contacts A1 are closed and contacts A2 are open, Figure 10–6C. In position K, all contacts are open, Figure 10–6D. In position L, contacts A1 are open and contacts A2 are closed, Figure 10–6E. The note under the truth table states, "I = contacts closed."

Author's Comment: J, K, and L are generic representations of functions depending on the application. For example, a common application is J = Hand (manual), K = Off, and L = Automatic. The Hand-Off-Auto application for a three-position selector switch is often called "HOA."

Three-position selector switches are commonly used with a 2-wire control circuit, where the motor starter is operated manually as well as automatically. For example, a sump-pump motor can be controlled automatically by a float switch, and manually by an HOA (Hand-Off-Automatic) selector switch. Figure 10–7

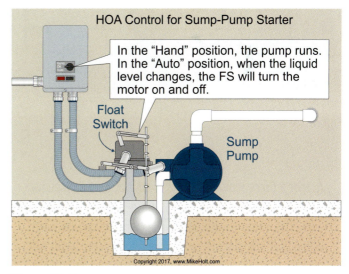

Figure 10–7

Understanding Basic Motor Controls | Mike Holt Enterprises

Figure 10–8A shows that when the selector switch is in the J (Hand or Manual) position, the starter coil is energized and the pump runs. While in the Manual position J, the motor runs regardless of the liquid level because the float switch is bypassed. When the selector switch is in the K (Off) position, Figure 10–8B, the coil is de-energized and can't be energized by the float switch. In the L (Automatic) position, Figure 10–9, the coil is energized when the liquid level rises to the point where the contacts in the float switch close, Figure 10–9C1, and the pump continues to run until the liquid level drops enough for the float switch contacts to open again. Figure 10–9C2

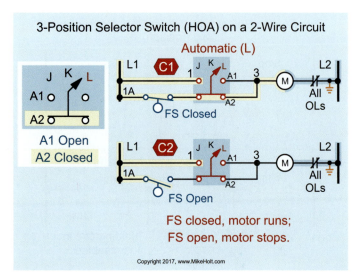

Figure 10–9

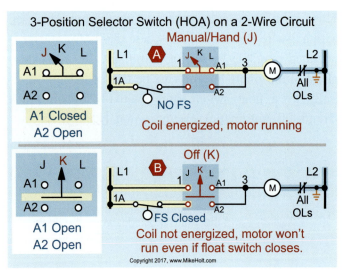

Figure 10–8

Author's Comment: In liquid level control, the sump pump is used to remove rising liquid from a room, pit, or other area. This same 2-wire circuit configuration can be used with a float switch that's set to operate the pump when the liquid level drops. For example, in a livestock-watering tank, as the animals drink the water, the float switch closes when the water drops to a predetermined level, and the pump motor starts to fill the tank. When the water level rises, the float switch opens and cuts off the pump.

10.4 Selector Switches—Variations

There are many different styles of two- and three- position selector switches. Here are some examples of other common types of selector switches frequently found in control circuits.

Variations for Two-Position Selector Switches

Figure 10–10 shows some common variations for two-position selector switch symbols. Some manufacturers use a "V" type basic symbol to represent their two-position selector switches. For example, Figure 10–10A1 shows the V type symbol representing a maintained-contact two-position selector switch. This selector switch was covered earlier in this unit. See Figure 10–1. Different symbols are added to the V to represent other types of two-position selector switches. Figures 10–10A2 and 10–10A3 represent momentary-contact selector switches. An arrow is added to the basic V symbol to represent the momentary-contact function of these types of selector switches.

Selector Switches and Truth Tables — Unit 10

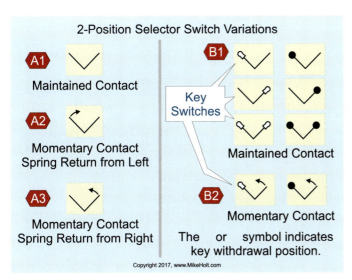

Figure 10–10

Figure 10–10A2 represents a momentary-contact selector switch with a spring return from the left. Figure 10–10A3 represents a momentary-contact selector switch with a spring return from the right.

A key-operated selector switch is another common method of operating a selector switch. Figure 10–10B1 shows several examples of key-operated maintained-contact selector switches. Figure 10–10B2 shows examples of key-operated momentary-contact selector switches. The operation of these momentary-contact selector switches is very similar to the operation of using a key to start a car.

The position of the key symbol (keyhole or black dot) indicates which position(s) the key must be in before it can be removed.

Author's Comment: These symbols aren't always found on control schematics. They're often found in manufacturer's literature or catalogs to help make the selection process for the type of selector switch needed easier. The symbols that manufacturers use can vary but they're excellent sources of information on most devices and components used in motor control circuits.

Another variation that can be found in a two-position selector switch is how the contacts are represented in a control circuit. Figures 10–11A and 10–11B represent the same selector switch. Figure 10–11A appears as a single-break maintained-contact selector switch used to toggle between coil F and coil R. Figure 10–11B is a similar selector switch incorporating a double-break device. Notice the jumper on the left side of the selector switch between the NC and NO contacts. Both representations are showing the same application.

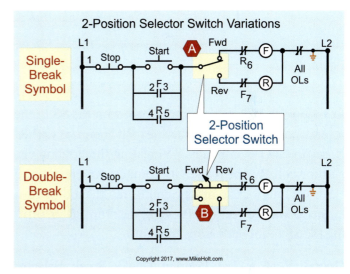

Figure 10–11

Operation of a Two-Position Single-Break Selector Switch. Figure 10–12A shows the ladder diagram with the motor off. In Figure 10–12B, with the SS in the forward position, pressing the start PB energizes coil F, closes the NO F contacts 2-3 creating the holding circuit for coil F, opens the NC contacts F7 creating an electrical interlock which disables coil R, and the motor runs in the forward direction. Pressing the stop PB or turning the SS to reverse stops the motor.

Understanding Basic Motor Controls | Mike Holt Enterprises

Unit 10 — Selector Switches and Truth Tables

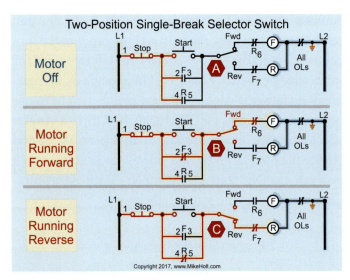

Figure 10–12

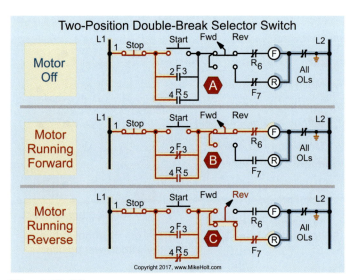

Figure 10–13

In **Figure 10–12C**, if the motor is off, with the SS in the reverse position, pressing the start PB energizes coil R, closes the NO R contacts 4-5 creating the holding circuit for coil R, opens the NC contacts R6 creating an electrical interlock to disable coil F, and the motor runs in the forward direction. Pressing the stop PB or turning the SS to forward stops the motor.

Operation of a Two-Position Double-Break Selector Switch. The operation of the circuit in **Figure 10–13** is identical to the one for the single-break selector switch in **Figure 10–12**. **Figure 10–13A** shows the ladder diagram with the motor off. In **Figure 10–13B**, with the SS in the forward position, pressing the start PB energizes coil F, closes the NO F contacts 2-3 creating the holding circuit for coil F, opens the NC contacts F7 creating an electrical interlock to disable coil R, and the motor runs in the forward direction. Pressing the stop PB or turning the SS to reverse stops the motor.

In **Figure 10–13C**, if the motor is off, with the SS in the reverse position, pressing the start PB energizes coil R, closes the NO R contacts 4-5 creating the holding circuit for coil R, opens the NC contacts R6 creating an electrical interlock to disable coil F, and the motor runs in the forward direction. Pressing the stop PB or turning the SS to forward stops the motor.

Variations for Three-Position Selector Switches

The V type symbol with added components can be used to represent the same operational features as a two-position selector switch in a three-position selector switch. The arrow still represents the momentary contacts, no arrow indicates maintained contacts. The black dot or keyhole represents a key-operated function. With three-position selector switches, it's possible to have maintained contacts, momentary contacts, and key operation all on the same device. **Figure 10–14** shows several examples of three-position selector switch symbols:

Selector Switches and Truth Tables — Unit 10

1. Maintained contacts in all three positions. See **Figure 10–14**.
2. Key operated, maintained contacts in all three positions.
3. Momentary contact—spring return from left, maintained contact to right.
4. Momentary contact—spring return from right, maintained contact to left.
5. Momentary contact—spring return to center from both sides.
6. Key operated, momentary contact—spring return to center from both sides.

Author's Comment: There are also four-position selector switches available with the same features.

Unit 10—Conclusion

This unit explained some of the uses for two- and three-position selector switches. It explained how to read a truth table to determine what the contacts do in each position of the selector switch. It explained how a selector switch can be used on a 3-wire control circuit in a jogging (inching) application. It also used a selector switch on a 2-wire circuit for an HOA application.

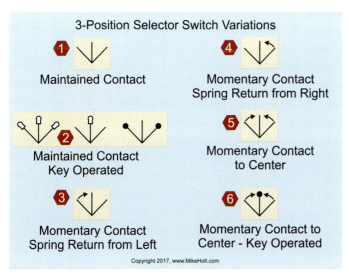

Figure 10–14

UNIT 10 Practice Questions

Unit 10—Practice Questions

10.1 Truth Tables

1. Selector switches use _____ to show the position of switch contacts in relation to the switch position.

   (a) truth tables
   (b) target tables
   (c) site maps
   (d) a or b

10.2 Two-Position Selector Switch

2. In **Figure 10–15**, when the maintained-contact selector switch is in position K, the _____.

   (a) A1 contacts are closed
   (b) A1 contacts are open
   (c) A2 contacts are closed
   (d) b and c

3. In **Figure 10–15**, when the maintained-contact selector switch is in position J, the _____.

   (a) A1 contacts are closed
   (b) A2 contacts are open
   (c) A1 contacts are open
   (d) a and b

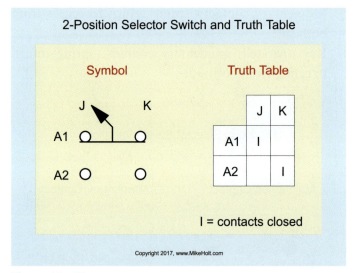

Figure 10–15

4. In **Figure 10–16**, letter C from the selector switch is connected to point _____.

   (a) 1
   (b) 2
   (c) 3
   (d) L2

5. In **Figure 10–16**, letter B from the start PB is connected to point _____.

   (a) 1
   (b) 2
   (c) 3
   (d) L2

Practice Questions — Unit 10

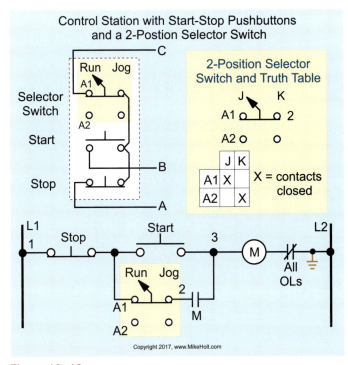

Figure 10–16

6. In **Figure 10–16**, letter A from the stop PB is connected to point _____.

   (a) 1
   (b) 2
   (c) 3
   (d) L2

7. In **Figure 10–16**, when the A2 contacts are closed, the 3-wire circuit _____.

   (a) is in a jogging mode
   (b) is in the normal run mode
   (c) won't function in any mode
   (d) will start the motor if the stop PB is pressed

8. In **Figure 10–16**, when the selector switch contacts A1 are in the closed position, pressing the start PB will _____.

   (a) start the motor normally
   (b) jog the motor
   (c) create a short circuit
   (d) stop the motor

Practice Questions—General

Note: The following questions are based on any part of this textbook up through this unit.

9. Based on **Figure 10–17**, which of the following statements is(are) correct?

   (a) In the jogging mode, the red pilot light will be on.
   (b) In the jogging mode, the green light will light as long as the start PB is pressed.
   (c) In the jogging mode, the A2 contacts of the selector switch are closed.
   (d) all of these

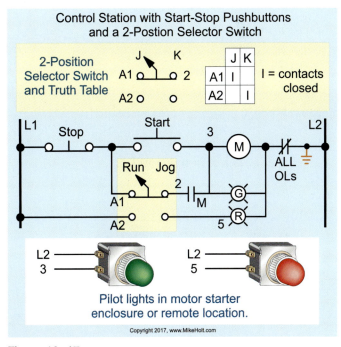

Figure 10–17

Understanding Basic Motor Controls | Mike Holt Enterprises

Unit 10 | Practice Questions

10. In **Figure 10–17**, if the selector switch is in the run position, the green pilot light will light as long as the motor is running.

    (a) True
    (b) False

11. In **Figure 10–17**, the A2 contacts of the selector switch are connected to points _____.

    (a) 2 and 3
    (b) L1 and 3
    (c) L1 and 5
    (d) L2 and 5

12. In **Figure 10–17**, if the motor is running with the NO start PB open, which of the following statements is(are) true?

    (a) The selector switch is in the K position.
    (b) The selector switch is in the J position.
    (c) The M contacts 2-3 are closed.
    (d) b and c

CHAPTER 3 — REVERSING CONTROLS

Many applications require motors to run both forward and backward. This chapter covers concepts, components, and schematic diagrams for reversing motor control circuits. It consists of the following units:

Unit 11—Reversing Controls for Three-Phase Motors

Unit 12—Reversing Controls with Indicator (Pilot) Lights for Three-Phase Motors

Unit 13—Reversing Controls with Limit Switches for Three-Phase Motors

Unit 14—Reversing Single-Phase Motors

Notes

UNIT 11 — Reversing Controls for Three-Phase Motors

Unit 11—Introduction

This unit introduces the subject of reversing motor controls. It covers forward and reverse contactors, interlocks that prevent those contactors from being energized at the same time (which will cause a phase-to-phase short), and control devices including reversing pushbutton stations and selector switches.

11.1 Reversing Three-Phase Motors

Reversing any two lines (power-supply conductors) to a three-phase motor causes the motor to run in the other direction. It's standard industry practice to interchange L1 and L3, Figure 11-1. A reversing motor starter can be used to interchange L1 and L3. The basic reversing starter has two contactors (one forward and one reverse), and an interlocking arrangement to prevent energizing the forward and reverse contactors at the same time.

> **Author's Comment:** When starting a three-phase motor for the first time, it should be uncoupled from the load and then jogged or bumped to ensure proper rotation.

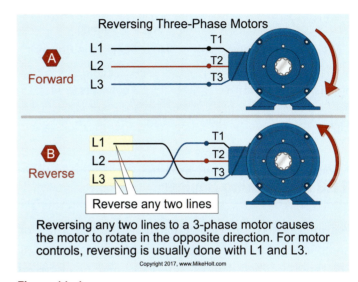

Figure 11–1

11.2 Forward and Reverse Contactors

Figure 11-2 shows just the forward and reversing contacts of a reversing starter (the coils and interlock aren't shown). When the forward contacts close, Figure 11-2A, L1 is connected to T1, L2 is connected to T2, and L3 is connected to T3. When the reverse contacts close, Figure 11-2B, L1 connects to T3, L2 connects to T2, and L3 connects to T1. The motor runs in the opposite direction.

Unit 11 Reversing Controls for Three-Phase Motors

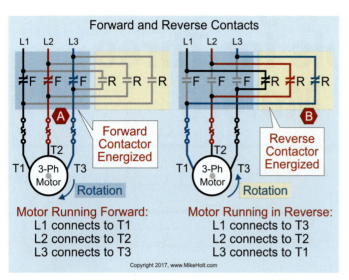

Figure 11–2

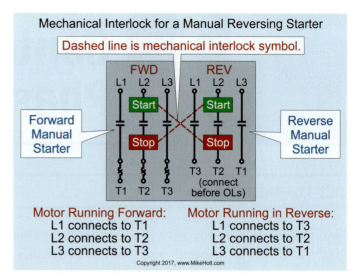

Figure 11–3

11.3 Interlocking Devices

An interlock is a device actuated by the operation of some other device to govern succeeding operations of the same or allied devices. Interlocks may be electrical or mechanical. Interlocking in reversing controls prevents the forward and reverse contactors from being energized at the same time, which will cause a phase-to-phase short.

Mechanical Interlock for a Manual Reversing Starter. A manual reversing starter is two individual 3-pole manual starters connected together. This type of reversing starter is often used for low-horsepower motors without automatic control. In some cases, the installer adds the manual interlock device between the start-stop pushbuttons of each starter, Figure 11-3. It may also be up to the installer to properly mark the starter enclosure "Forward" and "Reverse" because individual manual starter pushbuttons read start and stop.

Mechanical Interlock for Magnetic Reversing Controls. Most reversing magnetic starters contain a factory-installed interlock device between the forward and reverse contactors. The interlock device physically locks out one contactor at the beginning of the start cycle from the other contactor. Figure 11-4 shows a mechanical interlock symbol (dashed line) between the coils, which prevents the starter from closing all contacts simultaneously. When this type of reversing controller is used, the stop pushbutton must be pushed to de-energize the contactors before the motor can be reversed, allowing the interlock lever to reset.

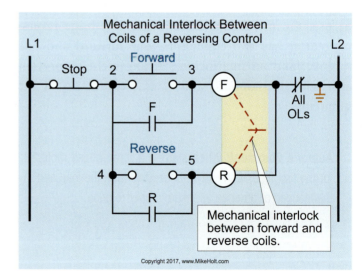

Figure 11–4

Reversing Controls for Three-Phase Motors — Unit 11

Figure 11–5A shows the voltage path when the F coil is energized. Coil R is blocked out by the interlock lever. When the motor is running in reverse, coil F is blocked out by the interlock lever. **Figure 11–5B**

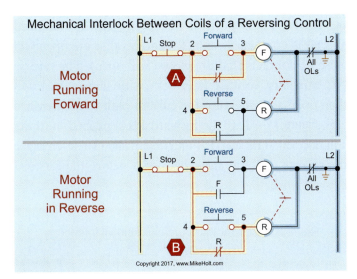

Figure 11–5

Figure 11-6 is the wiring diagram for the same control circuit as the one shown in **Figures 11-4 and 11–5**. Notice that each contactor has its own set of NO auxiliary contacts that serve as the holding circuit for each coil.

This is still an application of a basic 3-wire control circuit, even though there are five wires running to the pushbutton control station. Two 3-wire control circuits (with one shared conductor) are being used, one for each coil. Remember that a 3-wire control circuit has one wire from terminal 1 (L1 or other power source), a second wire that runs to one side of an auxiliary contact, and a third wire that runs to the other side of the auxiliary contact that connects to one side of the coil. The 3-wire circuit to the forward coil consists of control wires 1, 2, and 3.

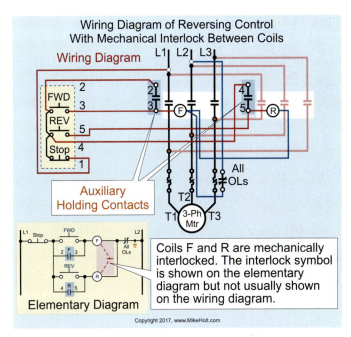

Figure 11–6

The 3-wire circuit to the reverse coil consists of control wires 1, 4, and 5. Whenever a control circuit makes use of holding contacts that drop out on power loss, it's called a "3-wire circuit" regardless of the actual number of conductors necessary to provide for all circuit options.

11.4 Electrical Interlock for Magnetic Reversing Controls

Electrical interlocking is accomplished by wiring the contacts of one circuit to control another circuit.

NC Auxiliary Contacts Electrical Interlock

It's common to use an extra set of NC auxiliary contacts at each coil to provide an electrical interlock for reversing controls. This is typically in addition to the mechanical interlock provided between the coils. New reversing starters commonly come prewired this way.

Unit 11 Reversing Controls for Three-Phase Motors

Figure 11-7 shows the ladder/elementary representation of this circuit, while Figure 11-8 shows the wiring diagram for the same controls. When the forward PB is pushed, the forward coil is energized and all F contacts switch (F contacts that are open will close, F contacts that are closed will open).

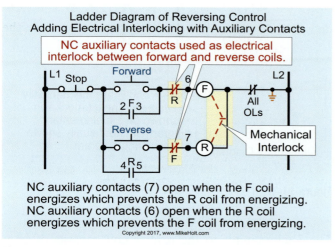

Figure 11–7

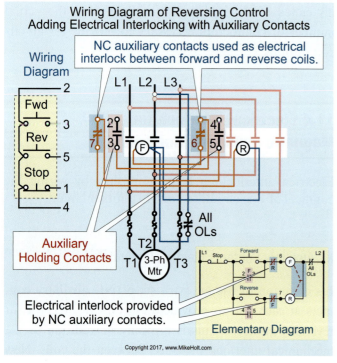

Figure 11–8

The forward NC auxiliary contact interlock (with terminal 7) opens and interrupts the current path to the reverse coil, Figure 11–9A. If the reverse PB is pushed, nothing happens. The stop PB must be pushed to de-energize the forward coil and the motor stops. Now if the reverse PB is pushed, the reverse coil is energized and all R contacts switch (R contacts that are open will close, R contacts that are closed will open). The reverse NC auxiliary contact interlock (with terminal 6) will then open and interrupt the current path to the forward coil, Figure 11–9B. If the forward PB is pushed, nothing will happen. The stop PB must be pushed to de-energize the reverse coil and stop the motor before the forward PB will work.

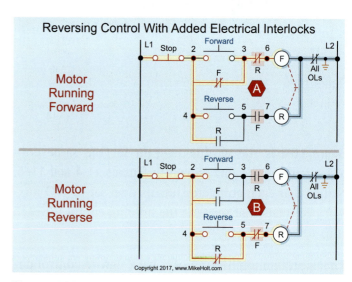

Figure 11–9

Author's Comment: Auxiliary contacts often come as two sets of contacts in a single device. This device can be two sets of NO contacts, two sets of NC contacts, or one set of NO contacts and one set of NC contacts.

132 | Mike Holt Enterprises | *Understanding Basic Motor Controls*

Reversing Controls for Three-Phase Motors — Unit 11

Pushbutton Electrical Interlock

In **Figure 11-10**, notice that both the forward and reverse pushbuttons have the mechanical interlock symbol. This gives the appearance that there are four individual pushbuttons for the forward and reverse controls (not counting the stop PB). But these are actually just two double-circuit momentary-contact pushbuttons, and the way these two pushbuttons are wired provides the electrical interlock method in this control circuit.

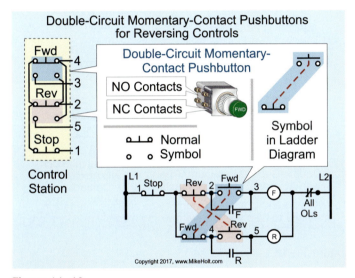

Figure 11–10

Remember that ladder/elementary diagrams show electrical functions and terminations rather than the physical location of devices. Each pushbutton has one set of NO contacts and one set of NC contacts, and when the button is pushed, both sets of contacts operate simultaneously.

The interlock symbol between the double-circuit pushbutton contacts represents the mechanical construction of the pushbuttons, but doesn't represent the electrical interlocking feature that the wiring of these double-circuit pushbuttons adds to the control circuit. Each of these pushbuttons contains two sets of contacts that operate when the pushbutton is pressed.

While each pushbutton controls the circuit it's connected to, it also operates a set of contacts that control another circuit, **Figure 11-11**. For example, the forward PB is part of the 3-wire circuit that controls the F coil. The NC contacts of the forward PB are the interlocking contacts of the reversing circuit and this set of NC contacts has a major role in controlling the 3-wire circuit for the R coil. The same features in the NC contacts of the reverse PB act exactly the same way on the 3-wire circuit for the F coil.

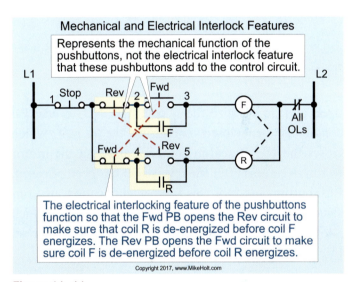

Figure 11–11

Figure 11-12A shows the standard method for using double-circuit pushbuttons as an electrical interlock in reversing controls. **Figure 11-12B** shows the same circuit configuration without using the dashed lines for the interlock symbol. Although this ladder diagram is seldom used, it shows the double-circuit pushbuttons and electrical interlocking features more clearly. When the forward PB is pressed, the NO forward PB contact is momentarily closed, which energizes the F coil through the NC reverse PB. The NO F holding contacts close, which allows the motor to continue to run forward after the forward PB has been released. When the reverse PB is pressed, the NC reverse PB contacts

Unit 11 Reversing Controls for Three-Phase Motors

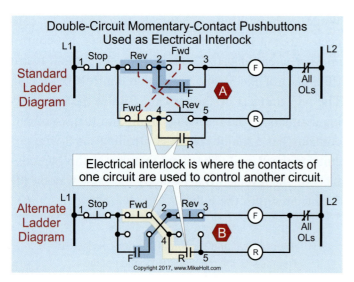

Figure 11–12

11.5 Combined Interlock Methods for Reversing Starters

Reversing starters that combine all three types of mechanical and electrical interlocks provide for maximum safety of operation. They're the most common reversing starter design. Figure 11-13

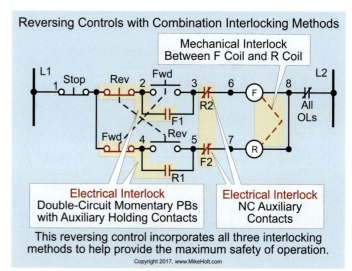

Figure 11–13

open and de-energize the F coil. The NO reverse PB contact is then closed, energizing the R coil, which closes the NO R seal-in contacts, allowing the motor to run in reverse after the reverse PB has been released. Pushbuttons used for this type of application are constructed with a "break-before-make" feature, which allows one set of contacts to open before the other set of contacts close.

Avoid Plugging Reversal. Pressing either the forward PB or the reverse PB to reverse direction while the motor is already running causes stress in it, and briefly causes a high current which produces abnormal heating in the motor. This is called a "plugging reversal." If this is done often it can damage the motor, especially if the motor isn't allowed to cool off between reversals, unless it's designed for such use. The repeated high currents may also cause fuses to blow, the circuit breaker to trip, or the overload relay to trip. It's preferable to push the stop PB and let the motor coast to a stop before reversing it. In some cases, it may be desirable to add a time-delay relay to the reversing process to allow the motor to come to a complete stop before allowing it to start in the opposite direction.

Operation from Rest

Pressing Forward PB. Figure 11–14A shows the same control circuit as Figure 11–13. The motor isn't running. When the forward PB is pressed, the NO forward PB contact closes and energizes coil F, Figure 11–14B1. In Figure 11–15B2, the NC forward PB momentarily opens the reverse portion of the control circuit. At the same time, the F1 contacts close providing the holding circuit to keep coil F energized and the NC F2 contacts open providing additional electrical interlock protection. The motor continues to run in a forward direction when the forward PB is released. Figure 11–15B3

134 | Mike Holt Enterprises | Understanding Basic Motor Controls

Reversing Controls for Three-Phase Motors — Unit 11

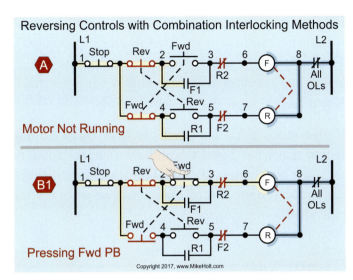

Figure 11–14

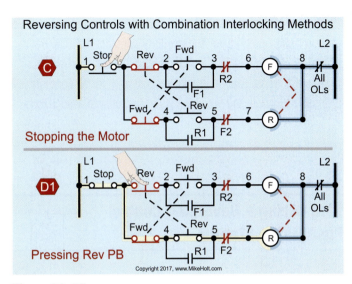

Figure 11–16

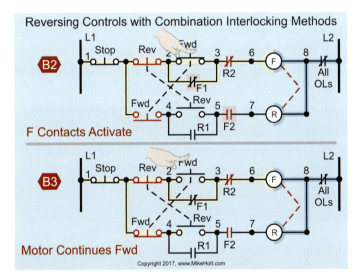

Figure 11–15

Pressing Reverse PB with Motor Running Forward. The control circuit in this example can run in the reverse direction by just pressing the reverse PB, but it's a good practice to stop a motor before reversing it. Since the motor is running in the forward direction, pressing the stop PB de-energizes coil F which opens contacts F1 and closes contacts F2, **Figure 11–16C**. Pressing the NC reverse PB interrupts the path to coil F and energizes coil R. **Figure 11–16D1**

When coil R energizes, contacts R1 close providing the reverse holding circuit, and contacts R2 open providing electrical interlock protection, **Figure 11–17D2**. When the reverse PB is released, the motor continues to run in a reverse direction. **Figure 11–17D3**

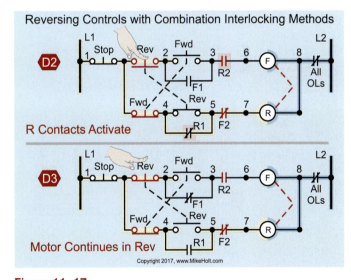

Figure 11–17

Understanding Basic Motor Controls | Mike Holt Enterprises

Unit 11 — Reversing Controls for Three-Phase Motors

Author's Comment: Most ladder and wiring diagrams don't use numbers for the auxiliary contacts (F1, F2, R1, or R2). We do this as a learning aid to make the schematic easier to read. You'll normally see just an F for all contacts associated with the F coil, an R for all contacts associated with the R coil, and so forth.

11.6 Wiring a Reversing Control Pushbutton Station

Figure 11-18 shows a comparison of the ladder diagram shown in Figure 11-18A to a wiring diagram, Figures 11-18B and 11-18C. As you can see, the wiring diagram is becoming more and more complicated as the control circuits become more complicated. This is the reason ladder diagrams are normally used instead of wiring diagrams. Many machines have wiring diagrams as well, but they're used more for troubleshooting.

It's important to remember that this is still the same two 3-wire control circuits used in previous examples. The forward 3-wire control circuit is control wires 1, 2, and 3, and the reverse 3-wire circuit is control wires 1, 4, and 5.

If this seems a bit confusing, look at Figure 11-18C. Notice that wires 2 and 4 both have a jumper going to the other pushbutton. If you follow these wires through the jumpers in the control station, it's easier to see the individual 3-wire circuits.

11.7 Wiring a Reversing Control with a Selector Switch

A two-position selector switch can be used with a regular start-stop pushbutton station to control a reversing starter. The momentary-contact start pushbutton is used for both the forward and reverse direction of a motor depending on the position of the selector switch. This control circuit also requires a set of NO and NC auxiliary contacts for both coils. This circuit is a little simpler than the circuits just covered. Figure 11-19

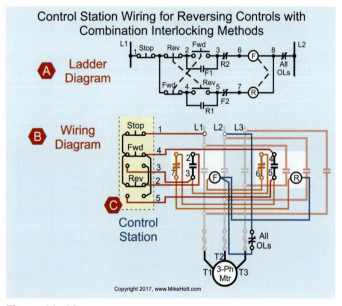

Figure 11-18

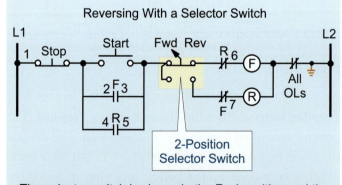

The selector switch is shown in the Fwd position and the reverse portion of the circuit is disconnected. When the selector switch is in the Rev position, the forward portion of the circuit is disconnected.

Figure 11-19

Reversing Controls for Three-Phase Motors — Unit 11

Operation from Motor Stopped—Forward Direction

The Selector Switch is in the Forward Position. Pressing the start PB energizes coil F, the NO auxiliary F contacts 2-3 close to hold in coil F, the NC auxiliary F contact 7 opens (electrical interlock), and the motor starts in the forward direction, Figure 11–20A. Pressing the stop PB de-energizes coil F, the NO auxiliary F contacts 2-3 open, the NC auxiliary F contact 7 closes, and the motor stops.

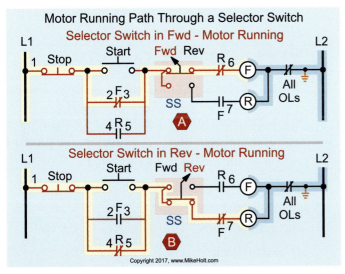

Figure 11–20

Safety Feature. An inherent safety feature is that when the selector switch is in the forward position, the reverse portion of the circuit is disconnected. When the selector switch is in the reverse position, the forward portion of the circuit is disconnected.

Operation from Motor Stopped—Reverse Direction

The Selector Switch is in the Reverse Position. Pressing the start PB energizes coil R, the NO auxiliary R contacts 4-5 close to hold in coil R, the NC auxiliary R contact 6 opens (electrical interlock), and the motor starts in the reverse direction, Figure 11–20B. Pressing the stop PB de-energizes coil R, the NO auxiliary R contacts 4-5 open, the NC auxiliary R contact 6 closes, and the motor stops.

Author's Comment: Turning the selector switch to the opposite position while the motor is running turns off the motor. It won't start running in the opposite direction until the start PB is pressed.

Unit 11—Conclusion

This unit covered basic concepts, components, and schematic diagrams used with reversing controls for three-phase motors. It made the important point that reversing motor controls are basically a variation of 3-wire control circuits, even though they may have four or five conductors.

Another important point made was that combining mechanical interlocking with electrical interlocking incorporates a greater degree of safety by reducing the possibility of phase-to-phase shorts.

Unit 11 — Practice Questions

Introduction

1. Reversing any two lines (power-supply conductors) to a three-phase motor causes the motor to run in the other direction.

    (a) True
    (b) False

2. Whenever a control circuit makes use of holding contacts that drop out on power loss, it's called a "____" circuit regardless of the actual number of conductors necessary to provide for all circuit options.

    (a) 1-wire
    (b) 2-wire
    (c) 3-wire
    (d) 4-wire

11.4 Electrical Interlock for Magnetic Reversing Controls

3. Pressing either the forward PB or the reverse PB to reverse direction while the motor is already running causes stress in the motor, and briefly causes a high current which produces abnormal heating in the motor. This is called a(n) ____.

    (a) plugging reversal
    (b) electrical interlock
    (c) mechanical interlock
    (d) reversing control

4. In the field, most ladder and wiring diagrams don't use numbers such as F1, F2, R1, or R3 for the auxiliary contacts.

    (a) True
    (b) False

11.7 Wiring a Reversing Control with a Selector Switch

5. When the selector switch of a forward-reverse control circuit is in the ____ position, the forward portion of the circuit is disconnected.

    (a) forward
    (b) backward
    (c) reverse
    (d) upside down

Practice Questions—General

Note: The following questions are based on any part of this textbook up through this unit.

6. In **Figure 11–21**, when the forward contactor contacts are closed, L1 connects to T1, L2 connects to T2, and L3 connects to T3.

    (a) True
    (b) False

7. In **Figure 11–21**, when the reverse contacts are closed ____.

    (a) L1 connects to T3
    (b) L2 connects to T2
    (c) L3 connects to T1
    (d) all of these

Practice Questions — Unit 11

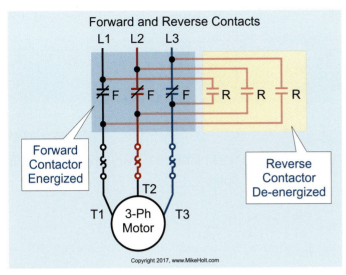

Figure 11–21

8. In **Figure 11–22**, letter A from the stop PB connects to point _____.

   (a) 1
   (b) 2
   (c) 3
   (d) 4

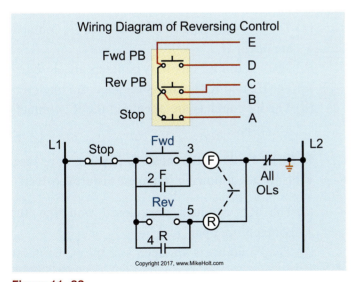

Figure 11–22

9. In **Figure 11–22**, letter B from the reverse PB connects to point _____.

   (a) 3
   (b) 4
   (c) 5
   (d) L2

10. In **Figure 11–22**, letter C from the reverse PB connects to point _____.

    (a) 2
    (b) 3
    (c) 4
    (d) 5

11. In **Figure 11–22**, letter D from the forward PB connects to point _____.

    (a) 1
    (b) 2
    (c) 3
    (d) 4

12. In **Figure 11–22**, letter E from the forward PB connects to point _____.

    (a) 2
    (b) 3
    (c) 4
    (d) 5

13. In **Figure 11–22**, there's one 3-wire control circuit for the forward coil, and one 3-wire control circuit for the reverse coil, even though there aren't six control conductors.

    (a) True
    (b) False

14. In **Figure 11–22**, the dashed line between the F coil and R coil represents _____.

    (a) an alternate wiring method
    (b) an electrical interlock
    (c) a mechanical interlock
    (d) a short circuit

Understanding Basic Motor Controls | Mike Holt Enterprises

Unit 11   Practice Questions

15. In **Figure 11–23**, the control circuit contains _____.

    (a) five separate pushbutton devices
    (b) one NC PB and two double-circuit momentary-contact PBs
    (c) one NC PB and two normally open PBs
    (d) three NC PBs and two NO PBs

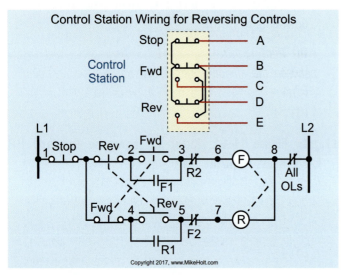

Figure 11–23

16. In **Figure 11–23**, letter A from the stop PB connects to point _____.

    (a) 1
    (b) 2
    (c) 3
    (d) 4

17. In **Figure 11–23**, letter B from the forward PB connects to point _____.

    (a) 1
    (b) 2
    (c) 3
    (d) 4

18. In **Figure 11–23**, letter C from the forward PB connects to point _____.

    (a) 1
    (b) 2
    (c) 3
    (d) 4

19. In **Figure 11–23**, letter D from the reverse PB connects to point _____.

    (a) 1
    (b) 2
    (c) 3
    (d) 4

20. In **Figure 11–23**, letter E from the reverse PB connects to point _____.

    (a) 1
    (b) 2
    (c) 3
    (d) 5

21. In **Figure 11–23**, if the motor is running forward, which of the following statements is correct?

    (a) The R1 contacts are closed and the F1 contacts are open.
    (b) The F2 and R2 auxiliary contacts are closed.
    (c) The F2 and R2 auxiliary contacts are open.
    (d) The F2 contacts are open and the R2 contacts are closed.

22. In **Figure 11–23**, if the motor is running in reverse, which of the following statements is(are) correct?

    (a) The R1 contacts are closed and the R2 contacts are open.
    (b) The F1 contacts are open and the F2 contacts are closed.
    (c) The R1 contacts are open and the R2 contacts are closed.
    (d) a and b

Unit 12: Reversing Controls with Indicator (Pilot) Lights for Three-Phase Motors

Unit 12—Introduction

Unit 11 introduced the subject of reversing motor controls. This unit discusses how pilot (indicator) lights are added to indicate the running status of the motor and its direction of operation.

12.1 Adding Forward and Reverse Pilot Lights

Pilot (indicator) lights have been added to the reversing control circuit with interlocks from the last unit. The forward and reverse indicator lights are connected in parallel with their corresponding coils. Each pilot (indicator) light comes on when its corresponding coil is energized, and goes off when its coil de-energizes. Figure 12-1

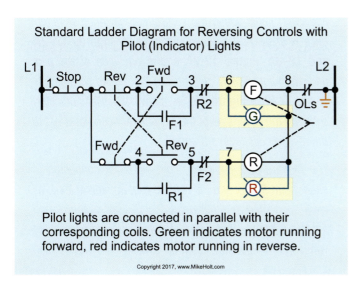

Figure 12–1

Example 1—Control Station for Reversing Controls with Pilot Lights. Figure 12-2 shows a comparison between the standard ladder diagram for the reversing control, Figure 12-1, and a simplified wiring diagram, Figure 12-2A. In order to simplify the wiring diagram, the main power contacts aren't shown.

Pilot (indicator) lights are typically installed in a remote location next to the PB control station, and aren't part of the actual forward or reverse control wiring. The lines with arrows drawn from the pilot (indicator) lights show that additional control wires need to be installed to points 7, L2, and 6 on the wiring diagram for the control station. Figure 12-2B

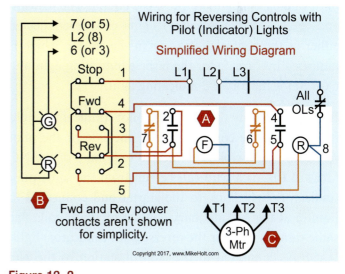

Figure 12–2

Understanding Basic Motor Controls | Mike Holt Enterprises 141

Unit 12 — Reversing Controls with Indicator (Pilot) Lights for Three-Phase Motors

12.2 Alternate Pilot Light Connection Points

In **Figure 12–2B**, the pilot (indicator) lights can be wired to points in the motor starter (7, L2, and 6) or alternate points of connection at the PB station. When wired to the PB station, wiring to points 7 and 6 are omitted. A wire to L2 is still required for both pilot (indicator) lights. The alternate wiring to the PB station is:

- Arrow line 6 to control panel wire terminal 3 (NO forward PB, omit wire to starter).

- Arrow line 7 to control panel wire terminal 5 (NO reverse PB, omit wire to starter).

- Arrow line L2 (point 8 on the diagram) must still run to L2 power.

Arrowed Lines on Schematics. Schematic diagrams sometimes use arrowed lines to indicate the connection of other devices to the basic control circuit. These arrowed lines represent connections made by the installer. Observe the arrowed lines in the control station for the pilot (indicator) lights and for the motor (T1, T2, and T3), **Figure 12-2**. In this case, we're adding pilot (indicator) lights to the basic circuit. The forward and reverse pilot (indicator) lights can be connected either at the control station or in the starter, which is indicated by 7 (or 5) for the reverse indicating light and 6 (or 3) for the forward indicating light.

For example, if the forward pilot (indicator) light is located in the control station, one side of the pilot (indicator) light can be connected to point 3 of the NO forward PB, or a wire can be run from the same pilot (indicator) light back to the starter and connected to point 6 at the NC auxiliary contact of the F coil. The same thing is true for the reverse pilot (indicator) light. It can be connected in the control station to the NO reverse PB, or a wire can be run from one side of the reverse pilot (indicator) light to point 7 at the NC auxiliary contact of the F coil.

Author's Comment: When the motor is running forward, wire 3 to the control station will remain energized because auxiliary holding contacts 2-3 are closed. This provides power to one side of the green pilot (indicator) light if wired at the control station. The same will be true if the motor is running in reverse. Wire 5 to the control station will remain energized because auxiliary holding contacts 4-5 are closed. This provides power to one side of the red pilot (indicator) light if wired at the control station. When the green and red pilot (indicator) lights are wired to control wires 3 and 5, they're wired to the two 3-wire circuits used for the Fwd and Rev PBs so the only additional wiring needed is one wire from L2 which is common to both lights.

Example 2—Control Station for Reversing Controls with Pilot Lights. **Figure 12-3** *is another version of the reversing control station from* **Figure 12-2**. *Instead of showing optional wiring (arrowed lines) for the pilot (indicator) lights. See* **Figure 12-2**. **Figure 12-3** *shows the pilot (indicator) light prewired into the control station. This diagram is a little easier to read.*

The wiring diagram in **Figure 12-2** *is more complicated because it provides information for wiring the pilot (indicator) lights from the control station or from the magnetic starter.* **Figure 12-3** *only shows the wiring for the pilot (indicator) lights within the control station. Another difference is seen on the ladder diagrams for* **Figures 12–2A and 12–3A**. **Figure 12-2A** *shows one side of the pilot (indicator) lights connected next to the related coils (points 6 and 7) while* **Figure 12-3A** *shows the pilot (indicator) lights on the other side of the NC auxiliary contacts next to the related coils (points 3 and 5).*

The forward pilot (indicator) light will work connected to either point 3 or 6, and the reverse pilot (indicator) light will work connected to either point 5 or 7. Part of the reason for this is simply that different manufacturers have slight variations in standard control circuits. Another reason

Reversing Controls with Indicator (Pilot) Lights for Three-Phase Motors — Unit 12

is that in **Figure 12-2**, if the pilot (indicator) lights are located in the magnetic starter or other location (not wired in the control station), the wiring will connect to points 6 or 7 in the starter.

In **Figure 12-3**, it's already been determined that the pilot (indicator) lights are to be wired in the control station. A wire from points 3 and 5 is already at the control station for the forward and reverse PBs, so additional wires aren't needed to run back to points 6 or 7. To simplify this, **Figure 12-3** shows the pilot (indicator) lights connected to points 3 and 5 only.

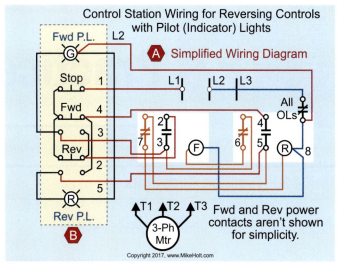

Figure 12–3

Unit 12—Conclusion

This short unit explained how pilot (indicator) lights are used with reversing controls for three-phase motors. Subjects covered here included control schematics, motor starter auxiliary contacts, and the additional conductors needed to add pilot (indicator) lights to these motor control circuits.

UNIT 12 Practice Questions

Unit 12—Practice Questions

12.2 Alternate Pilot Light Connection Points

1. In **Figure 12–4**, if the motor is running in reverse, the electrical interlocks that prevent the F coil from energizing is(are) _____.

   (a) auxiliary contacts 5-7
   (b) auxiliary contacts 3-6
   (c) auxiliary contacts marked F2
   (d) the forward PB

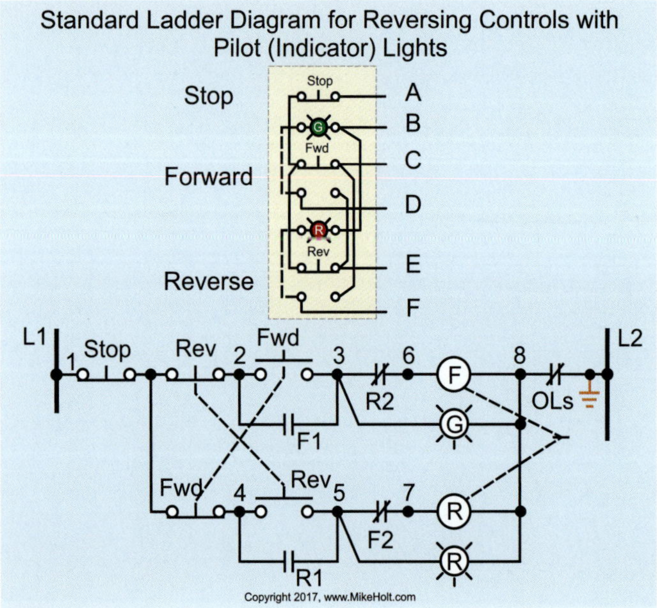

Figure 12–4

2. In **Figure 12–4**, the pilot lights are connected in _____ with the associated coils.

   (a) series
   (b) parallel
   (c) series-parallel
   (d) a and b

3. In **Figure 12–4**, letter A from the stop PB connects to point _____.

   (a) 1
   (b) 2
   (c) 3
   (d) 4

4. In **Figure 12–4**, letter B from the forward pilot light connects to point _____.

   (a) 1
   (b) 4
   (c) 6
   (d) 8

5. In **Figure 12–4**, letter C from the forward PB connects to point _____.

   (a) 1
   (b) 2
   (c) 3
   (d) 4

Practice Questions — Unit 12

6. In **Figure 12–4**, letter D from the forward PB connects to point _____.

   (a) 1
   (b) 2
   (c) 3
   (d) 4

7. In **Figure 12–4**, letter E from the reverse PB connects to point _____.

   (a) 1
   (b) 2
   (c) 3
   (d) 4

8. In **Figure 12–4**, letter F from the reverse PB connects to point _____.

   (a) 3
   (b) 4
   (c) 5
   (d) L2

9. In **Figure 12–4**, the green pilot light is used to indicate when the ____

   (a) motor is running in reverse
   (b) motor is running forward
   (c) motor is stopped
   (d) power is off.

Notes

UNIT 13
Reversing Controls with Limit Switches for Three-Phase Motors

Unit 13—Introduction

While motors often run continuously for long periods of time, other applications require them to start and stop, run briefly, and change direction (raising and lowering a motorized door is a common example). This unit covers the use of limit switches in conjunction with other components to control the duration and direction of motor operation.

13.1 Reversing Controls with Limit Switches Used to Automatically Stop a Motor

Another variation to the standard forward and reverse control circuit is the use of limit switches to automatically stop a motor when it's reached a predetermined amount of travel or torque.

Figure 13-1 is a standard ladder diagram of a reversing control with forward and reverse pilot (indicator) lights. Notice that limit switches are added as an option to the basic schematic with dashed lines and sometimes a note about the limit switches such as "Limit Switch if Used" or "Omit Jumper if Limit Switch is Used."

Figure 13-2 shows a simplified wiring diagram of the same reversing control with optional wiring for limit switches. In this case, the jumpers to be removed have letter designations to help make it easier to read.

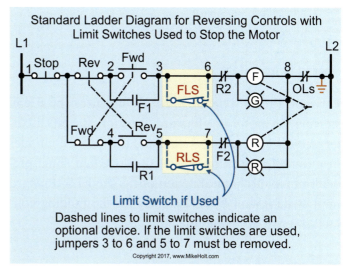

Figure 13–1

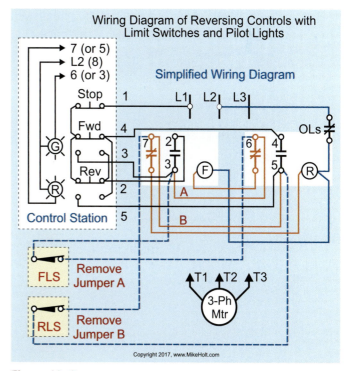

Figure 13–2

Understanding Basic Motor Controls | Mike Holt Enterprises

Unit 13 — Reversing Controls with Limit Switches for Three-Phase Motors

Author's Comment: There's more than one way to wire limit switches for a Stop function in reversing control circuits. Both schematics shown in **Figures 13-1 and 13-2** show the limit switches connected between the pushbuttons and the NC auxiliary contacts. It's also common to see limit switches connected between the NC auxiliary contacts and the coil. A Stop function can be accomplished by installing a NC device wired in series with the control circuit.

Operation from Rest

Forward. Pressing the forward PB energizes the F coil starting the motor in a forward direction, the NO auxiliary holding contacts 2-3 close and the motor continues in a forward direction, **Figure 13–3A**. When some predetermined mechanical action opens the FLS (forward limit switch), coil F will de-energize, the holding contacts 2-3 will open, and the motor will stop.

Reverse. Pressing the reverse PB energizes the R coil starting the motor in a reverse direction, the NO auxiliary holding contacts 4-5 close, and the motor continues in a reverse direction, **Figure 13–3B**. When some predetermined mechanical action opens the RLS (reverse limit switch), coil R will de-energize, the holding contacts 4-5 will open, and the motor will stop.

13.2 Reversing Controls—Limit Switches for Automatic Forward and Reverse

When limit switches are used for automatic forward and reversing circuits on machinery such as conveyors, precision grinding machines, chain feeds, and so forth, double-circuit limit switches are generally used. **Figure 13-4**

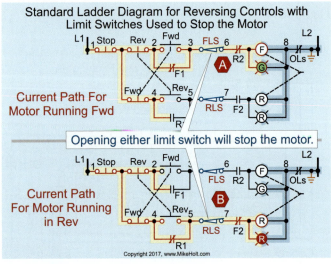

Figure 13–3

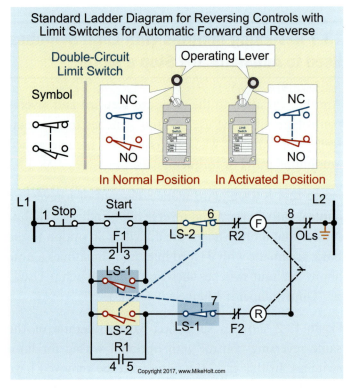

Figure 13–4

148 Mike Holt Enterprises | *Understanding Basic Motor Controls*

Reversing Controls with Limit Switches for Three-Phase Motors — Unit 13

As with many other devices shown in a ladder diagram, the dashed line between the limit switches indicates function rather than location. LS-1 is a limit switch with one set of NO contacts and one set of NC contacts. LS-2 is the same type of switch. The operating lever operates both sets of contacts in the limit switch at the same time when pressure is applied. When pressure is removed from the operating lever, it returns to its original position. This function is similar to a momentary-contact device that operates the contacts only when "pushed."

In this example, a regular start-stop pushbutton station is used with each PB having only one set of contacts. The forward and reverse function is provided by the double-circuit limit switches.

Operation from Rest

Figure 13-5A. Pushing the start PB completes the circuit through the NC LS-2 contacts and the NC R2 interlock contacts to energize the F coil closing the F1 holding contacts. The motor runs forward. The NC F2 contacts open to provide electrical interlock protection.

Figure 13-5B. The motor runs forward until the LS-2 operating lever is moved, **Figure 13-5B2**. The NC LS-2 contacts open, de-energizing the F coil, and the forward motion stops. At the same time, the NO LS-2 contacts close completing the circuit through the NC LS-1 contacts and the F2 interlock contacts (which closed when the F coil de-energized) to energize the R coil. Reverse motion starts. The R1 holding contacts close.

Figure 13-6C. As the reverse motion starts, the LS-2 contacts return to their normal position. The R1 holding contacts remain closed to provide a complete circuit to the R coil.

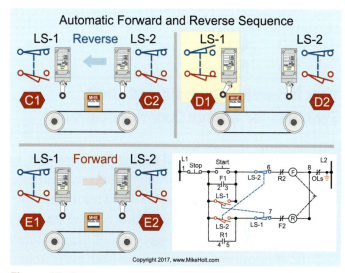

Figure 13–6

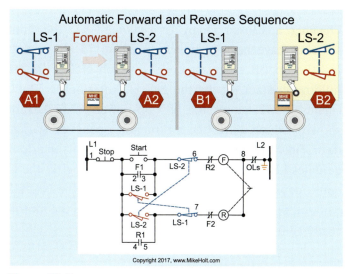

Figure 13–5

Figure 13-6D. The motor runs in reverse until the LS-1 operating lever is moved, **Figure 13-6D1**. The NC LS-1 contact opens and de-energizes the R coil, and the motor stops. The R1 holding contacts open and the R2 interlock contacts return to their NC position. At the same time, the NO LS-1 contacts close, completing the circuit through the NC LS-2 contacts and the now-closed R2 interlock contacts to energize the F coil starting the forward motion again.

Unit 13 — Reversing Controls with Limit Switches for Three-Phase Motors

Figure 13-6E. As the forward motion continues, the LS-1 contacts return to their normal position but the forward motion is maintained by the now-closed F1 holding contacts.

This sequence continues until the stop PB is pushed or the power goes off. After the motor stops, pushing the start PB will start the motor running forward, even if the motor was running in reverse when the stop PB was pushed.

Break-Before-Make. The contacts in a device with both NO and NC contacts commonly operate on a "break-before-make" principle, so that one set of contacts open a small fraction of an instant before the other set of contacts close.

13.3 Reversing Controls and Limit Switches for Garage Door Applications

A garage door opening and closing operation can be accomplished by using a reversing starter with an electrical interlock between the up and down coils, and two NC limit switches, **Figure 13-7**. This type of reversing control was discussed earlier, but without limit switches, and the forward and reversing labels on the pushbuttons have been changed to Up and Down. The ladder diagram for this control circuit, **Figure 13-7A**, is combined with the wiring diagrams for the pushbutton station and the two limit switches. **Figures 13-7B and 13-7C**

This is a common arrangement found in many schematics. Notice that limit switches LS-1 and LS-2 have additional instructions for connecting them. For example, the note for LS-1 says that if it's used, it will connect to points 3 and A of the control circuit, but the jumper between these points must be removed.

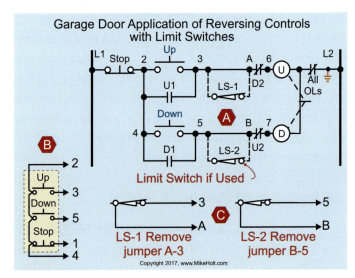

Figure 13–7

Author's Comment: It's common to use microswitches located in the gear case of the door opener mechanism instead of limit switches. As the name implies, a microswitch is simply a small switch. There are many different types and they're frequently used in equipment for numerous types of control features.

Operation from Rest

Opening a Closed Door. In **Figure 13–8A**, the limit switches have been installed. In **Figure 13–8B1**, pressing the up PB energizes coil U, which closes the U1 holding contact, opens the NC U2 interlock contact, **Figure 13–9B2**, closes the NO up-power contacts (not shown), which starts the motor and opens the garage door, **Figure 13–9C**. At a predetermined point, the door actuates LS-1, **Figure 13–10D1**, which de-energizes the U coil, opens the U1 holding contact, closes the NC U2 contact, opens the power contacts, and stops the motor. **Figure 13–10D2**

Reversing Controls with Limit Switches for Three-Phase Motors — Unit 13

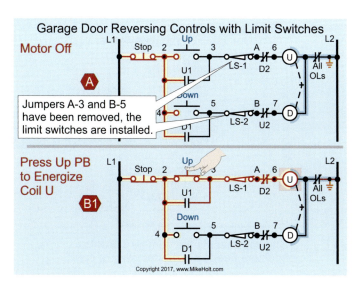

Figure 13–8

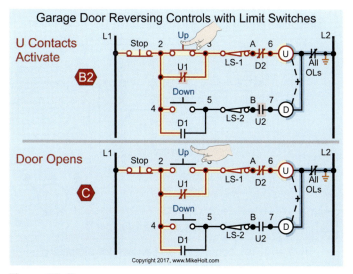

Figure 13–9

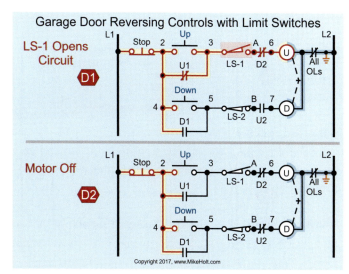

Figure 13–10

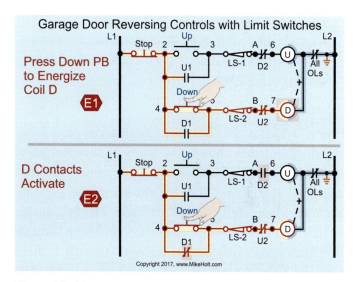

Figure 13–11

Closing an Open Door. In **Figure 13–11E1**, pressing the down PB energizes coil D, closes the D1 holding contact, opens the NC D2 interlock contact, **Figure 13–11E2**, closes the NO down-power contacts (not shown), which starts the motor and closes the garage door. **Figure 13–12F**

At another predetermined point, the door actuates LS-2, which de-energizes coil D, opens the D1 holding contact, closes the NC D2 contact, **Figure 13–12G1**, opens the power contacts, and stops the motor. **Figure 13–12G2**

Understanding Basic Motor Controls | Mike Holt Enterprises

Unit 13 — Reversing Controls with Limit Switches for Three-Phase Motors

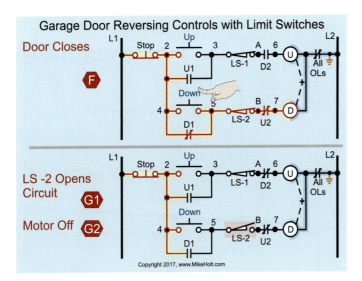

Figure 13–12

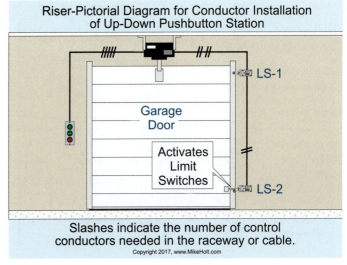

Figure 13–13

Author's Comment: Pushing the stop PB any time the door is moving up or down de-energizes either coil and stops the motor. The door stays at the position it's in when the stop PB is pushed.

Figure 13-13 is a riser diagram (combined with a pictorial diagram) that shows how many conductors go to each component of the garage door control system, based on the wiring diagram shown in the previous example when limit switches are used. The five slashes on the line from the motor-starter enclosure indicate that five conductors are required to the PB station. The line from the motor-starter enclosure to the first limit switch shows that two pairs (four conductors) are required. Each limit switch needs two conductors. A riser diagram isn't usually found with schematics, but they can sometimes be found on blueprints for a building. It might be helpful for the installer to make his or her own riser diagram to help layout the job.

Wiring Diagram. The wiring diagram for this control circuit is shown in Figure 13-14. Previous examples of reversing starters showed the two contactors in a side-by-side arrangement. This example uses an over-under arrangement.

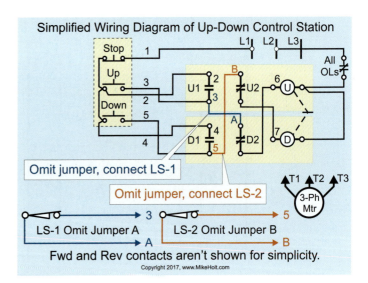

Figure 13–14

Reversing Controls with Limit Switches for Three-Phase Motors — Unit 13

13.4 Forward-Reverse Control With 2-Wire Circuits

2-Wire Control Station

A 2-wire forward-reverse PB station can be used with this reversing contactor, Figure 13-15. Notice that the 2-wire control station has three wires, which can be confusing. There are two 2-wire circuits here, one 2-wire circuit for each coil with a common conductor (wire 1) to both circuits. The 2-wire circuit for the forward PB is 1 and 3. The 2-wire circuit for the reverse PB is 1 and 5.

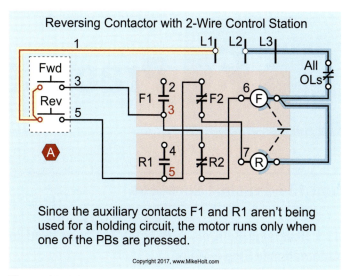

Figure 13–16

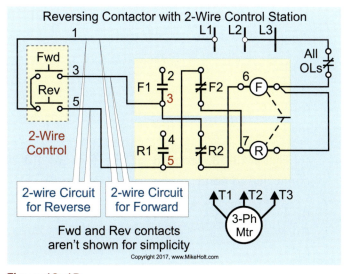

Figure 13–15

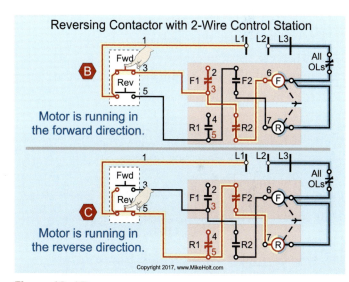

Figure 13–17

Because this is a 2-wire circuit, auxiliary holding contacts aren't used, Figure 13–16A. The motor runs forward only when the momentary-contact forward PB is being pushed and stops when the forward PB is released, Figure 13–17B. The motor runs in a reverse direction only when the reverse PB is being pushed and stops when the momentary-contact reverse PB is released, Figure 13–17C.

Unit 13—Conclusion

This unit explained the use of limit switches in reversing motor control circuits, discussed control schematics and the wiring of pushbutton stations, and mentioned the use of microswitches for control applications such as raising and lowering garage doors. A reversing control using 2-wire circuits was also introduced.

Unit 13 Practice Questions

Unit 13—Practice Questions

13.1 Reversing Controls with Limit Switches Used to Automatically Stop a Motor

1. In **Figure 13–18**, the dashed lines on the limit switch symbols indicate _____.

   (a) a mechanical interlock
   (b) an electrical interlock
   (c) optional wiring if limit switches are used
   (d) which pilot light to connect to

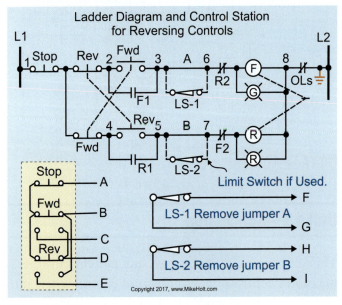

Figure 13–18

2. In **Figure 13–18**, the instructions state that in order to install LS-1, remove jumper _____.

   (a) B and connect points H and I to 5 and 7
   (b) B and connect points H and I to 7 and 8
   (c) A and connect points F and G to 3 and 6
   (d) A and connect points F and G to 4 and 5

3. In **Figure 13–18**, letter A of the stop PB is connected to point _____.

   (a) 1
   (b) 2
   (c) 3
   (d) 4

4. In **Figure 13–18**, letter B of the forward PB is connected to point _____.

   (a) 1
   (b) 2
   (c) 3
   (d) 4

5. In **Figure 13–18**, letter C of the forward PB is connected to point _____.

   (a) 2
   (b) 3
   (c) 4
   (d) 5

Practice Questions — Unit 13

6. In **Figure 13–18**, letter D of the reverse PB is connected to point _____.

   (a) 1
   (b) 2
   (c) 3
   (d) 4

7. In **Figure 13–18**, letter E of the reverse PB is connected to point _____.

   (a) 2
   (b) 3
   (c) 4
   (d) 5

8. In **Figure 13–18**, if jumper A is removed and letter G is connected to point 3, then letter F is connected to point _____.

   (a) L1
   (b) L2
   (c) 4
   (d) 6

9. In **Figure 13–18**, if the optional limit switches are installed as shown, and the motor is running forward, when the NC LS-1 opens, the _____.

   (a) motor will run in a reverse direction
   (b) R coil will energize
   (c) the stop PB will open
   (d) the motor will stop

10. In **Figure 13–18**, the red pilot light will be on if the _____.

    (a) motor is running in the forward direction
    (b) motor is running in the reverse direction
    (c) stop PB is pressed
    (d) motor protection device opens

11. In **Figure 13–18**, which of the following devices is(are) connected to one side of the OLs (point 8)?

    (a) The forward coil.
    (b) The reverse coil.
    (c) The red and green pilot lights.
    (d) all of these

13.2 Reversing Controls—Limit Switches for Automatically Forward and Reverse

12. In **Figure 13–19**, there are _____ limit switches.

    (a) four different
    (b) two double-circuit
    (c) two single-circuit
    (d) four NC

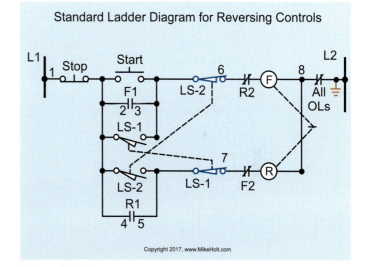

Figure 13–19

13. In **Figure 13–19**, if the motor is running forward, and LS-2 is activated, the motor will _____.

    (a) continue running in the forward direction
    (b) stop running
    (c) run in the reverse direction
    (d) energize the F coil

Unit 13 Practice Questions

14. In **Figure 13–19**, if the motor is running in the reverse direction, the motor will stop if the _____.

    (a) stop PB is pressed
    (b) overloads open
    (c) the power goes off
    (d) all of these

15. In **Figure 13–19**, when the motor is running in the reverse direction, contacts _____ will be open.

    (a) F1
    (b) R1
    (c) R2
    (d) both a and c

16. Based on **Figure 13–19**, which of the following statements is(are) correct?

    (a) The R2 and F2 contacts provide electrical interlock protection.
    (b) Forward coil F and reverse coil R have mechanical interlock protection.
    (c) Contacts F1 and R1 are auxiliary contacts used as holding circuits.
    (d) all of these

17. In **Figure 13–19**, if the motor is running in the forward direction, and the stop PB is pressed, the next time the start PB is pressed, the motor will run in the forward direction.

    (a) True
    (b) False

UNIT 14 Reversing Single-Phase Motors

Unit 14—Introduction

The previous three units covered a variety of reversing controls for three-phase motors. The rotation of some single-phase motors can also be reversed. This unit explains the process, components, and schematic diagrams, which are similar to three-phase motor controls but are generally simpler.

14.1 Types of Motors

The most common types of motors used for single-phase reversing are capacitor-start motors, which range from 1/8 hp to 10 hp, and split-phase (fractional hp) motors. Both types have a "start" winding and a "run" winding. The run winding alone can't start the motor from a standstill, so a separate start winding that's out-of-phase with the run winding is required to provide starting torque. **Figure 14-1**

Author's Comment: A single-phase motor that sits and hums without starting when energized will draw excessive current and quickly burn up. This often happens because the start winding isn't working due to a bad capacitor or a malfunctioning centrifugal starting switch.

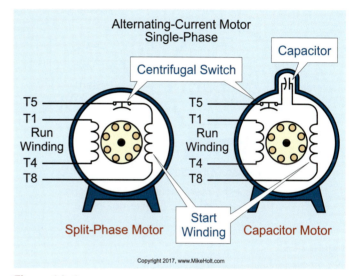

Figure 14–1

When a single-phase motor starts, both the run winding and the start winding are energized. In the capacitor-start motor, the start capacitor is in series with the start winding to aid in starting the motor. This is accomplished because of the out-of-phase characteristics introduced into the start winding by the capacitor. When the motor reaches approximately 65 to 70 percent of its full speed, the centrifugal starting switch opens due to the centrifugal force exerted by the rotation of the shaft. The start winding and capacitor are de-energized, allowing the motor to operate on the run winding only.

Unit 14 | Reversing Single-Phase Motors

The motor leads for the start winding are usually marked T5 and T8, are frequently red and black in color, and are usually a heavier gauge wire than the run winding leads. The run windings are usually marked T1 and T4. **Figure 14-2**

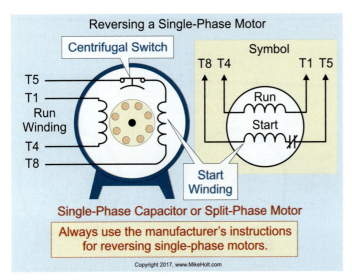

Figure 14–2

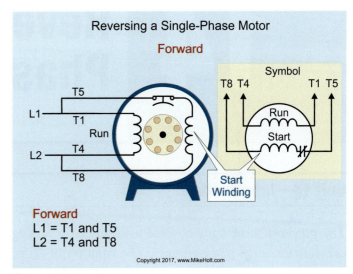

Figure 14–3

To reverse a single-phase capacitor-start or split-phase motor, either the run winding leads are interchanged or the start winding leads are interchanged, but not both. **Figures 14–3 and 14–4**

Figure 14-5A shows a set of contacts that are interchanging the run windings in order to reverse a single-phase motor.

Figure 14-5A shows the contacts when the motor is off. **Figure 14-6B** shows the motor running in the forward direction with L1 connected to T1 and T5, and L2 connected to T4 and T8. In **Figure 14-6C**, the motor is running in the reverse direction because the run winding leads are interchanged so that L1 is connected to T4 and T5, while L2 is connected to T1 and T8.

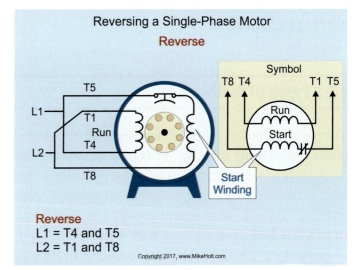

Figure 14–4

CAUTION: *Always use the manufacturer's instructions for reversing single-phase motors. There are several variations for making the connections to reverse single-phase motors. Dual-voltage motors will have more leads, but reversing is done following the same principles. Motors from different manufacturers or different countries may have different schemes for labeling or coloring the motor leads. Instructions for making motor terminations and reversing, if reversing is an option, are usually included with the equipment.*

Reversing Single-Phase Motors   Unit 14

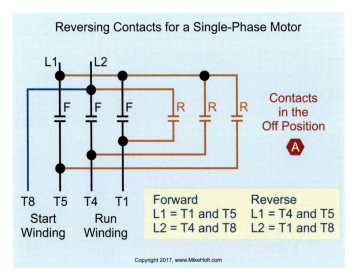

Figure 14–5

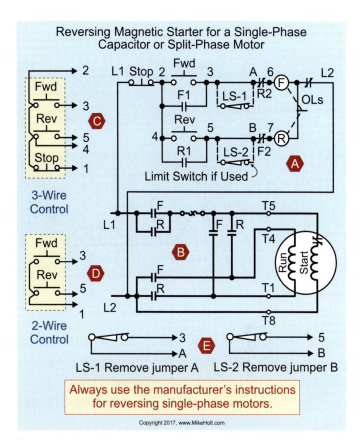

Figure 14–7

Figure 14-7 also shows two common ways to wire the control circuit which includes a 3-wire control station, **Figure 14-7C**, and a 2-wire control station, **Figure 14-7D**. It also shows how limit switches are normally connected if used with this reversing contactor. **Figure 14-7E**

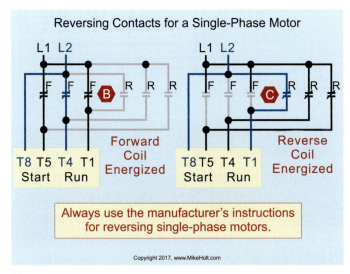

Figure 14–6

14.2 Reversing Control Circuit

Figure 14-7 takes the up-down control circuit used in the last unit on a three-phase motor (see **Figure 13-7**), and uses it for a single-phase motor, **Figure 14-7A**. This circuit can be applied to the set of contacts from **Figure 14-5** that's been redrawn into a ladder diagram, **Figure 14-7B**. Note that this schematic still interchanges the run winding leads to change motor directions.

14.3 Sequence of Operation

Figure 14-8 is taking the control circuit from **Figure 14-7** and connecting it to the 3-wire control circuit. **Figure 14-8** shows the 3-wire control circuit tapped from L1 and L2. When the motor isn't running, the forward and reverse power contacts are all open. This reversing contactor arrangement will interchange motor leads T1 and T4 between L1 and L2 to make the motor run in a forward and reverse direction.

Unit 14 — Reversing Single-Phase Motors

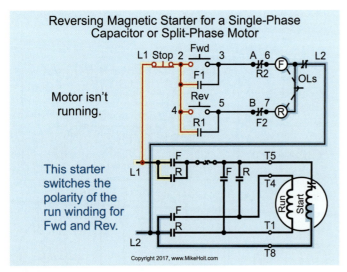

Figure 14–8

Motor Running Forward. After the forward PB is pressed, Figure 14–9, the F power contacts close and connect L1 to T1 of the run winding, and T5 of the start winding. L2 connects to T4 of the run winding and T8 of the start winding.

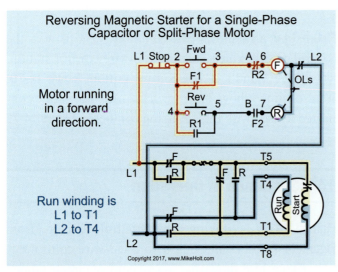

Figure 14–9

Motor Running Reverse. After the reverse PB is pressed, Figure 14–10, the R power contacts close and connects L1 to T4 of the run winding, and T5 of the start winding. L2 connects to T1 of the run winding and T8 of the start winding.

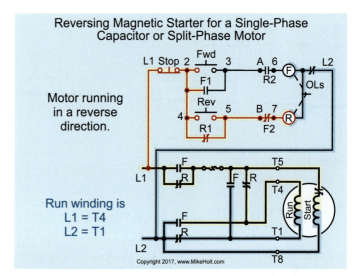

Figure 14–10

Author's Comment:

- There are no contacts shown opening or closing the connection from L2 to T8 for this type of motor. The *NEC* doesn't require that all conductors be opened by a controller unless it also serves as a disconnecting means [430.84], but for safety considerations, many installers prefer to use a controller that disconnects all line conductors.

- Switching the start winding leads only creates the phase relationship difference compared to the run windings while starting. If the circuit is reversed before the motor stops (or at least slows enough for the centrifugal switch to drop out) the motor will continue to run in the current running direction.

Alternate Configurations. There are many variations of single-phase reversing motors and controls that we aren't able to cover in this unit. But they're all based on the principle of interchanging the relative "polarity" of the start winding(s) with reference to run winding(s).

Unit 14—Conclusion

This unit explained reversing controls for single-phase motors. It made the important point that manufacturer's instructions should always be followed when reversing single-phase motors, because there are variations in making the connections. Dual-voltage motors, or those from different manufacturers or different countries, may not use the same schemes for identifying the motor leads.

UNIT 14 Practice Questions

Unit 14—Practice Questions

14.1 Types of Motors

1. The most common types of motors used for single-phase reversing are capacitor-start motors and split-phase motors.

   (a) True
   (b) False

14.3 Sequence of Operation

2. In **Figure 14–11**, letter A of the up PB is connected to point _____.

   (a) 1
   (b) 2
   (c) 3
   (d) L1

3. In **Figure 14–11**, letter B of the up PB is connected to point _____.

   (a) 1
   (b) 2
   (c) 3
   (d) 4

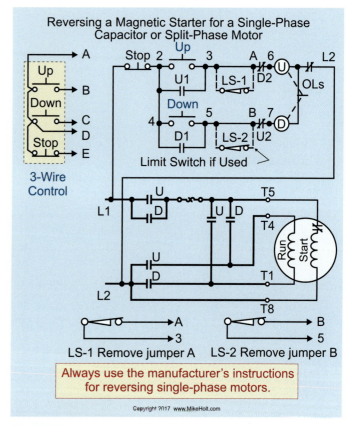

Figure 14–11

4. In **Figure 14–11**, letter C of the down PB is connected to point _____.

   (a) 2
   (b) 3
   (c) 5
   (d) L2

Practice Questions | Unit 14

5. In **Figure 14–11**, letter D of the down PB is connected to point _____.

   (a) 1
   (b) 2
   (c) 3
   (d) 4

6. In **Figure 14–11**, letter E of the stop PB is connected to point _____.

   (a) L1
   (b) L2
   (c) L3
   (d) B

7. In **Figure 14–11**, if limit switch LS-1 is connected, the jumper between _____ must be removed.

   (a) 2 and 3
   (b) 3 and A
   (c) 4 and 5
   (d) 5 and B

8. In **Figure 14–11**, if both limit switches are installed, and the motor is running in the down direction, the NC LS-1 contacts are used to automatically stop the motor.

   (a) True
   (b) False

9. In **Figure 14–11**, pressing the Up PB causes L1 to energize motor leads _____.

   (a) T1 and T5
   (b) T1 and T8
   (c) T2 and T3
   (d) T4 and T5

10. In **Figure 14–11**, pressing the up PB causes L2 to energize motor leads _____.

    (a) T1 and T4
    (b) T1 and T5
    (c) T2 and T3
    (d) T4 and T8

11. In **Figure 14–11**, pressing the down PB causes L1 to energize motor leads _____.

    (a) T1 and T5
    (b) T1 and T8
    (c) T2 and T3
    (d) T4 and T5

12. In **Figure 14–11**, pressing the down PB causes L2 to energize motor leads _____.

    (a) T1 and T4
    (b) T1 and T8
    (c) T2 and T3
    (d) T4 and T8

13. In **Figure 14–11**, the control circuit is configured to reverse the leads T1 and T4 of the run winding of the motor between L1 and L2.

    (a) True
    (b) False

14. Based on **Figure 14–11**, which of the following statements is correct?

    (a) There are two sets of NC auxiliary contacts for each coil.
    (b) There are two sets of NO auxiliary contacts for each coil.
    (c) Each coil has one set of NO and one set of NC auxiliary contacts.
    (d) Each coil has two sets of NO auxiliary contacts.

Understanding Basic Motor Controls | Mike Holt Enterprises

Unit 14 — Practice Questions

15. In **Figure 14–11**, electrical interlock is provided by _____.

   (a) contacts D2 and U2
   (b) coils U and D
   (c) the up and down PB switches
   (d) the stop PB

CHAPTER 4
CONTROLS FOR MULTIPLE MOTORS

Some applications, such as assembly lines, use multiple motors, which must be started or stopped in a certain sequence. A lubricating or hydraulic pump that must be operating before a manufacturing machine can start is one example. This unit explains control schemes involving more than one motor. It consists of the following units:

Unit 15—Sequencing Control

Unit 16—Master Stop Function

Notes

UNIT 15 Sequencing Control

Unit 15—Introduction

This unit explains how the control circuits of magnetic motor starters can be interconnected so that one must be started before the second one is energized. It covers components, control devices such as pushbutton stations, and schematic diagrams.

15.1 Sequencing Control

Sequence control is a method by which the control circuits of magnetic starters are interconnected so that one must be started before the second one is energized. This type of control is often required for auxiliary equipment, such as high-pressure lubricating and hydraulic pumps that are associated with some types of machinery and must be operating before the machine itself can operate. Sequence control is frequently used with assembly line and conveyor installations. In electric heating and air-conditioning, air-handler blower motors must be running in order for heating elements to energize or compressors to operate. The possible applications for this type of control are almost endless.

Figures 15–1 and 15–2 represent a ladder and connection diagram of the same sequencing control circuit. Coil M1, which causes motor 1 to start, must be energized before coil M2 can be energized. This is accomplished by using an additional set of normally open auxiliary contacts on the magnetic starter of M1, indicated on the drawing by terminal connections 4 and 5.

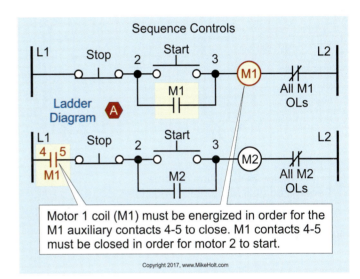

Figure 15–1

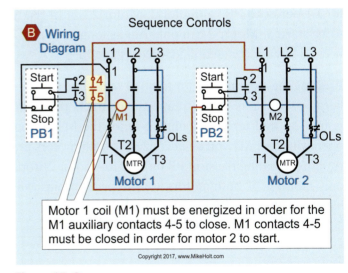

Figure 15–2

Understanding Basic Motor Controls | Mike Holt Enterprises 167

Unit 15 Sequencing Control

In this example, motor M1 represents a lubricating pump that must be running before the main equipment motor M2 can be started. This is a form of motor interlocking. **Figure 15-3**

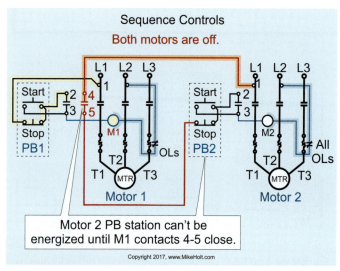

Figure 15–3

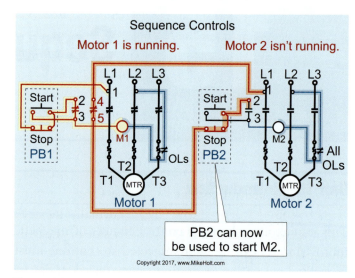

Figure 15–4

Figure 15–4 shows that when motor 1 is running, auxiliary contacts 4-5 at motor 1 are closed providing a path for L1 power to PB2 at motor 2. Motor 2 is now ready to be started. Motor 2 can only run as long as coil M1 keeps auxiliary contacts 4-5 closed. **Figure 15–5**

Pressing the stop on PB1 for motor 1 stops both motors because both sets of NO auxiliary contacts (terminal points 2-3 and terminal points 4-5) for the M1 starter open when the M1 coil de-energizes. If both motors are running, pressing the stop PB on PB2 for motor 2 stops only motor 2. If both motors are stopped, nothing will happen if the start PB is pressed on PB2.

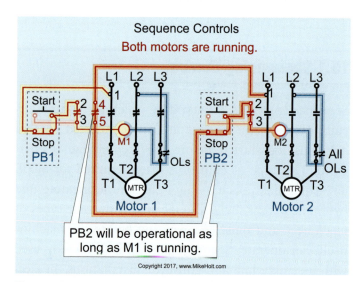

Figure 15–5

Sequencing Control — Unit 15

Figures 15–6 and 15–7 represent a ladder and connection diagram of the same sequencing control circuit using a 120V, Class 1 separate control circuit. Any connections from the main power in each motor starter to the control circuit must be removed before connecting the Class 1 circuit. A 120V starter coil must be installed if this starter comes with a coil rated for any other voltage. The hot conductor from the Class 1 control circuit replaces L1 (point 1) in the starter that we normally use, and the neutral conductor of the Class 1 control circuit is used where starter L2 is normally in series with the overload contacts to the other side of the coil.

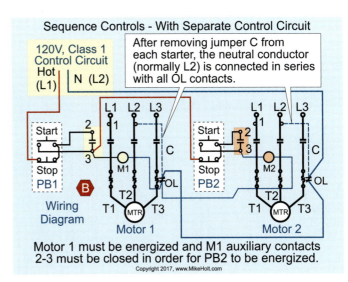

Figure 15–7

Motor 1 auxiliary contact terminal 3, which only energizes when motor 1 is energized, is used to supply PB2 for motor 2. This way, motor 2 can't start until motor 1 is started. **Figure 15–8**

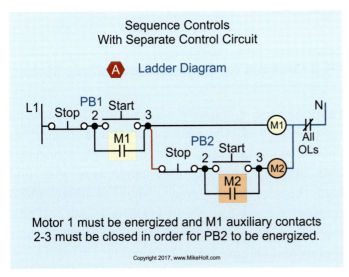

Figure 15–6

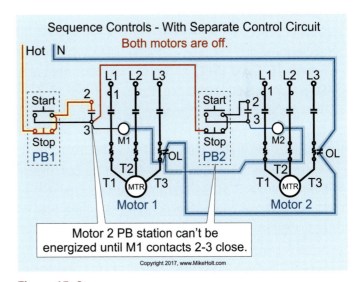

Figure 15–8

In this example, the neutral conductor is wired in series with all of the OL contacts of both motors, and jumper C is removed from each starter. If any OL to any of the motors opens, both coils de-energize. If the OLs in motor 2 open, the neutral from motor 2 to motor 1 interrupts the power to the motor 1 coil. If the OLs in motor 1 open, the M1 coil de-energizes, auxiliary contacts 2-3 open and interrupt power to the control circuit for coil M2.

If motor 1 de-energizes, motor 2 will also de-energize. The stop PB of PB2 can be used to stop motor 2, but motor 1 will continue running.

Unit 15 | Sequencing Control

Since the OLs for M1 are wired in series with the OLs for M2, if any OL opens, both coil M1 and coil M2 will de-energize. **Figure 15–9**

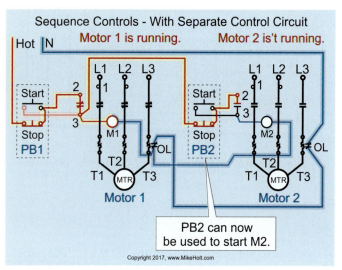

Figure 15–9

Author's Comment: Figure 15-10 shows four jumpers that frequently come with motor starters. Point A is a jumper that provides power from L1 of the branch circuit to a convenient terminal (terminal 1) for a common control circuit. See **Figures 15–1 and 15–2**. This terminal isn't used when a Class 1 circuit is being used. See **Figures 15–6 and 15–7**. Point B is showing a jumper between terminal 3 of the auxiliary contact and one side of the coil, and it must stay for the control circuit we're using in both examples. Point C is providing power from L2 to the coil through the OLs. This must be removed if a Class 1 control circuit is being used. In **Figure 15-7**, this is referred to as "Jumper C." There must be a 120V rated coil used when the 120V, Class 1 control circuit is being used. Point D is a jumper between the OL assembly and the coil terminal. This jumper stays when (1) only one motor starter is involved or (2) when more than one motor starter is used as shown in **Figures 15–6 and 15–7**, but the OLs aren't wired in series. When more than one motor starter is being used with the OLs wired in series as shown in **Figures 15–6 and 15–7**, that jumper must stay in motor starter 1, but must be removed in motor starter 2.

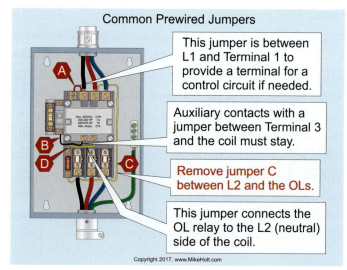

Figure 15–10

15.2 Controls for Sequencing Multiple Motors

Figure 15-11 is a common application for sequencing multiple motors. The machine press and its controls are oversimplified in this example. Most press machines have large control boxes, with hundreds of wires and many contactors and relays. Many of these added devices are safety features while others are parts of various controls already covered in this textbook, such as jogging and multiple control stations.

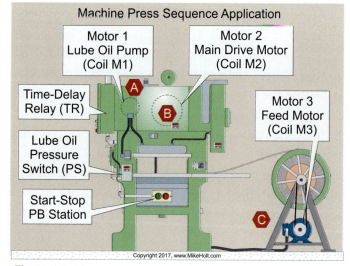

Figure 15–11

170 | Mike Holt Enterprises | *Understanding Basic Motor Controls*

Sequencing Control — Unit 15

Figure 15–12 is a ladder diagram for the application shown in Figure 15–11. From this machine press, we'll take three motors that need to be sequenced and add a control circuit. Motor 1 is a lube oil pump, motor 2 is the main drive motor for the machine, and motor 3 is the feed motor. Motor 2 can't operate until motor 1 is running and the oil pressure reaches its predetermined value. Motor 3 (the feed motor) can't start until motor 2 is running. **Figure 15–12A**

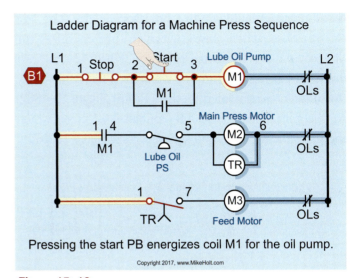

Figure 15–13

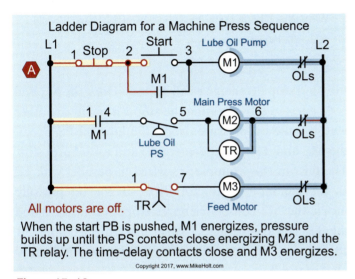

Figure 15–12

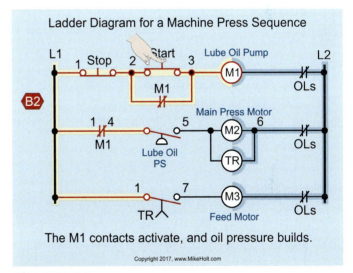

Figure 15–14

Operation Sequence (From Rest). Pressing the start PB energizes the M1 coil, Figure 15–13B1, closes the M1 holding contacts 2-3 and closes the additional NO auxiliary contacts 1-4, which supplies L1 current to the lube oil PS (pressure switch) in series with coil M2. **Figure 15–14B2**

Unit 15 — Sequencing Control

As oil pressure builds up to a predetermined setting, the NO pressure switch closes, which in turn energizes the M2 coil and the TR (time relay) coil, Figure 15–15C1. At this point, motor 2 is running while the TDC (time-delay close) switch is activated by the TR coil, Figure 15–15C2. At the preset delay, the TR contacts 1-7 close which energizes the M3 coil, and motor 3 runs. Figure 15–16D

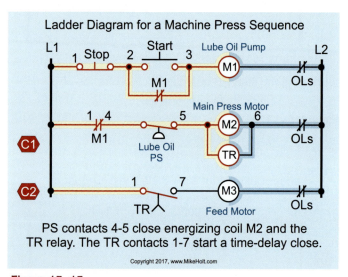

Figure 15–15

Author's Comment: The TR coil and the TDC switch are contained in a single device. This ladder diagram shows the electrical function of the circuit, not the physical locations of components, so it's possible to see the simplified effect of the TR device as it impacts this circuit. The up arrow in the schematic indicates that there's an on-delay function incorporated into the TR contacts. These contacts are called "NOTC" which stands for "Normally Open, Timed Closing." In other words, a time delay is required after the TR coil is energized and before the TR NO contacts close. When the TR coil is de-energized, the TR NOTC contacts open immediately.

Pressing stop de-energizes all motors. Once the M1 coil is de-energized by pressing the stop PB or by any other method, the oil pressure drops, the lube oil PS opens, the M2 and TR coils de-energize, and all motors stop. The OLs in this example are wired in parallel with L2 as the common conductor. Also, if the oil pressure drops, the M2 coil de-energizes stopping motor 2 and the TR coil de-energizes, which in turn opens the TR contacts 1-7 immediately, and de-energizes M3 stopping motor 3.

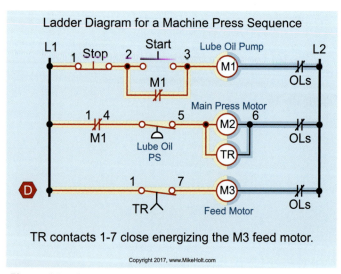

Figure 15–16

Author's Comment: The OLs can also be connected in series so that if any one motor stops due to an overload condition in the OLs, all of the motors stop. This is often done for safety reasons.

Figure 15-17 is the same machine press and control circuit in a wiring diagram. Connections from the TR and PS devices, as well as the actual power contacts for the motors, show terminal numbers rather than conductors to simplify the drawing. Notice that in this diagram, there's a set of NO contacts with the pressure switch. One side terminates to the pressure switch (point 4) while the other side has an arrow line indicating it connects to point 1 or some other source of power.

Sequencing Control Unit 15

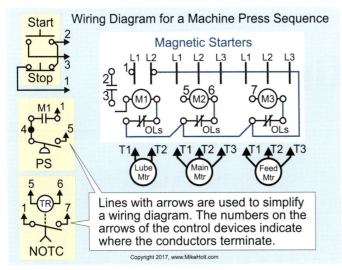

Figure 15–17

These contacts are an additional set of NO auxiliary contacts that operate from coil M1 and aren't part of the pressure switch.

Unit 15—Conclusion

This unit explained sequence controls for multiple motors, such as those used in many industrial applications. While the motor control concepts are logical extensions of those discussed throughout this textbook, real-life applications involving industrial machines can be quite complex, with hundreds of wires and many contactors and relays.

Today, many sequencing functions are handled by computers. Nevertheless, the control wiring must be configured such that the system will still function safely if the control computer fails. This necessitates interlocking the systems just as you've learned in the last few units.

Understanding Basic Motor Controls | Mike Holt Enterprises 173

UNIT 15 Practice Questions

Unit 15—Practice Questions

15.1 Sequencing Control

1. Sequence control is the method by which the control circuits of magnetic starters are interconnected so that one must be started before the second one is energized.

   (a) True
   (b) False

2. In **Figure 15–18**, the magnetic starter for motor 1 contains _____ set(s) of auxiliary contacts.

   (a) one
   (b) two
   (c) three
   (d) four

3. Based on **Figure 15–18**, which of the following statements is correct?

   (a) M1 auxiliary contacts 2-3 must be open for coil M2 to energize.
   (b) Motor 2 must be running in order for motor 1 to start.
   (c) M1 auxiliary contacts 4-5 must be closed in order for motor 2 to start.
   (d) M2 auxiliary contacts 4-5 must be closed in order for motor 2 to start.

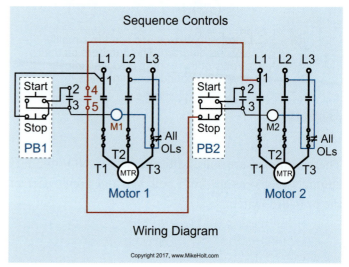

Figure 15–18

4. Based on **Figure 15–18**, which of the following statements is(are) correct?

   (a) Pressing the stop PB for motor 2 stops both motors.
   (b) Pressing the stop PB for motor 1 stops both motors.
   (c) Pressing the stop PB for motor 2 stops motor 2 only.
   (d) b and c

5. In **Figure 15–19**, letter A is connected to _____.

   (a) L1
   (b) point 2 of auxiliary contact M1
   (c) point 2 of auxiliary contact M2
   (d) the neutral

Practice Questions — Unit 15

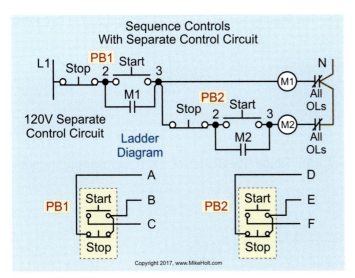

Figure 15–19

6. In **Figure 15–19**, letter B is connected to _____.

   (a) L1
   (b) point 2 of auxiliary contact M1
   (c) point 2 of auxiliary contact M2
   (d) the neutral

7. In **Figure 15–19**, letter C is connected to _____.

   (a) L1
   (b) point 2 of auxiliary contact M1
   (c) point 3 of auxiliary contact M1
   (d) point 3 of auxiliary contact M2

8. In **Figure 15–19**, letter D is connected to _____.

   (a) L1
   (b) point 2 of auxiliary contact M1
   (c) point 3 of auxiliary contact M1
   (d) point 3 of auxiliary contact M2

9. In **Figure 15–19**, letter E is connected to _____.

   (a) L2
   (b) point 3 of auxiliary contact M1
   (c) point 2 of auxiliary contact M1
   (d) point 2 of auxiliary contact M2

10. In **Figure 15–19**, letter F is connected to _____.

    (a) L2
    (b) point 2 of auxiliary contact M2
    (c) point 3 of auxiliary contact M1
    (d) point 3 of auxiliary contact M2

11. In **Figure 15–19**, if both motors are running, pressing the stop PB in PB1 _____.

    (a) only de-energizes the M1 coil
    (b) only de-energizes the M2 coil
    (c) de-energizes both the M1 and M2 coils
    (d) allows both coils to stay energized

15.2 Controls for Sequencing Multiple Motors

12. In **Figure 15–20**, letter A is connected to point _____.

    (a) 1
    (b) 2
    (c) 3
    (d) 4

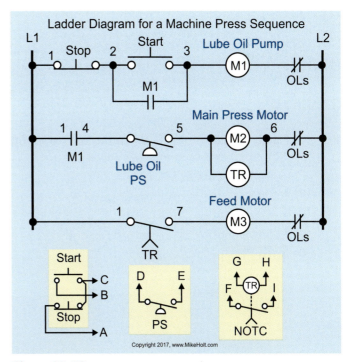

Figure 15–20

Unit 15 | Practice Questions

13. In **Figure 15–20**, letter B is connected to point _____.

    (a) 2
    (b) 3
    (c) 4
    (d) 5

14. In **Figure 15–20**, letter C is connected to point _____.

    (a) 2
    (b) 3
    (c) 4
    (d) 5

15. In **Figure 15–20**, letter D is connected to point _____.

    (a) 1
    (b) 2
    (c) 3
    (d) 4

16. In **Figure 15–20**, letter E is connected to point _____.

    (a) 1
    (b) 4
    (c) 5
    (d) 6

17. In **Figure 15–20**, letter F is connected to point _____.

    (a) 1
    (b) 2
    (c) 4
    (d) 5

18. In **Figure 15–20**, letter G is connected to point _____.

    (a) 1
    (b) 2
    (c) 4
    (d) 5

19. In **Figure 15–20**, letter H is connected to point _____.

    (a) 1
    (b) 2
    (c) 6
    (d) 7

20. In **Figure 15–20**, letter I is connected to point _____.

    (a) 4
    (b) 5
    (c) 6
    (d) 7

21. In **Figure 15–20**, which coil needs to be de-energized in order for all motors to stop running in the machine press?

    (a) M1
    (b) M2 or TR
    (c) M2 or M3
    (d) Any of the coils will stop all motors in the machine press.

UNIT 16 Master Stop Function

Unit 16—Introduction

This unit explains wiring motor controllers together so that one or more stop pushbuttons can be used to shut down several motors simultaneously.

16.1 Master or Emergency Stop Controls for Multiple Motors

It's often desirable to have several motors in a system shut down at the same time. **Figure 16-1** is a ladder diagram of a machine consisting of three motors. Each has its own start-stop PB station, and there's one master PB that stops all motors at the same time. This installation also uses overload contacts (OLs) for all of the motors. They're wired in series to stop all motors if any one of the three overload contacts opens. The power for all three PB stations comes from one motor starter (or a separate source). When using this method, it's important to remove any relevant factory-installed jumpers within the starters before wiring this control circuit.

An example of a master (emergency) stop application is where an assembly-line conveyor feeds sheet steel to a machine press that cuts or shapes the steel, then ejects the pieces to another conveyor for an additional process. If the press stops out of sequence with the other motors, the steel on the conveyor will still be fed into the system, creating many problems. A master (emergency) stop PB can help prevent this type of problem.

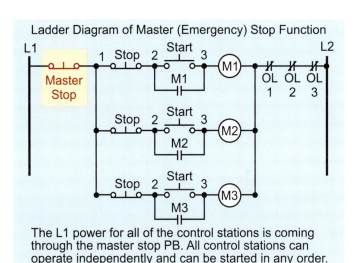

Figure 16–1

Most machine presses are equipped with hydraulic and high-pressure oil cooling pumps. If either of these pumps stops working, damage to the equipment can result and injuries to personnel can occur. Wiring all OL contacts in series is one method that can help prevent this.

Figure 16-2 is a connection (wiring) diagram of the installation shown in **Figure 16-1**. Although harder to read than the control circuit line diagram, this diagram clearly shows the relationship between the different motors and their controllers. In this application, start-stop stations can control each motor individually as long as the master stop switch is closed and all of the OLs are closed.

Unit 16 Master Stop Function

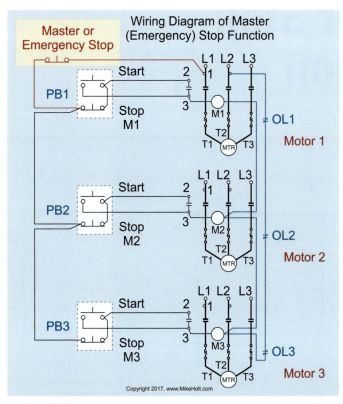

Figure 16–2

Additional master (emergency) stop switches can be added. They must be connected in series with the first master stop switch. They must also be connected into the control circuit before the first individual start-stop station.

16.2 Factory Installed Jumpers

Some starters arrive from the factory with a jumper installed from terminal 3 of the holding contact to one side of the coil. Jumpers from the L2 terminal to one side of the overload contact, and from the other side of the NC overload contact to the starter coil may also be installed.

When wiring controls for multiple motors, it's important to remember that these factory-installed jumpers between L2 and the coil must be removed from the OL contacts in order to connect them in series, **Figures 16–1 and 16–2**. In these diagrams, the OLs for all of the motors are connected in series. This method is used to stop all motors if any one of them fails due to an overload condition.

In other types of controls, the jumper from the holding contact terminal 3 to the coil, and the OL jumpers may need to be removed. Because there are so many possible combinations of controls, each application and installation needs to be considered carefully before energizing the system.

16.3 Types of Pushbuttons

The master stop examples shown in **Figures 16–1 and 16–2** use a momentary-contact pushbutton. It's also common to use a maintained-contact pushbutton, such as a mushroom-head emergency stop pushbutton, or some other maintained-contact switch (such as a toggle switch) for the master stop function. When a maintained-contact device is used, the motors on this control circuit can't operate until the master stop switch is reset.

Unit 16—Conclusion

This unit explained how to implement a master stop function for multiple motors. It also described how motor overload units (OLs) can be connected in series so that if any motor stops due to an overload condition, all related motors will stop.

UNIT 16 Practice Questions

Unit 16—Practice Questions

16.1 Master or Emergency Stop Controls for Multiple Motors

1. Based on **Figure 16–3**, which of the following statements is correct?

   (a) A master stop switch is wired between L1 and L3.
   (b) A master stop switch is wired between L1 and the PB1 start PB.
   (c) A master stop switch is wired between L1 and the PB1 stop PB.
   (d) A master stop switch is wired between PB1 and PB3.

2. In **Figure 16–3**, if OL3 opens, which of the following motors will stop?

   (a) 1
   (b) 2
   (c) 3
   (d) 1, 2, and 3

3. In **Figure 16–3**, an additional emergency switch can be added between the L1 terminal of motor 1 and the NC PB emergency stop switch.

   (a) True
   (b) False

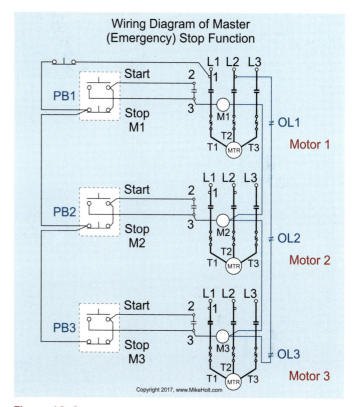

Figure 16–3

4. In **Figure 16–3**, if the stop PB is pressed for motor 1, which of the following motors will stop?

   (a) 1
   (b) 2
   (c) 3
   (d) 1, 2, and 3

Unit 16 — Practice Questions

5. Based on **Figure 16–3**, which of the following statements is correct?

   (a) Motor 1 must be running in order for the other motors to run.
   (b) The OLs for all three motors are wired in parallel to each other.
   (c) Motor 3 can start if motors 1 and 2 are off.
   (d) Motor 2 must be on before motor 3 can be started.

6. In **Figure 16–3**, a NC PB installed between the NC PB in PB1 and the NC PB in PB2 will stop _____ when pressed.

   (a) motor 1 only
   (b) motors 1 and 2 only
   (c) motors 2 and 3 only
   (d) all three motors

ANNEX A — MISCELLANEOUS REQUIREMENTS

Chapter 1 of this textbook contained general information related to motor controls, including definitions, abbreviations, and drawing symbols. Chapters 2, 3, and 4 covered control theory, components, and schematic directions for many different motor control applications. This annex presents technical reference information that's useful when working on motor controls. It consists of the following units:

Unit 17—Motor and Controller Disconnecting Means in Schematics

Unit 18—Miscellaneous Motor Control Circuits

Unit 19—Motor Winding Connections

Unit 20—Miscellaneous Control and Signaling Circuits

Notes

UNIT 17 — Motor and Controller Disconnecting Means in Schematics

Unit 17—Introduction

In most cases, the *NEC* requires that a motor have a disconnecting means within sight of the motor. The *Code* also requires that the motor controller has a disconnecting means within sight of the motor controller. In some cases, a single disconnect can be used for both.

Author's Comment: The *Code* defines "In Sight From (Within Sight)" as being visible and within 50 ft. See the Article 100 definition in the *NEC*. **Figure 17–1**

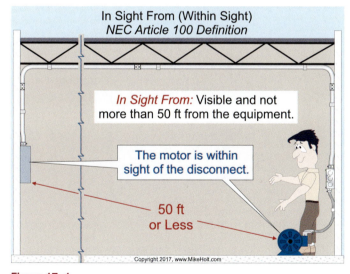

Figure 17–1

Most motor control schematics don't show the disconnecting means for the motor or the motor controller. It's up to the designer or installer to understand the *Code* requirements for both the motor and motor controller disconnecting means.

This part explains what the *NEC* considers a motor controller. One example of a motor controller is the magnetic starter we've been using for many of the control circuits covered in this textbook. What can be a little confusing is that the PB stations we've been discussing aren't considered motor controllers in the *Code*. They're just devices used in a control circuit. The key to understanding the difference between a control device and a motor controller is the motor controller actually makes-and-breaks the branch-circuit conductors that supply the motor.

17.1 Motor Controllers and Disconnects

This part discusses some of the *NEC* terminology related to motor control circuits.

Author's Comment: Annex B of this textbook contains text on Article 430 of the *NEC* (Motors, Motor Circuits, and Controllers) extracted from Mike Holt's *Illustrated Guide to Understanding the National Electrical Code, Volume 1*.

Unit 17 — Motor and Controller Disconnecting Means in Schematics

Disconnecting Means. A device, group of devices, or other means by which the conductors of a circuit can be disconnected from their source of supply [Article 100]. **Figure 17–2**

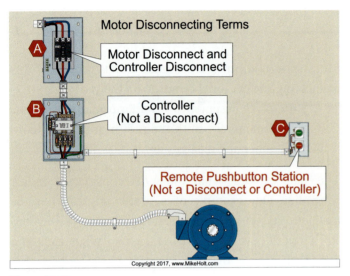

Figure 17–2

The disconnecting means in **Figure 17-2A** is a circuit breaker that, when opened, disconnects the branch-circuit conductors from the controller. A fusible disconnect switch can also be used. An unfused safety switch can also be used if short-circuit and ground-fault protection for the motor is provided elsewhere. The *NEC* requires that a motor controller has a disconnecting means, and also requires that a motor have a disconnecting means. Because the controller disconnect in this illustration is located right next to the controller but also close to the motor, it's used as both a controller disconnect and a motor disconnect. The *Code* generally requires a disconnect for a motor or a motor controller to be located within sight of the equipment it serves.

Controller. A motor controller is any switch or device that's normally used to start and stop a motor by making-and-breaking the motor-circuit current [430.2]. In **Figure 17-2B**, the magnetic starter is the controller because the main motor power contacts carry the motor current and are normally closed and opened to start and stop the motor. The disconnecting means shown in **Figure 17-2A** isn't a controller because it's not normally used to turn the motor off and on.

The start-stop station, shown in **Figure 17-2C** isn't a motor disconnect or a motor controller because it doesn't carry the actual motor current. It's simply a control device and part of the motor control circuit. Start-stop stations are often confused with controllers because they're used to start and stop motors. But since they don't actually make-and-break the power contacts to the motor, by definition they aren't motor controllers. The definition in 430.2 of the *NEC* states that a motor control circuit is the circuit of a control apparatus or system that carries the electrical signals directing the performance of the controller, but doesn't carry the main power current. **Figure 17–3**

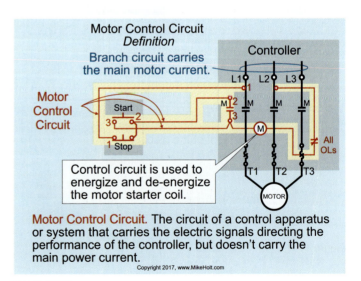

Figure 17–3

Motor and Controller Disconnecting Means in Schematics — Unit 17

It's important to understand that although pushing the start-stop PB station causes the power contacts to open and close, the power contacts aren't actually located in the start-stop PB station, so the PB station itself isn't the controller. In cases where a magnetic motor starter has the start-stop PBs located in the same enclosure, the magnetic contactor is still the controller, and the start-stop PBs are just control devices.

Author's Comment: A device used to control a motor, such as a drum switch or pressure switch, will often carry the main power to a motor as well as being used to turn the motor on and off. Under these conditions, by definition, these devices are considered controllers. If these same devices are used to energize a coil instead of carrying the main power to the motor, they will simply be control devices.

Controller and Disconnect. The definitions of "Controller Disconnect" and "Motor Controller" are similar in some aspects. They both carry motor current in some way. It's possible for the motor disconnect and the motor controller to be the same device. For example, small motors are often controlled by the simple operation of a switch which disconnects the circuit conductors from the motor instead of the motor starter. This switch meets the definition of a disconnect, but it's also the normal method of turning the motor on and off and carries the motor current which makes it a controller as well. **Figure 17-4**

Author's Comment: A general-use ac snap switch can be used as a motor disconnect or controller for stationary motors rated 2 hp or less, and 300V or less providing the requirements of 430.83(C) or 430.109(C)(2) of the *NEC* are met.

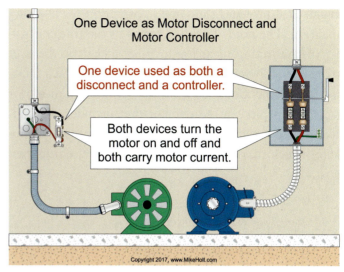

Figure 17–4

Disconnects in Schematics. Many control schematics don't show the motor or controller disconnecting means. When they do show the disconnecting means, it's often just a box with a notation. **Figure 17-5** demonstrates how a disconnecting means can be shown in a ladder diagram.

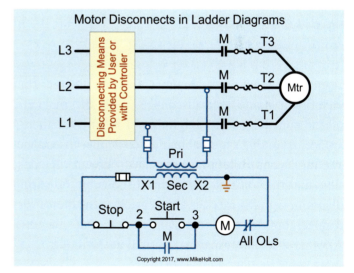

Figure 17–5

Unit 17 — Motor and Controller Disconnecting Means in Schematics

Figure 17-6 provides the same information for a wiring diagram. The note in the box indicates that the controller disconnecting means is to be provided by the user (which usually means the installer), or it can be a built-in part of the motor controller. A combination motor starter is a piece of equipment that includes the controller disconnect and the controller in the same enclosure, which may save installation time and equipment cost.

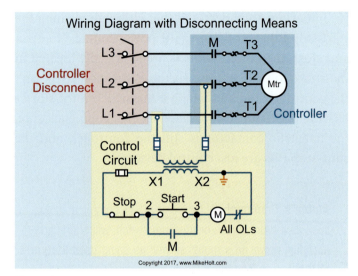

Figure 17–7

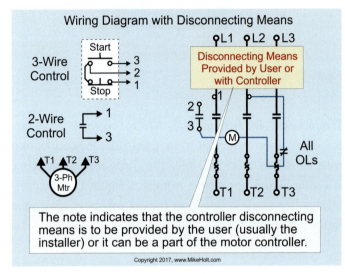

Figure 17–6

Figure 17–7 shows an example of a wiring diagram that includes a nonfusable disconnect with the magnetic motor controller. The diagram can mean that there's an enclosure that's a combination controller disconnect and motor controller (magnetic motor starter). It's possible that the controller disconnect shown in the wiring diagram, in many cases, is also serving as the motor disconnect, but don't automatically assume that's the case. Another disconnect may be required at the motor.

Author's Comment: Motors and motor controllers both require disconnects. Sometimes a single disconnect can be used for both depending on the conditions and locations of the equipment [430.102(B)]. **Figure 17–8**

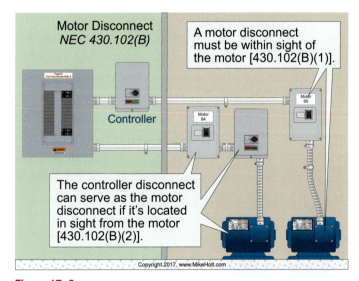

Figure 17–8

186 | Mike Holt Enterprises | *Understanding Basic Motor Controls*

17.2 Disconnect for Separate Control Circuit

A disconnect for the motor control circuit is required when the control circuit isn't tapped from the controller disconnect. The control circuit disconnect and the controller disconnect must be adjacent to each other [450.75(A)]. **Figure 17–9**

Additional information on disconnects can be found in Annex B of this textbook.

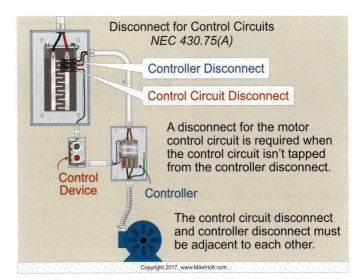

Figure 17–9

Unit 17—Conclusion

This unit discussed *NEC* requirements for disconnecting means used with motor and motor controllers. It also explained why the PB controls aren't usually the actual motor controller or disconnect.

Unit 17—Practice Questions

17.1 Motor Controllers and Disconnects

1. A _____ is any switch or device that's normally used to start and stop a motor by making-and-breaking the motor-circuit current.
   (a) motor circuit
   (b) controller disconnect
   (c) motor controller
   (d) motor starter

2. A general-use ac snap switch can be used as a motor disconnect or controller for stationary motors rated 2 hp or less and _____ or less providing the requirements of 430.83(C) or 430.109(C)(2) of the *NEC* are met.
   (a) 120V
   (b) 240V
   (c) 300V
   (d) 600V

3. Which of the following can be considered control devices rather than motor controllers?
   (a) A start-stop PB station.
   (b) A pressure switch.
   (c) A limit switch.
   (d) all of these

4. Which of the following can be considered a motor controller?
   (a) A magnetic starter.
   (b) A drum switch.
   (c) A snap switch.
   (d) all of these

5. Based on **Figure 17–10**, which of the following statements is correct?
   (a) The controller disconnecting means is shown on the wiring diagram.
   (b) A 2-wire control circuit won't work with this motor controller.
   (c) The controller disconnect is provided by the user or installer.
   (d) The main power contacts aren't shown in this wiring diagram.

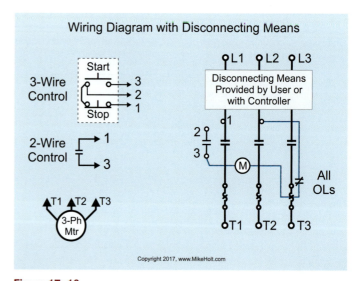

Figure 17–10

Practice Questions — Unit 17

6. In **Figure 17–10**, if a 2-wire control circuit is used, which of the following statements is correct?

    (a) The auxiliary contacts 2-3 are necessary for the 2-wire circuit to operate.
    (b) The auxiliary contacts 2-3 will remain open after the contacts on the 2-wire circuit close.
    (c) The circuit is connected to L1 and one side of the coil.
    (d) The circuit is connected to both sides of the auxiliary contacts.

7. In **Figure 17–10**, the start-stop PB station with a 3-wire circuit can be used as the motor disconnecting means required by the *NEC*.

    (a) True
    (b) False

8. In **Figure 17–10**, the start-stop PB station with a 3-wire circuit can be used as the motor controller disconnecting means required by the *NEC*.

    (a) True
    (b) False

9. In **Figure 17–10**, the start-stop PB station is just a control device and not considered a motor disconnect or a controller disconnect.

    (a) True
    (b) False

10. In **Figure 17–10**, if the 2-wire circuit is wired with a snap switch and connected to the motor starter, it will be considered _____.

    (a) a controller disconnect as required by the *NEC*
    (b) a motor disconnect as required by the *NEC*
    (c) just a control circuit with a control device
    (d) a or b

Notes

UNIT 18 | Miscellaneous Motor Control Circuits

Unit 18—Introduction

The basic control functions described in this textbook can be combined and expanded into more complex and sophisticated control schemes. This unit explains how to combine some of the equipment covered earlier to add different functions to motor control circuits.

18.1 Combining Devices and Functions for Motor Control Circuits

Basic motor control circuits can be expanded by combining circuits and components, and adding functions to create more sophisticated control schemes. This results in more complex control circuit diagrams. Remember to break down a complex control diagram into the individual functions found in basic control schematics, and carefully evaluate the relationship of the various components and functions to understand the overall operation.

18.2 Control Relay (CR)

Control relays (see Unit 3) are frequently used to expand the capability of basic 2- or 3-wire control circuits.

Example: Control Relay for Jogging. Figure 18-1A illustrates a control relay (CR) being used to add a jogging (inching) feature to a basic start-stop station and 3-wire circuit. The wiring diagram illustrates a control relay with two NO contacts. Although the control relay is shown directly above the PB station, it can be located in other enclosures such as the magnetic starter enclosure, if there's enough room. Placing the control relay directly above the pushbutton station in the diagram makes it easier to see the wiring between these two components. An NO momentary-contact pushbutton has been added to the pushbutton station, Figure 18-1B. The magnetic starter with the M coil and auxiliary contacts 2-3 is shown in Figure 18-1C.

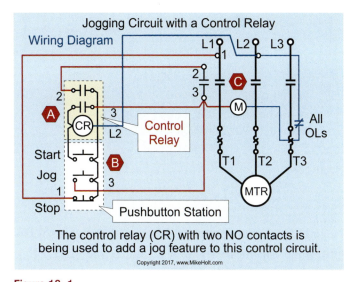

Figure 18–1

Unit 18 — Miscellaneous Motor Control Circuits

Author's Comment: A two-position momentary-contact switch can be used for the jogging (inching) feature of the circuit shown in **Figure 18–1B**. The wiring will be the same.

The ladder diagram for the same control circuit and motor is provided in **Figure 18-2**. The wiring diagram of this circuit, **Figure 18-1**, makes it easier to see how to wire the control relay and pushbutton station while the ladder diagram, **Figure 18-2**, makes it easier to see how the circuit works. Although the control relay has been installed to add a jogging feature to this circuit, the NO CR contacts are wired in series with the holding circuit. During jogging operations, the holding circuit must be disabled so the starter will only run as long as the jog PB is depressed. Adding the CR NO contacts in series with the M holding contacts accomplishes this.

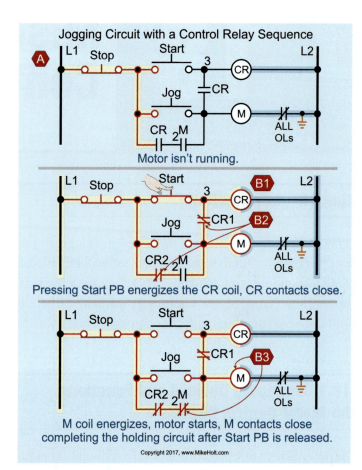

Figure 18–3

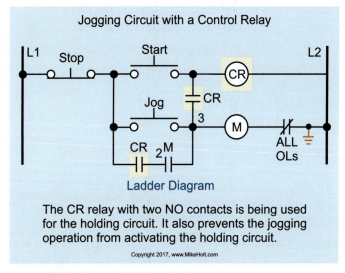

Figure 18–2

At this point, the CR1 contact energizes the M coil while the CR2 contact creates a path to terminal 2 of the auxiliary contacts. When the M coil energizes, the auxiliary contacts close providing the last component of the holding circuit and the motor stays running. **Figure 18-3B3**

At this point, pushing the jog PB while the holding circuit is activated has no effect on the motor's running condition. Pressing the stop PB de-energizes the M and CR coils, the auxiliary contacts and both CR contacts open, and the motor stops.

Normal Operation. Figure 18-3A depicts the control circuit while the motor is at rest. When the start PB is pushed, **Figure 18-3B1**, the CR coil energizes and closes both NO CR contacts. **Figure 18-3B2**

Miscellaneous Motor Control Circuits — Unit 18

Jog Operation. The jog function only works when the motor is stopped or at rest, **Figure 18-4A**. When the jog PB is pushed, the M coil energizes and the motor runs, **Figure 18-4B**. The auxiliary contacts M close while the jog PB is pressed but the holding circuit can't be maintained because the NO CR2 contacts prevent a complete circuit during the jogging operation, **Figure 18–4C**. Also, the NO CR1 contacts prevent the control relay from being energized. Releasing the jog PB de-energizes the M coil and the motor stops.

18.3 Selector Switch Pushbutton

A maintained-contact selector switch (see Unit 10) can be combined with a momentary-contact pushbutton. This combination allows maintained contacts (depending on the position of the switch) to be used with the spring return feature of a momentary-contact pushbutton. This allows several possible wiring combinations with a single device. **Figure 18-5**

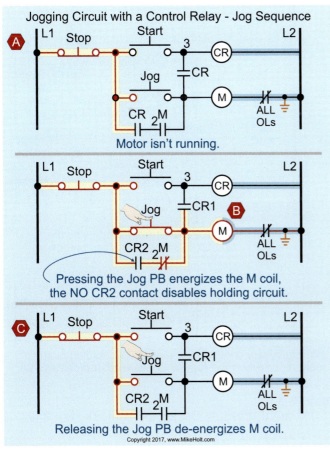

Figure 18–4

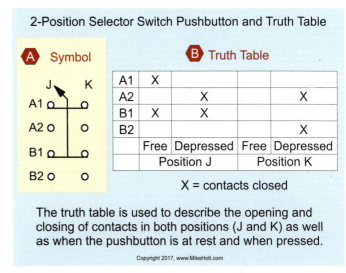

Figure 18–5

The truth table illustrates how this device functions in each position, **Figure 18-6**. In position J and with the PB not pressed (free), contacts A1 are closed, A2 are open, B1 are closed, and B2 are open, **Figure 18-6A**. Still in position J, but with the PB pressed, contacts A1 are open, A2 are closed, B1 stay the same (closed), and B2 stay the same (open), **Figure 18-6B**. When the selector switch is in position K, and when the PB isn't pressed (free), all four sets of contacts are open, **Figure 18-6C**. Still in position K, but with the PB pressed, the A1 contacts remain open, the A2 contacts close, B1 remain open, and B2 close. **Figure 18-6D**

Unit 18 — Miscellaneous Motor Control Circuits

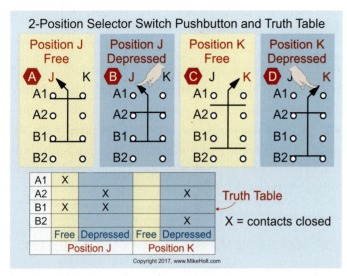

Figure 18–6

Example: The ladder diagram in **Figure 18-7** *provides an example of a two-position selector switch pushbutton used to add a jog feature to a 3-wire motor control circuit.*

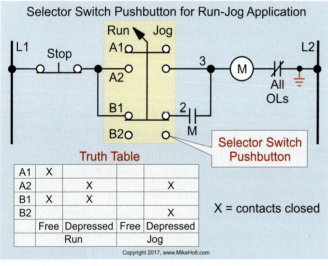

Figure 18–7

Normal Operation. **Figure 18-8A** depicts the control circuit line diagram when the motor is at rest and the selector switch pushbutton is in the run position. In this position, the control circuit works just like a normal start-stop station on a 3-wire circuit (run being the same as start). When the run PB is pressed, **Figure 18-8B**, coil M energizes, auxiliary contacts 2-3 close, and the motor runs. When the run PB is released, **Figure 18-8C**, the holding circuit stays energized through the closed B1 contacts of the run-jog selector switch PB, and the motor continues to run.

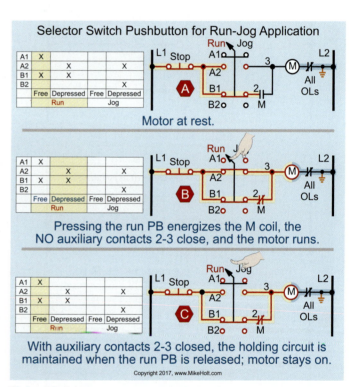

Figure 18–8

Jog Operation. The selector switch can be turned to the jog function at any time using this control circuit, even when the motor is running. If the motor is running, setting the selector switch PB to the jog position opens the holding circuit through the B1 contacts and de-energizes the coil and motor. **Figure 18-9A**

194 | Mike Holt Enterprises | *Understanding Basic Motor Controls*

Miscellaneous Motor Control Circuits — Unit 18

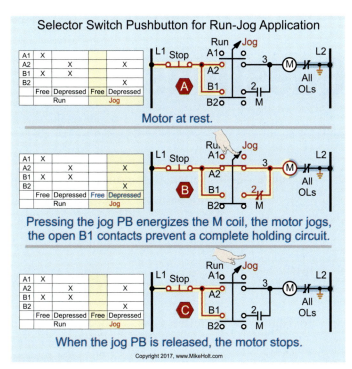

Figure 18–9

When the jog PB is pushed, Figure 18-9B, the M coil energizes, the auxiliary contacts 2-3 close, and the motor runs only as long as the jog PB is being pressed. Because the B1 contacts in series with the auxiliary contacts 2-3 are open, the holding circuit can't achieve continuity. When the jog PB is released, Figure 18-9C, the M coil and the motor both de-energize.

Unit 18—Conclusion

This unit explained how control relays and selector switch PBs are used to expand the capability of a basic 2- or 3-wire motor control circuit by combining equipment used in previous units.

UNIT 18 Practice Questions

Unit 18—Practice Questions

18.2 Control Relay (CR)

1. In **Figure 18–10**, letter A is connected to point _____.

   (a) 2
   (b) 3
   (c) L1
   (d) L2

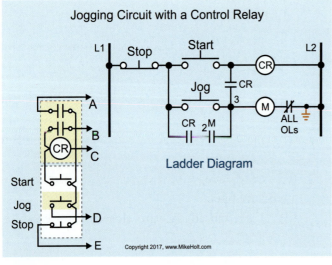

Figure 18–10

2. In **Figure 18–10**, letter B is connected to point _____.

   (a) 2
   (b) 3
   (c) 4
   (d) L1

3. In **Figure 18–10**, letter C is connected to point _____.

   (a) 3
   (b) 4
   (c) L1
   (d) L2

4. In **Figure 18–10**, letter D is connected to point _____.

   (a) 2
   (b) 3
   (c) L1
   (d) L2

5. In **Figure 18–10**, letter E is connected to point _____.

   (a) 2
   (b) 3
   (c) L1
   (d) L2

18.3 Selector Switch Pushbutton

6. In **Figure 18–11**, the word "free" on the truth table means that the PB is _____.

   (a) being pressed in the J position
   (b) being pressed in the K position
   (c) not closing any contacts
   (d) not being pressed while in the J or K position

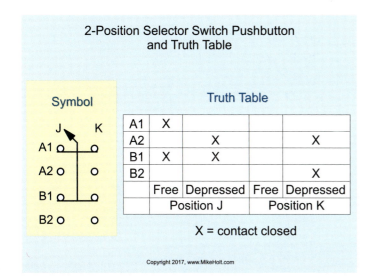

Figure 18–11

7. In **Figure 18–11**, if the switch is in the K position, and the PB is pressed, contacts _____.

   (a) A1 are open, A2 are closed, B1 are open, and B2 are closed
   (b) A1 are closed, A2 are open, B1 are closed, and B2 are open
   (c) A1 are open, A2 are closed, B1 are closed, and B2 are open
   (d) A1 are closed, A2 are closed, B1 are closed, and B2 are closed

8. In **Figure 18–11**, if the switch is in the K position and the PB isn't being pressed, contacts _____.

   (a) A1 are open, A2 are closed, B1 are open, and B2 are closed
   (b) A1 are closed, A2 are open, B1 are closed, and B2 are open
   (c) A1 are open, A2 are open, B1 are open, and B2 are open
   (d) A1 are closed, A2 are closed, B1 are closed, and B2 are closed

9. In **Figure 18–11**, if the switch is in the J position, and the PB is pressed, contacts _____.

   (a) A1 are open, A2 are closed, B1 are open, and B2 are closed
   (b) A1 are closed, A2 are open, B1 are closed, and B2 are open
   (c) A1 are open, A2 are closed, B1 are closed, and B2 are open
   (d) A1 are closed, A2 are closed, B1 are closed, and B2 are closed

10. In **Figure 18–11**, if the switch is in the J position, and the PB isn't being pressed, contacts _____.

    (a) A1 are open, A2 are closed, B1 are open, and B2 are closed
    (b) A1 are closed, A2 are open, B1 are closed, and B2 are open
    (c) A1 are open, A2 are closed, B1 are closed, and B2 are open
    (d) A1 are closed, A2 are closed, B1 are closed, and B2 are closed

Notes

UNIT 19 Motor Winding Connections

Part 19—Introduction

Three-phase motors are available in many different designs and configurations, including dual-voltage motors. They may have up to nine different terminals or leads, numbered T-1 through T-9. This unit explains lead designations for different types of three-phase motors.

19.1 Three-Phase Motors

Three-phase motors are typically used in commercial and industrial applications. Three-phase motors are available in most nominal voltage ranges and many can be field-connected to operate on either of two possible voltages (typically called a high- or low-voltage level). These types of motors are referred to as dual-voltage motors.

All three-phase motors are constructed with a number of individual, internally wound coils. Regardless of how many separate coils there are in a three-phase motor, the coils of each phase are always wired together in series or in parallel to produce three distinct windings, which are called "phases." Each phase is always equal to one-third of the total number of coils. The phases are usually referred to as "Phase A," "Phase B," and "Phase C."

Wye (Y) three-phase and delta (Δ) three-phase refer to the way the windings are connected together in three-phase motors. Many of the construction and installation requirements are the same for wye- and delta-connected, three-phase motors. The external branch-circuit wiring is the same. The windings of some three-phase motors are internally connected together to form either a wye or delta connection, with only three motor leads accessible to the installer; T1, T2, and T3. Other motors have more than three leads brought out from the internal windings, typically nine leads, which need to be properly connected in the field. **Figure 19-1**

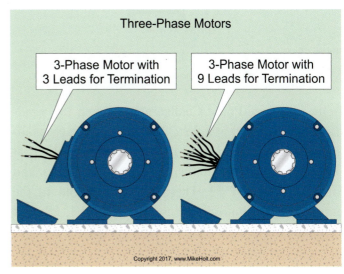

Figure 19–1

Unit 19 — Motor Winding Connections

Wye (Y) Three-Phase Configuration. When the windings are connected in a wye configuration, one end of each of the three phases is connected together internally. The other ends of the three phases are marked T1, T2, and T3 and are brought out to the motor terminal housing for connection to L1, L2, and L3 of the circuit supplying the motor, **Figure 19-2**. A wye configuration is also called a "Star Configuration" or "Star Connection."

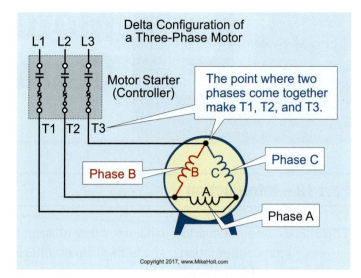

Figure 19–3

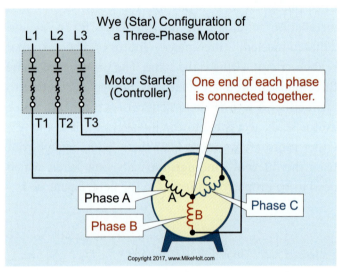

Figure 19–2

Delta (Λ) Three-Phase Configuration. When the windings are connected in a delta configuration, each winding is connected end-to-end to make a closed loop at the point where two of the phases come together and form T1, T2, and T3. These are brought out to the motor terminal housing for connection to L1, L2, and L3 of the circuit supplying the motor. **Figure 19-3**

Author's Comments:

- There's also a wye/delta- (star/delta-) connected motor, which is commonly used where reduced inrush currents or reduced starting torque is needed. In effect, the motor starts as a wye-connected motor, which produces less torque and draws less starting current. After coming up-to-speed, a contactor changes the connections so the motor runs as a delta-connected motor to produce full power. This is one of many specialized motors which aren't covered in detail in this unit.

- When starting a three-phase motor for the first time, it should be uncoupled from the load and then jogged or bumped to ensure proper rotation.

19.2 Dual-Voltage, Nine Lead, Three-Phase Motors

The most common three-phase motor is the nine-lead, dual-voltage motor. The windings are connected in either a wye (Y) or delta (Δ) configuration. The most common nominal dual-voltage rating for both types is 230V (low) and 460V (high). Each phase is made up of two windings (or two groups of windings). Some of the windings are connected internally and nine leads are brought out to the motor terminal housing. The internal connection of the winding leads depends on whether the motor is wye-connected or delta-connected. The nine leads are typically numbered T1 through T9.

Motor Winding Connections Unit 19

A dual-voltage motor has the same hp rating at both voltages. Also, the motor uses the same amount of power (VA) at either voltage. At the lower voltage, the motor draws twice as much current as it does at the higher voltage. Dual-voltage motors connected to the higher voltage often have smaller conductor and raceway sizes, which can reduce the installation cost.

Author's Comment: There are numerous other voltage ratings for motors. Small commercial buildings commonly use 208V three-phase motors, which aren't dual-voltage. There are specialized motors that operate at higher voltages including 550V and 575V that may be encountered in industrial installations. Examples of these higher-voltage specialized motors are deep well pumps in oil fields where higher-voltage distribution systems are used to combat voltage drop. Occasionally machinery imported from other countries may have a different operating voltage. Always check the nameplate voltage before wiring a motor.

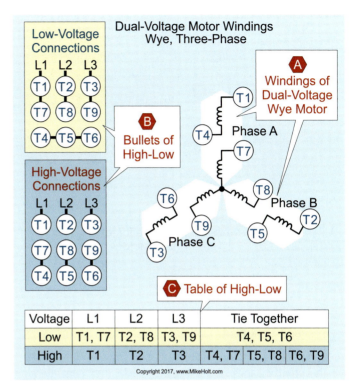

Figure 19–4

Wye- (Star-) Connected, Three-Phase, Dual-Voltage Motors

Figure 19-4 shows motor windings connected in a wye (Y) configuration. One end of each of the three phases is connected to the other phases at a common point inside the motor. The remaining end of each phase is then brought out and connected to the power-supply conductors. Each phase is split between two windings to allow the individual windings to be connected in series for high voltage, or in parallel for low voltage, **Figure 19-4A**. This creates the nine terminals referred to as T1 through T9. The information provided on the terminal connection chart is usually provided on the motor nameplate, or sometimes in the motor terminal housing. The connection chart is either bullets with lines, **Figure 19-4B**, or a table. **Figure 19-4C**

Low-Voltage Wye Connection (Usually 230V, Three-Phase). The individual coils of each phase (A, B, and C) are connected in parallel so each coil receives 100 percent of the voltage. This is accomplished by connecting power L1 to motor leads T1 and T7, power L2 to motor leads T2 and T8, and power L3 to motor leads T3 and T9. The remaining motor leads are connected together (T4, T5, and T6). **Figures 19–4 and 19–5A**

High-Voltage Wye Connection (Usually 460V, Three-Phase). The individual coils of each phase (A, B, and C) are connected in series so each coil receives 50 percent of the voltage. This is accomplished by connecting power L1 to motor lead T1, power L2 to motor lead T2, and power L3 to motor lead T3. Both coils of each phase are then connected together. In phase A, motor leads T4 and T7 are connected together; in phase B, motor leads T5 and T8 are connected together; and in phase C, motor leads T6 and T9 are connected together. **Figures 19–4 and 19–5B**

Unit 19 | Motor Winding Connections

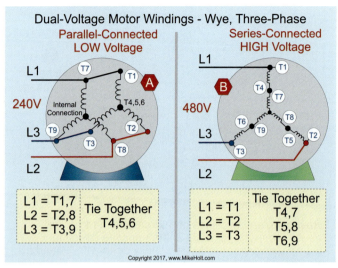

Figure 19–5

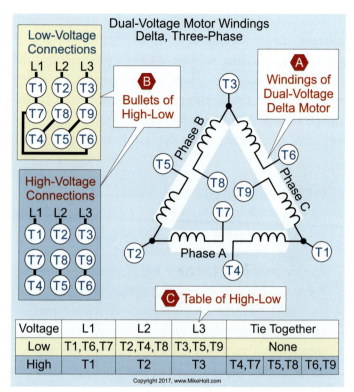

Figure 19–6

Author's Comment: Common system nominal voltages include 120/240V, 120/208V, and 277/480V, which are the rated voltages of the electrical service or separately derived system to the building or facility. Common motor rated voltages are lower (115V, 230V, and 460V) to allow for voltage drop from the electrical source.

Delta-Connected, Three-Phase, Dual-Voltage Motors

Figure 19-6 shows delta-connected motor windings with nine leads. Both high- and low-voltage connections are pictured.

Figure 19-6A shows a three-phase motor wired in a delta (Δ) configuration. Like wye-connected motors, delta dual-voltage motors have nine leads marked T1 through T9 (terminals 1 through 9). Also, like wye-connected motors, each phase has two coils (windings). The information provided on the terminal connection chart is usually provided on the motor nameplate, or sometimes in the motor terminal housing. The connection chart is either bullets with lines, Figure 19-6B, or a table. Figure 19-6C

Low Voltage (Usually 230V, Three-Phase). The coils are connected in parallel so each of the six windings receives 100 percent of the voltage, Figure 19-7A. This is accomplished by connecting power L1 to motor leads T1, T6, and T7.

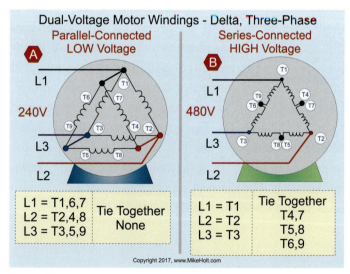

Figure 19–7

202 | Mike Holt Enterprises | *Understanding Basic Motor Controls*

Motor Winding Connections — Unit 19

Author's Comment: In **Figure 19-7A**, L1 is connected to four points of the windings, so it's a bit confusing to say it's connected to only three points (T1, T6, and T7). Remember that point T1 is made up of two points internally with one lead brought out. See **Figure 19-6A**. This is where the fourth point comes from. This explanation also applies to points T2 and T3.

Continuing with the low-voltage connection points, L2 is connected to T2, T4, and T8, and L3 is connected to T3, T5, and T9. There are no leads to be tied together.

High Voltage (Usually 460V, Three-Phase). The individual coils of each phase (A, B, and C) are connected in series so each coil receives 50 percent of the voltage. This is accomplished by connecting power L1 to motor lead T1, power L2 to motor lead T2, and power L3 to motor lead T3. Both coils of each phase are then connected together. In phase A, motor leads T4 and T7 are connected together; in phase B, motor leads T5 and T8 are connected together; and in phase C, motor leads T6 and T9 are connected together. **Figure 19-7B**

Author's Comment: The high-voltage connection terminal numbers are the same for wye-connected and delta-connected motors. Even though the terminal numbers are the same, the configuration of the interior windings is different for each motor.

Rotation of Nine-Lead Motors. In order to change the direction of rotation in both wye (Y) and delta (Δ) three-phase, nine-lead motors, the industry standard is to interchange power leads L1 and L3, **Figure 19-8**. This can be easily accomplished by installing either a drum switch or a reversing starter. All the other motor leads shown in **Figures 19–4 through 19–7** remain the same.

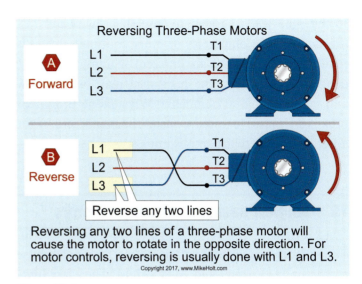

Figure 19–8

Connection Information on Nine-Lead Motors. It's not possible to determine whether a three-phase motor is wye- or delta-connected just by looking at it. All that's visible is the motor housing with coils of wire inside and nine motor leads in a terminal or connection box. However, the nameplate should provide the necessary information required for properly connecting the motor to the power leads.

For low-voltage connections, the way in which the nine leads connect identifies the motor as delta- or wye-connected. This isn't the case for high-voltage connections. Both wye-connected motors and delta-connected motors have the same high-voltage terminal number combinations, (L1-T1, L2-T2, L3-T3, tie together T4-T7, T5-T8, and T6-T9). See **Figures 19–4 and 19–6**.

Author's Comment: Notice that the high-voltage connection terminal numbers are the same for wye and delta nine-lead motors. But the numbering of the connections for the lower-voltage terminals are different for wye and delta.

Unit 19 | Motor Winding Connections

If the nine leads happen to lose their markings (T1 through T9), an ohmmeter or other continuity tester is required to isolate the six different windings. In some delta-wound motors, the resistance may be very low and require a digital ohmmeter, Wheatstone Bridge, or other very sensitive tester. Consult the manufacturer for a test procedure to accomplish this.

19.3 Single-Phase, Dual-Voltage Motors

The most common dual-voltage rating for single-phase motors is 115V (low) and 230V (high). There are literally hundreds of configurations for single-phase motor wiring, so it's very important to use the manufacturer's wiring diagrams for any single-phase motor.

A dual-voltage motor has the same hp rating at both voltages. Also, the motor uses the same amount of power (VA) at either voltage. The difference is that at the lower voltage, the motor draws twice as much current than it does at the higher-voltage connection. Dual-voltage motors connected to the higher voltage often have smaller conductor and raceway sizes, which can reduce the installation cost.

Single-phase, dual-voltage motors have two field windings that are each rated 115V. When the motor is operating at low voltage (115V), the windings are connected in parallel, **Figure 19–9A**. When the motor is operating at high voltage (230V), the windings are connected in series. **Figure 19-9B**

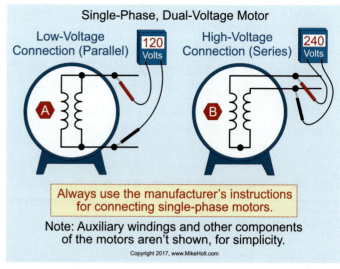

Figure 19–9

Unit 19—Conclusion

This unit explained wiring configurations for different types of three-phase motors and how to reverse three-phase motors by interchanging the L1 and L3 power leads.

UNIT 19 Practice Questions

Unit 19—Practice Questions

19.1 Three-Phase Motors

1. Most three-phase motors are used in commercial and industrial applications.

   (a) True
   (b) False

2. All of the windings of three-phase motors are always wired together to produce three distinct windings called Phases.:

   (a) True
   (b) False

3. A wye configuration for a three-phase motor is also called a _____-configured or connected motor.

   (a) triangle
   (b) star
   (c) square
   (d) circle

4. A wye/delta-connected motor is commonly used where reduced inrush current or reduced starting torque is needed.

   (a) True
   (b) False

19.2 Dual-Voltage, Nine Lead, Three-Phase Motors

5. In a dual-voltage, three-phase motor, the VA of the motor if connected for the lower voltage is _____.

   (a) one-half that of the higher voltage
   (b) double that of the higher voltage
   (c) one-third higher than the higher voltage
   (d) the same as that of the higher voltage

6. When connected at the lower voltage, a dual-voltage, three-phase motor draws _____ than when connected at the higher voltage.

   (a) one-half as much current
   (b) twice as much current
   (c) one-third as much current
   (d) the same amount of current

7. In **Figure 19–10**, if the low-voltage connections are being used, L1 will be connected to _____.

   (a) T1 and T2
   (b) T1 and T7
   (c) T1 only
   (d) T3 only

8. In **Figure 19–10**, if the low-voltage connections are being used, L2 will be connected to _____.

   (a) T1 and T7
   (b) T2 and T3
   (c) T2 and T8
   (d) T2 only

Unit 19 | Practice Questions

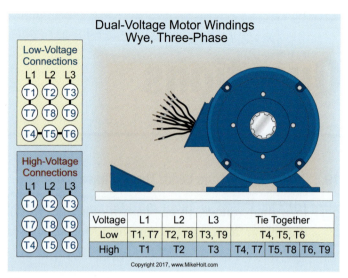

Figure 19–10

9. In **Figure 19–10**, if the low-voltage connections are being used, L3 will be connected to _____.

   (a) T3 and T4
   (b) T3 and T6
   (c) T3 and T9
   (d) T3 only

10. In **Figure 19–10**, if the low-voltage connections are being used, which motor leads not connected to the branch circuit are tied together?

    (a) T1, T2, and T3
    (b) T2, T3, and T4
    (c) T3, T4, and T5
    (d) T4, T5, and T6

11. In **Figure 19–10**, if the high-voltage connections are being used, L1 will be connected to _____.

    (a) T1 and T7
    (b) T1 only
    (c) T2 and T3
    (d) T2 only

12. In **Figure 19–10**, if the high-voltage connections are being used, L2 will be connected to _____.

    (a) T2 and T3
    (b) T2 and T6
    (c) T2 only
    (d) T3 only

13. In **Figure 19–10**, if the high-voltage connections are being used, and the motor leads are connected properly to the branch circuit, then _____ will be connected together.

    (a) T4 and T7
    (b) T5 and T8
    (c) T6 and T9
    (d) all of these

14. In **Figure 19–11**, if the high-voltage connections are being used, L1 will be connected to _____.

    (a) T1 and T2
    (b) T1 and T7
    (c) T1 only
    (d) T3 only

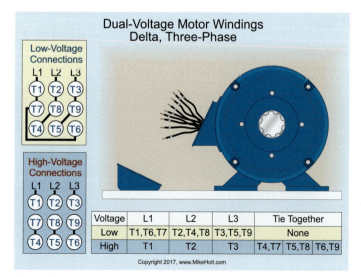

Figure 19–11

15. In **Figure 19–11**, if the low-voltage connections are being used, L1 will be connected to _____.

    (a) T1 and T2
    (b) T1, T2, and T3
    (c) T1, T6, and T7
    (d) T4 and T7

Practice Questions—General

Note: The following question is based on any part of this textbook up through this unit.

16. In **Figure 19–12**, the reversing motor starter is configured to interchange _____ to reverse the three-phase motor.

    (a) L1 and L2
    (b) L1 and L3
    (c) L2 and L3
    (d) T1 and T2

17. In **Figure 19–12**, if the motor is running in the reverse direction, which of the following statements is correct?

    (a) L1 connects to T1, L2 connects to T2, and L3 connects to T3.
    (b) L1 connects to T3, L2 connects to T2, and L3 connects to T1.
    (c) L1 connects to T2, L2 connects to T3, and L3 connects to T1.
    (d) The F coil is energized and the R coil isn't energized.

18. In **Figure 19–12**, if the FWD PB has been pressed and released, which of the following is(are) correct?

    (a) The NO contacts 2-3 remain closed.
    (b) The NO contacts 4-5 remain open.
    (c) Coil F is energized and coil R isn't energized.
    (d) all of these

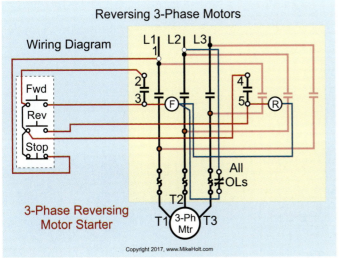

Figure 19–12

Notes

UNIT 20

Miscellaneous Control and Signaling Circuits

Unit 20—Introduction

This section contains miscellaneous control and signaling circuits that are very common in most buildings. Most electricians should have a basic understanding of how to wire these circuits. In many cases, wiring and connection instructions come with the equipment being installed.

20.1 Doorbells

Doorbells are very common in dwelling units. In addition to being installed at front doors, they're also used for back doors or delivery doors for businesses. Many consist of a small transformer, one or more doorbell buttons, and one or more chimes, bells, or buzzers.

Transformers. Many doorbell transformers have a 120V, 2-wire primary with a 16V, 2-wire secondary. There are also 18V and 24V transformers. This makes them a Class 2 device according to the *NEC* and they must comply with Article 725. The line side connections of the transformer (120V) must be in an enclosure [725.127], **Figure 20–1**. The load side of the transformer is a Class 2 circuit and the wiring isn't permitted in the same raceway or enclosure with power or Class 1 conductors [725.136(A)]. **Figure 20–2**

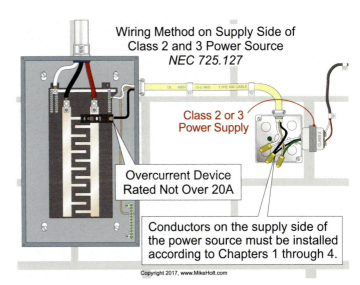

Figure 20–1

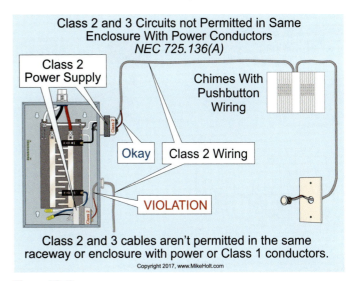

Figure 20–2

Understanding Basic Motor Controls | Mike Holt Enterprises

Unit 20 — Miscellaneous Control and Signaling Circuits

The cables can be run inside closed walls but all terminations and splices must be accessible. See Article 725, Part III of the *NEC* for Class 2 wiring method requirements.

Doorbells. There are hundreds of different doorbell arrangements that start with a simple buzzer. Chimes can sound a variety of tones from a basic "ding-dong" to electronic versions that play different sounds or music. There are also a large variety of wireless doorbell systems available.

Doorbell Buttons. A doorbell button is a momentary-contact pushbutton switch. Some of these pushbuttons are also illuminated. The illuminated pushbuttons are wired in the same manner as those that aren't illuminated. They're available in many different styles and colors.

Doorbell Circuits

Diagram 1. The following diagram shows an installation that includes one pushbutton and one bell, buzzer, or chime. **Figure 20–3**

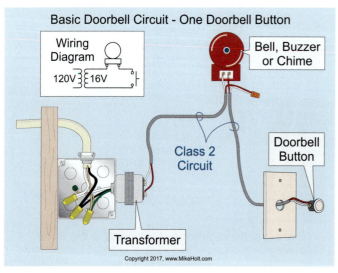

Figure 20–3

Diagram 2. The following diagram shows one set of chimes with two doorbell buttons. This type of chime can have one sound for the first door (such as ding-dong), and a different sound for the second door (such as dong-ding). **Figure 20–4**

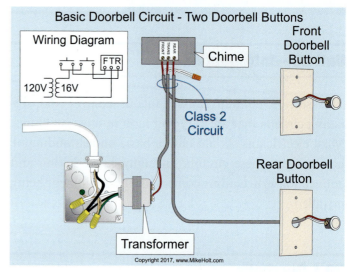

Figure 20–4

Diagram 3. The following diagram shows two sets of chimes with two doorbell buttons. This is the same circuit as the one shown in **Figure 20–4**, but with the additional set of chimes connected in parallel with the first set of chimes using a 3-wire cable. This application will work well in a two-story house or a house with a basement to allow the occupants to hear the chime in any part of the building. **Figure 20–5**

Diagram 4. This diagram shows the same circuit for wiring two doorbell buttons and two sets of chimes. This arrangement uses a 5-wire cable to take the 2-wire transformer circuit, and 3-wire chime extension circuit to the junction box for the other set of chimes. **Figure 20–6**

Miscellaneous Control and Signaling Circuits — Unit 20

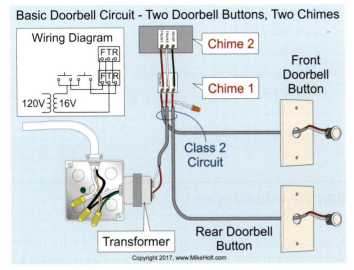

Figure 20–5

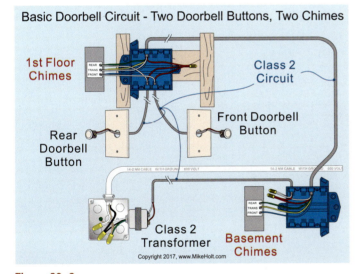

Figure 20–6

20.2 Thermostats for Air-Conditioning and Heat

Nearly every building has some form of air-conditioning that can include cooling, heat, or a combination of both. There are dozens of ways to combine heating and cooling equipment. The thermostat controls for this can be extremely complicated. We'll just touch on the most basic type such as those you might find in a small house or other type of small building. Different manufacturers use different control schemes, so always check the manufacturer's instructions before connecting control circuits.

Thermostat Terminal Codes

In 1972, NEMA standardized the labels on thermostat terminals. The following industry standards specify alphanumeric codes to be used for specific functions in thermostats:

- R, or RH for heat or RC for cool (red): hot side of transformer
- W (white): heat control
- W2 (pink or other color): heat, second stage
- Y2 (blue or pink): cool, second compressor stage
- C or X (black): common side of transformer (24 V)
- G (green): fan
- O (orange): energize to cool (heat pumps)
- L (tan, brown, gray, or blue): service indicator lamp
- X2 (blue, brown, gray, or tan): heat, second stage (electric)
- B (blue or orange): energize to heat
- B or X (blue, brown, or black): common side of transformer
- E (blue, pink, gray, or tan): emergency heat relay on a heat pump
- T (tan or gray): outdoor anticipator reset

Thermostat Diagrams

Some equipment has schematics fastened on the inside of the access panel or some other location inside the unit. For every installation, use the manufacturer's instructions for all electrical connections.

Unit 20 | Miscellaneous Control and Signaling Circuits

Diagram 1. Figure 20–7 shows one of many ways to wire a one-stage thermostat for an air-handling unit that contains the circulating fan and electric heat strips plus a compressor unit located outside the building. Since this application is using Class 2 cables instead of raceways for the thermostat wiring, the colors of the conductor insulation won't always match up with the NEMA terminal color codes.

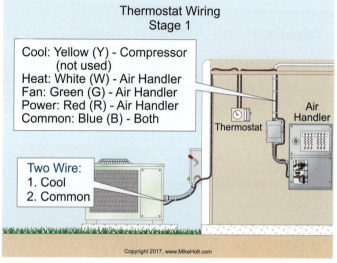

Figure 20–7

Author's Comment: There are no standard wiring diagrams for thermostats. There are dozens of possible ways to combine electric and gas/oil heating and air-conditioning equipment, so many installations have custom designed control wiring. In most cases, wiring diagrams are provided with equipment.

Unit 20—Conclusion

This unit discussed some different ways to wire doorbell circuits. It also explained that it's very important to use the manufacturer's wiring diagrams to wire the controls for heating and cooling equipment.

UNIT 20 Practice Questions

Unit 20—Practice Questions

Introduction

1. In many cases, equipment for control and signaling comes with the manufacturer's instructions.

    (a) True
    (b) False

20.1 Doorbells

2. Residential type doorbell circuits are typically _____.

    (a) 16V
    (b) 48V
    (c) 240V
    (d) 480V

3. Some chimes _____.

    (a) are electronic
    (b) can play music
    (c) go ding-dong
    (d) all of these

4. Illuminated doorbell pushbuttons can be wired in the same way as doorbell pushbuttons that aren't illuminated.

    (a) True
    (b) False

5. In **Figure 20-8**, which of the following statements is(are) correct?

    (a) The primary transformer terminations are in an enclosure.
    (b) There are two sets of chimes.
    (c) The wiring on the secondary side of the transformer is Class 2.
    (d) all of these

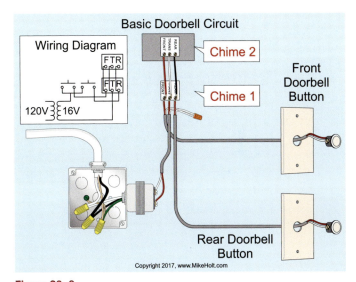

Figure 20–8

6. In **Figure 20–8**, chime 2 is wired in parallel with chime 1.

    (a) True
    (b) False

Unit 20 | Practice Questions

7. In **Figure 20–8**, the control circuit shown can be used for a _____.

   (a) house or business with a front and back door
   (b) location with only one door
   (c) location with only one room
   (d) b or c

8. In **Figure 20–8**, different tones sound depending on whether the front or rear doorbell button is pressed.

   (a) True
   (b) False

20.2 Thermostats for Air-Conditioning and Heat

9. In thermostat conductor termination, the color red is typically used for the _____.

   (a) power from the transformer
   (b) heat control
   (c) fan
   (d) compressor

10. In thermostat conductor termination, the color green is typically used for the _____.

    (a) power from the transformer
    (b) heat control
    (c) fan
    (d) compressor

ANNEX B

Bonus Material: Article 430—Motors, Motor Circuits, and Controllers

Introduction to Annex B—Bonus Material: Article 430—Motors, Motor Circuits, and Controllers

Article 430 contains the specific rules for conductor sizing, overcurrent protection, control circuit conductors, controllers, and disconnecting means for electric motors. The installation requirements for motor control centers are covered in Part VIII, and air-conditioning and refrigeration equipment are covered in Article 440.

Article 430 is one of the longest articles in the *NEC*. It's also one of the most complex, but motors are also complex equipment. They're electrical and mechanical devices, but what makes motor applications complex is the fact that they're inductive loads with a high-current demand at start-up that's typically six, or more, times the running current. This makes overcurrent protection for motor applications necessarily different from the protection employed for other types of equipment. So don't confuse general overcurrent protection with motor protection—you must calculate and apply them differently using the rules in Article 430.

You might be uncomfortable with the allowances for overcurrent protection found in this article, such as protecting a 10 AWG conductor with a 60A overcurrent protection device, but as you learn to understand how motor protection works, you'll understand why these allowances aren't only safe, but necessary.

NOTICE: The requirements contained in this Annex B edition of Article 430 are based on the 2020 *NEC* and you should always consult your *Code* book for current requirements.

Notes

ARTICLE 430 Motors, Motor Circuits, and Controllers

Introduction to Article 430—Motors, Motor Circuits, and Controllers

Article 430 contains the specific rules for conductor sizing, overcurrent protection, control circuit conductors, controllers, and disconnects for electric motors. The installation requirements for motor control centers are covered in Part VIII, and air-conditioning and refrigeration equipment are covered in Article 440.

This is one of the longest articles in the *NEC*. It is also one of the most complex, but motors are complex equipment. They are electrical and mechanical devices, but what makes motor applications complex is the fact that they are inductive loads with a high-current demand at start-up that is typically six (or more) times the running current. This makes overcurrent protection for motor applications necessarily different from the overcurrent protection employed for other types of equipment. So, do not confuse general overcurrent protection with motor protection—you must calculate and apply them differently using the rules in Article 430.

You might be uncomfortable with the allowances for overcurrent protection found in this article, such as protecting a 10 AWG conductor with a 60A overcurrent protective device. As you progress through Article 430, you will learn to understand how motor overcurrent protection works and realize just why these allowances are not only safe, but necessary.

Part I. General

430.1 Scope

Article 430 covers motors, motor branch-circuit and feeder conductors and their protection, motor overload protection, motor control circuits, motor controllers, and motor control centers. ▶Figure 430–1

▶Figure 430–1

Author's Comment:

▸ This article is divided into several parts; the most important being: ▶Figure 430–2

  ▸ General—Part I
  ▸ Conductor Sizing—Part II
  ▸ Overload Protection—Part III
  ▸ Branch-Circuit Short-Circuit and Ground-Fault Protection—Part IV
  ▸ Feeder Short-Circuit and Ground-Fault Protection—Part V
  ▸ Motor Control Circuits—Part VI
  ▸ Motor Controllers—Part VII
  ▸ Motor Control Centers—Part VIII
  ▸ Disconnecting Means—Part IX

Note 1: Article 440 contains the installation requirements for hermetic air-conditioning and refrigeration motor-compressors [440.1].

Article 430 Bonus Material: Article 430—Motors, Motor Circuits, and Controllers

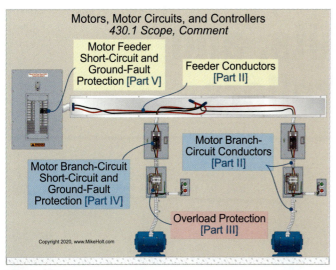

▶Figure 430-2

430.2 Definitions

Controller. Any switch or device used to start and stop a motor by making and breaking the motor circuit current. ▶Figure 430-3

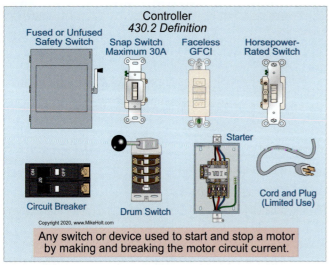

▶Figure 430-3

Author's Comment:

▸ A controller can be a horsepower-rated switch, snap switch, or circuit breaker. A pushbutton that operates an electromechanical relay is not a controller because it does not meet the controller rating requirements of 430.83. Devices such as start-stop stations and pressure switches are often control devices rather than motor controllers. When these devices control the coil of the motor starter they usually do not carry all the current of the motor branch circuit. ▶Figure 430-4

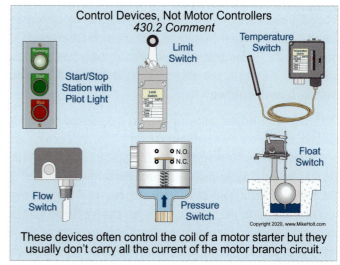

▶Figure 430-4

Electronically Protected (as applied to motors). A motor that is provided with electronic control that is an integral part of the motor and protects the it against dangerous overheating due to failure of the electronic control, overload, and failure to start.

430.6 Table FLC versus Motor Nameplate Current Rating

The size of conductors supplying equipment covered by Article 430 must be selected from the ampacity tables in accordance with 310.15 or be calculated in accordance with 310.14(B). Where flexible cord is used, the size of the conductor must be selected in accordance with 400.5.

(A) General Requirements. Motor current ratings used for the application of this article are determined by (A)(1) and (A)(2). ▶Figure 430-5

Bonus Material: Article 430—Motors, Motor Circuits, and Controllers | Article 430

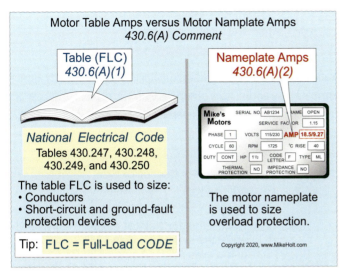

▶Figure 430–5

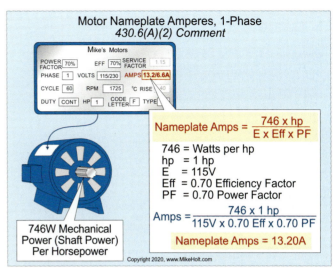

▶Figure 430–6

(1) Table Full-Load Current (FLC). The motor full-load current ratings contained in Tables 430.248 and 430.250 are used to determine conductor sizing [430.22] and the branch-circuit short-circuit and ground-fault overcurrent protection size [430.52 and 430.62].

Author's Comment:

▸ The motor full-load amperes (FLA) identified on the motor nameplate [430.6(A)(2)] is not permitted to be used to determine the conductor size and the motor short-circuit and ground-fault overcurrent protective device except for other than continuous duty motor applications as covered in 430.22(E).

(2) Motor Nameplate Current Rating (FLA). Overload devices and conductor sizing for intermittent duty motors must be sized based on the motor nameplate full-load ampere (FLA) rating in accordance with 430.31.

Author's Comment:

▸ The motor nameplate current rating is identified as full-load amperes (FLA). The FLA rating is the current in amperes the motor draws while producing its rated horsepower load at its rated voltage, based on its rated efficiency and power factor. ▶Figure 430–6

Author's Comment:

▸ The actual current drawn by the motor's FLA depends on the load on the motor and the actual operating voltage at the motor terminals. If the load increases, the current also increases, or if the motor operates at a voltage below its nameplate rating, the operating current will increase.

Caution

To prevent damage to motor windings from excessive heat (caused by excessive current), never load a motor above its horsepower rating and be sure the applied voltage is within 10 percent of the motor's voltage rating.

430.14 Location of Motors

(A) Ventilation and Maintenance. Motors must be located so adequate ventilation is provided and maintenance can be readily accomplished.

430.17 Highest Rated Motor

When sizing motor circuits for a group of motors, the highest rated motor of the group will be the motor with the largest full-load current (FLC) rating as listed in Tables 430.248 and 430.250.

Article 430 — Bonus Material: Article 430—Motors, Motor Circuits, and Controllers

▶ **Example**

Question: Which of the following motors has the highest FLC rating: a 10 hp, 208V, three-phase motor; a 5 hp, 208V, single-phase motor; or a 3 hp, 115V, single-phase motor? ▶Figure 430–7

(a) A 3 hp, 115V, single-phase motor.
(b) A 5 hp, 208V, single-phase motor.
(c) A 10 hp, 208V, three-phase motor.
(d) none of these

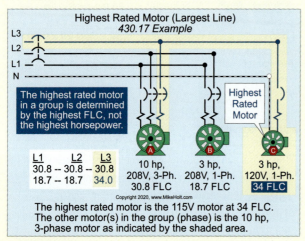

▶Figure 430–7

Solution:

10 hp, 208V, Three-Phase Motor = 30.80A [Table 430.250]

5 hp, 208V, Single-Phase Motor = 30.80A [Table 430.248]

3 hp, 115V, Single-Phase Motor = 34.00A [Table 430.248]

Answer: (a) A 3 hp, 115V, single-phase motor.

Author's Comment:

▸ Determining the highest rated motor of a group is used for calculating conductor size and the short-circuit ground-fault protective device where the conductors are supplying more than one motor [430.24].

Part II. Conductor Size

430.22 Single Motor Conductor Size

Branch-circuit conductors to a single motor in a continuous duty application must have an ampacity of not less than 125 percent of the motor's full-load current (FLC) as listed in Tables 430.248 and 430.250 [430.6(A)(1) and 430.22]. ▶Figure 430–8

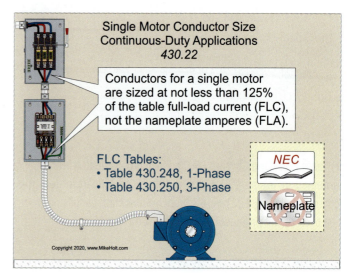

▶Figure 430–8

Author's Comment:

▸ When selecting motor current from one of these tables, note that the last sentence above each table allows us to use the ampacity columns for a range of system voltages without any adjustment. The actual conductor size must be selected from Table 310.16 according to the terminal temperature rating (60°C or 75°C) of the equipment [110.14(C)(1)].

▸ The motor nameplate full-load amperes (FLA) [430.6(A)(2)] is not permitted to be used to determine the motor conductor size.

▸ Motor applications are considered continuous duty unless the nature of the control or apparatus the motor drives is designed so the motor will not operate continuously under load [Table 430.22(E) Note]. When a motor is not continuous duty because of this type of application, the conductors are sized using the percentages of Table 430.22(E). If a motor must stop when performing its function (such as in the case of an elevator motor) it is a good sign the motor is intermittent duty.

Bonus Material: Article 430—Motors, Motor Circuits, and Controllers | Article 430

▶ **Example 1**

Question: What size branch-circuit conductor is required for a 3 hp, 230V, single-phase motor in a continuous duty application, where the conductor terminals are rated 75°C? ▶Figure 430-9

(a) 14 AWG (b) 12 AWG (c) 10 AWG (d) 8 AWG

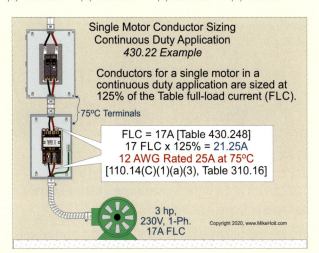

▶Figure 430-9

Solution:

Determine the branch-circuit conductor size based on 125 percent of the motor's FLC.

3 hp, 230V Motor FLC = 17A [Table 430.248]

Conductor = 17A × 125% = 21.25A

Conductor = 12 AWG rated 25A at 75°C [110.14(C)(1)(a)(3) and Table 310.16]

Answer: (b) 12 AWG

▶ **Example 2**

Question: What size branch-circuit conductor is required for a 7½ hp, 230V, three-phase motor? ▶Figure 430-10

(a) 14 AWG (b) 12 AWG (c) 10 AWG (d) 8 AWG

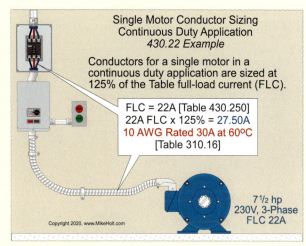

▶Figure 430-10

Solution:

Determine the branch-circuit conductor size based on the motor's FLC [430.6(A)(1), 430.22, and Table 310.16].

Motor FLC = 22A [Table 430.250]

Conductor Size = 22A × 125%

Conductor Size = 27.50A

Conductor Size = 10 AWG rated 30A at 60°C [110.14(C)(1)(a) and Table 310.16]

Answer: (c) 10 AWG

(E) Single Motor in Duty-Cycle Application—Conductor Sizing. Conductors for a motor used in a short-time, intermittent, periodic, or varying duty application must have an ampacity of not less than the percentage of the motor nameplate full-load ampere (FLA) rating shown in Table 430.22(E).

Article 430 — Bonus Material: Article 430—Motors, Motor Circuits, and Controllers

▶ **Example**

Question: *What size branch-circuit conductors are required for a 10 hp, 208V, three-phase, motor with a nameplate FLA of 29A, rated for 5-minute service, used for intermittent duty, and with terminals rated 75°C?* ▶Figure 430–11

(a) 14 AWG (b) 12 AWG (c) 10 AWG (d) 8 AWG

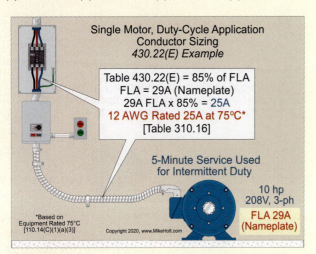

▶Figure 430–11

Solution:

The motor nameplate FLA is used for duty-cycle service.

The conductor must be sized no less than 85 percent of the motor FLA [Table 430.22(E)]

Conductor Ampacity = 29A × 85%
Conductor Ampacity = 25A

Use 12 AWG conductors rated 25A at 75°C [110.14(C)(1)(a)(3) and Table 310.16]

Answer: (b) 12 AWG

430.24 Several Motors—Conductor Size

Conductors that supply several motors must be sized not smaller than the sum of the following: ▶Figure 430–12

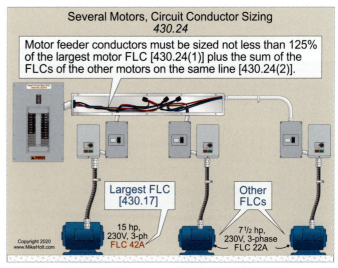

▶Figure 430–12

(1) 125 percent of the highest rated motor's full-load current (FLC) as listed in Tables 430.248 and 430.250.

(2) The full-load current (FLC) of the other motors as listed in Tables 430.248 and 430.250.

Author's Comment:

▸ The motor nameplate full-load ampere (FLA) rating [430.6(A)(2)] is not permitted to be used to determine the motor conductor size.

▶ **Example**

Question: *What size feeder conductors are required for a 2 hp, single-phase, 230V motor and a 5 hp, single-phase, 230V motor with terminals rated 75°C?* ▶Figure 430–13

(a) 10 AWG (b) 8 AWG (c) 6 AWG (d) 4 AWG

Solution:

2 hp FLC = 12A [Table 430.248]
5 hp FLC = 28A [Table 430.248]

Feeder Size = Ampacity of not less than 125 percent of the highest rated motor's FLC, plus the sum of the FLCs of the other motors.
Feeder Size = (28A × 125%) + 12A
Feeder Size = 47A

Use 8 AWG rated 50A at 75°C [110.14(C)(1)(a)(3) and Table 310.16].

Bonus Material: Article 430—Motors, Motor Circuits, and Controllers | Article 430

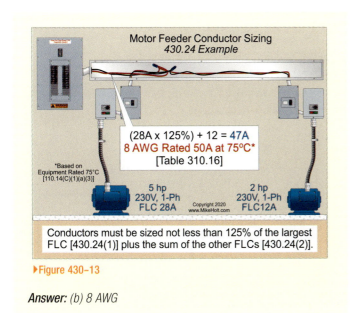
▶Figure 430–13

Answer: (b) 8 AWG

Part III. Motor and Branch-Circuit Overload Protection

430.31 Overload

Part III contains the requirements for overload devices, which are intended to protect motors, motor control equipment, and motor branch-circuit conductors against excessive heating due to motor overloads and failure to start, but not against short circuits or ground faults.

Author's Comment:

▸ Overload devices can be: ▶Figure 430–14

▸ **Thermal Overloads.** Thermal overloads (heaters) located in an overload relay of a motor contactor (starter). These heater units are selected using a chart or size given by the manufacturer.

▸ **Solid-State (Electronic) Overloads.** Solid-state overload devices have an adjustment dial that can be used to set the trip level. They are installed in an overload relay of a motor contactor (starter).

▸ **Inverse Time Circuit Breaker and DE Fuses.** Inverse time circuit breakers and dual-element fuses are permitted to serve as both motor overload protection and the motor short-circuit ground fault protection if the requirements of 430.32 are met [430.55].

▸ **Fuses.** Fuses can be used for overload protection when sized in accordance with 430.32(A) [430.36].

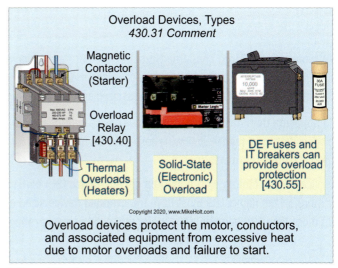
▶Figure 430–14

Note 2: An overload is a condition where equipment is operated above its current rating, or where the current exceeds the conductor ampacity. When an overload condition persists for a long time, equipment failure or a fire from damaging or dangerous overheating can result. A fault, such as a short circuit or ground fault, is not an overload [Article 100]. ▶Figure 430–15

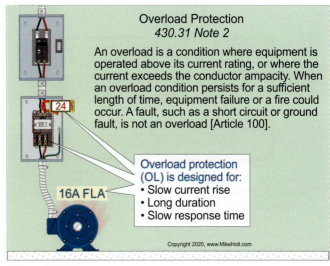
▶Figure 430–15

Overload protection is not required where it might introduce additional or increased hazards, as in the case of fire pumps [Article 695].

Note: See 695.7 for the overcurrent protection requirements for fire pump supply conductors.

Article 430 Bonus Material: Article 430—Motors, Motor Circuits, and Controllers

430.32 Overload Sizing for Continuous-Duty Motors

(A) Motors Rated More Than One Horsepower. Motors rated more than 1 hp, used in a continuous-duty application without integral thermal protection, must have the overload device(s) sized as follows:

(1) Separate Overload Device. An overload device must be selected to open at no more than the following percent of the motor nameplate full-load current (FLA) rating:

Service Factor. Motors with a marked service factor (SF) of 1.15 or more on the nameplate must have the overload device sized at not more than 125 percent of the motor nameplate current rating.

Author's Comment:

▸ Motor service factors are safety factors; they indicate how much the motor capacity can be exceeded for short periods without overheating. For example, a motor with a service factor of 1.15 can operate at 15 percent more than its rated output without overheating. This is important for motors where loads vary and may peak slightly above the rated torque. ▸Figure 430–16

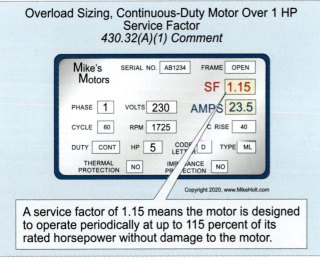

▸Figure 430–16

▸ Example

Question: If a dual-element time-delay fuse is used for overload protection, what size fuse is required for a 5 hp, 230V, single-phase motor, with a service factor of 1.15, if the motor nameplate current rating is 29A? ▸Figure 430–17

(a) 25A   (b) 30A   (c) 35A   (d) 40A

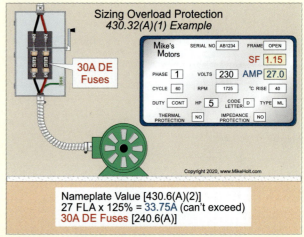

▸Figure 430–17

Solution:

Overload protection is sized to the motor nameplate current rating [430.6(A), 430.32(A)(1), and 430.55].

Overload Protection = 29A × 125%
Overload Protection = 36.25A, 35A dual-element time-delay fuse

When using a fuse for overload protection, the values of 430.32(C) aren't to be exceeded, so we must round down to the next smaller fuse. Standard fuse sizes are listed in 240.6(A).

Answer: (c) 35A

Temperature Rise. Motors with a nameplate temperature rise of 40°C or less must have the overload device sized no more than 125 percent of the motor nameplate current rating.

Bonus Material: Article 430—Motors, Motor Circuits, and Controllers | Article 430

Author's Comment:

▸ A motor with a nameplate temperature rise of 40°C means the motor is designed to operate so it will not heat up more than 40°C above its rated ambient temperature when operated at its rated load and voltage. Studies have shown that when the operating temperature of a motor is increased 10°C above its rating, the motor winding insulating material's anticipated life is reduced by 50 percent. ▸Figure 430–18

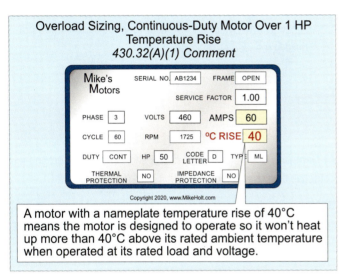

▸Figure 430–18

▶ **Example**

Question: A motor has a nameplate that specifies the following: The service factor is 1.12 with a temperature rise of 41°C and a nameplate full load current rating of 25A. What size dual-element time-delay fuse is required when used for the overload protection of this motor? ▸Figure 430–19

(a) 20A   (b) 25A   (c) 30A   (d) 40A

Solution:

Since the service factor of 1.12 is less than 1.15, and 41°C is over 40°C, the overload protection is sized based on 115 percent of the motor nameplate ampere rating [430.6(A)(2)].

Overload Protection = 25A × 115%

Overload Protection = 28.75A; use a 25A dual-element time-delay fuse [240.6(A)]

Answer: (b) 25A

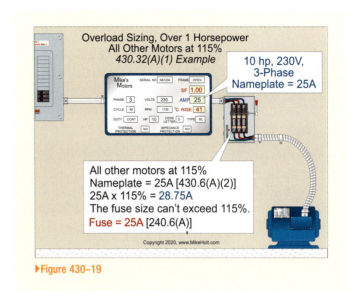

▸Figure 430–19

Other Motors. No more than 115 percent of the motor "nameplate current rating."

Part IV. Branch-Circuit Short-Circuit and Ground-Fault Protection

430.51 General

A branch-circuit short-circuit and ground-fault protective device protects the motor, the motor control equipment, and the conductors against short circuits or ground faults, but not against overload. ▸Figure 430–20

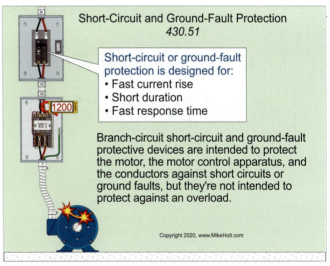

▸Figure 430–20

Understanding Basic Motor Controls | Mike Holt Enterprises | 225

Article 430 — Bonus Material: Article 430—Motors, Motor Circuits, and Controllers

Author's Comment:

- **Motor-Starting Current.** When voltage is first applied to the field winding of an induction motor, only the conductor resistance opposes the flow of current through the motor winding. Because the conductor resistance is so low, the motor will have a very large inrush current. ▶Figure 430–21

- **Motor-Running Current.** Once the rotor reaches its rated speed, the starting current reduces to running current due to counter-electromotive force (CEMF). ▶Figure 430–22

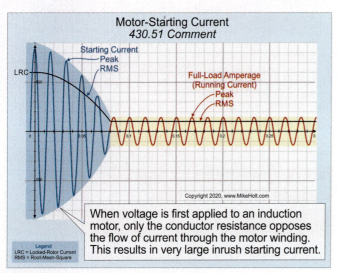

▶Figure 430–21

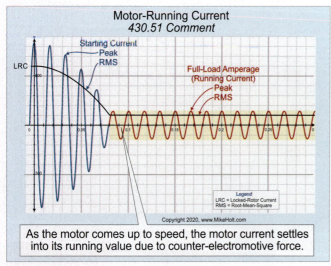

▶Figure 430–22

Author's Comment:

- **Motor Locked-Rotor Current (LRC).** If the rotating part of the motor winding (armature) becomes jammed so it cannot rotate, no counter-electromotive force (CEMF) will be produced in the motor winding. This results in a decrease in conductor impedance to the point that it is effectively a short circuit. The motor then operates at locked-rotor current (often six times the full-load ampere rating) depending on the motor's Code letter rating [430.7(B)]. This condition will cause the motor winding to overheat and be destroyed if the current is not quickly reduced or removed.

430.52 Branch-Circuit Short-Circuit and Ground-Fault Protection

(A) General. The motor branch-circuit short-circuit and ground-fault protective device must comply with 430.52(B) and 430.52(C).

(B) Motor Starting Current. A motor branch-circuit short-circuit and ground-fault protective device must be capable of carrying the motor's starting current. ▶Figure 430–23

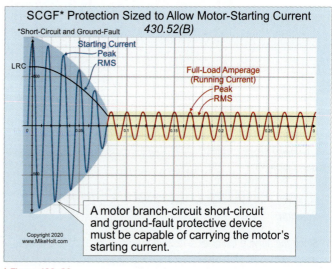

▶Figure 430–23

(C) Rating or Setting.

(1) The motor branch circuit must be protected against short circuits and ground faults by a protective device sized no greater than the percentages contained in Table 430.52. ▶Figure 430–24

Bonus Material: Article 430—Motors, Motor Circuits, and Controllers | Article 430

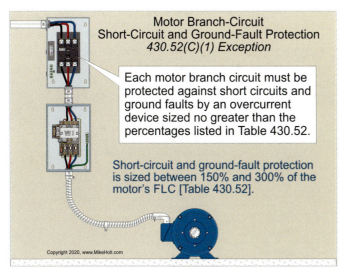

▶Figure 430–24

Author's Comment:

▸ The motor nameplate full-load amperes (FLA) rating [430.6(A)(2)] is not permitted to be used to determine the motor short-circuit and ground-fault overcurrent protection.

Table 430.52 Maximum Rating or Setting of Motor Branch-Circuit Short-Circuit and Ground-Fault Protective Devices			
Motor Type	Nontime Delay Fuse	Dual-Element (Time-Delay) Fuse	Inverse Time Breaker
Wound Rotor	150%	150%	150%
Direct Current	150%	150%	150%
Other Motors	300%	175%	250%

▶ Example

Question: What size conductor and inverse time circuit breaker are required for a 1 hp, 115V, single-phase motor with terminals rated 75°C? ▸Figure 430–25

(a) 14 AWG, 30A breaker (b) 14 AWG, 35A breaker
(c) 14 AWG, 40A breaker (d) 14 AWG, 45A breaker

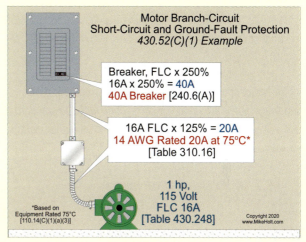

▶Figure 430–25

Solution:

Step 1: Determine the branch-circuit conductor at 125 percent of the motor's FLC [430.22 and Table 430.248].

Branch-Circuit Conductor = 16A × 125%
Branch-Circuit Conductor = 20A

Use 14 AWG rated 20A at 75°C [110.14(C)(1)(a)(3) and Table 310.16].

Step 2: Determine the branch-circuit protection at 250% of the motor's FLC [430.52(C)(1) and Table 430.248].

Branch-Circuit Protection = 16A × 250%
Branch-Circuit Protection = 40A [240.6(A)]

Answer: (c) 14 AWG, 40A breaker

Article 430 — Bonus Material: Article 430—Motors, Motor Circuits, and Controllers

Author's Comment:

- I know it bothers many in the electrical industry to see a 14 AWG conductor protected by a 40A circuit breaker, but branch-circuit conductors are protected against overloads by the overload device which is sized between 115 and 125 percent of the motor's nameplate current rating [430.32]. See 240.4(G) for details.

- The rule that limits 15A overcurrent protection for 14 AWG conductors does not apply to motor circuit protection, see 240.4(D) and 240.4(G).

Ex 1: If the motor short-circuit and ground-fault protective device values derived from Table 430.52 do not correspond with the standard overcurrent device ratings listed in 240.6(A), the next higher overcurrent device rating can be used. ▶Figure 430–26

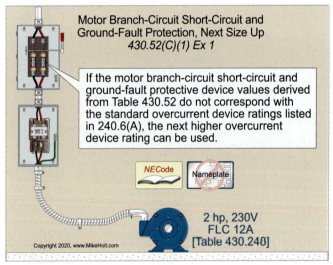

▶Figure 430–26

▶ Example

Question: What size inverse time circuit breaker is required for a 5 hp, 208V, single-phase motor? ▶Figure 430–27

(a) 35A   (b) 40A   (c) 60A   (d) 80A

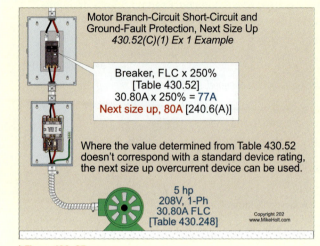

▶Figure 430–27

Solution:

Determine the branch-circuit protection at 250% of the motor's FLC [430.52(C)(1) and Table 430.248].

Branch-Circuit Protection = 30.80A × 250%

Branch-Circuit Protection = 77A; next size up 80A circuit breaker 240.6(A)

Answer: *(d) 80A*

Author's Comment:

- Remember that the 80A circuit breaker is providing short-circuit and ground-fault protection and the motor overload protective device (set at 125 percent or 115 percent of the motor's FLA) will protect the motor, motor equipment, and motor circuit conductors against overloads.

430.55 Combined Overcurrent Protective Device

A motor can be protected against overload, short circuit, and ground fault by a single overcurrent protective device sized to the overload requirements contained in 430.32.

▶ Example

Question: What is the maximum size dual-element fuse that can be used to provide overload, short-circuit and ground-fault protection for a 5 hp, 230V, single-phase motor with a service factor of 1.20 and a nameplate current rating of 28A? ▶Figure 430–28

(a) 30A   (b) 35A   (c) 40A   (d) 50A

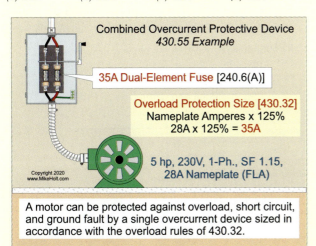

▶Figure 430–28

Solution:

A single overcurrent device must be sized in accordance with the percentages contained in 430.32. For this application, the single overcurrent device must be sized not greater than 125 percent of the motor's nameplate current rating.

Overcurrent Protection = 28A FLA × 125%

Overcurrent Protection = 35A [240.6(A)]

Answer: (b) 35A

Part V. Feeder Short-Circuit and Ground-Fault Protection

430.62 Motor Feeder Protection

(A) Motors Only. Feeder conductors must be protected against short circuits and ground faults by a protective device sized not greater than the largest rating of the branch-circuit short-circuit and ground-fault protective device for any motor, plus the sum of the full-load currents (FLC) of the other motors in the group as listed in Tables 430.248 and 430.250. ▶Figure 430–29

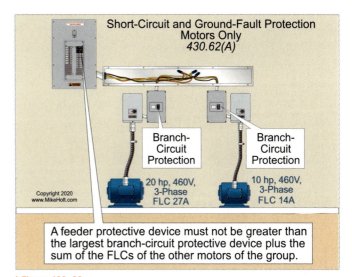

▶Figure 430–29

Article 430 — Bonus Material: Article 430—Motors, Motor Circuits, and Controllers

▶ Example

Question: What size feeder overcurrent protection (inverse time breaker) and conductors are required for the following two motors where the conductor terminals are rated 75°C? ▶Figure 430–30

- Motor 1–20 hp, 460V, Three-Phase = 27A FLC [Table 430.250]
- Motor 2–10 hp, 460V, Three-Phase = 14A FLC [Table 430.250]

(a) 10 AWG/30A
(b) 10 AWG/40A
(c) 10 AWG/50A
(d) 8 AWG/80A

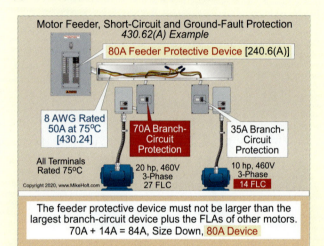

▶Figure 430–30

Solution:

Step 1: Determine the feeder conductor size [430.24]. Largest motor FLC of the group at 125 percent plus FLC of other motors.

Conductor = (27A × 125%) + 14A
Conductor = 48A
Conductor = 8 AWG rated 50A at 75°C [110.14(C)(1)(a)(3) and Table 310.16]

Step 2: Feeder overcurrent protection [430.62(A)] is not greater than the largest branch-circuit ground-fault and short-circuit protective device plus the other motors' FLC.

Determine the largest branch-circuit ground-fault and short-circuit protective device [240.6(A) and 430.52(C)(1) Ex].

20 hp Motor = 27A × 250%
20 hp Motor = 68; use the next size up, 70A

10 hp Motor = 14A × 250%
10 hp Motor = 35A

Determine the feeder protection size.

Feeder Protection = Not more than 70A + 14A
Feeder Protection = 84A; use the next size down, 80A [240.6(A)]

Answer: (d) 8 AWG/80A

Author's Comment:

- The "next size up protection" rule for branch circuits [430.52(C)(1) Ex 1] does not apply to motor feeder overcurrent protective devices.

- In some cases where there are three-phase and single-phase motors on the same feeder, the current on L1, L2, and L3 (or Phase 1, Phase 2, and Phase 3) will be different. The "group" is determined by balancing out the motor currents between different phases (lines) of the motor feeder. ▶Figure 430–31

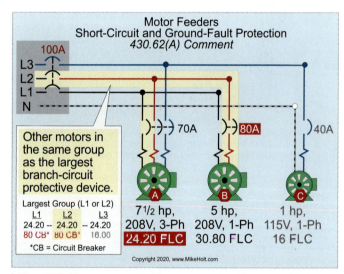

▶Figure 430–31

Bonus Material: Article 430—Motors, Motor Circuits, and Controllers | Article 430

▶ Example

Question: What size feeder overcurrent protective device (inverse time breaker) and conductors are required for the following three motors where all terminals are rated 75°C? ▶Figure 430–32

▸ Motor 1–7½ hp, 208V, three-phase = 24.20A FLC [Table 430.250]
▸ Motor 2–5 hp, 208V, single-phase = 30.80A FLC [Table 430.250]
▸ Motor 3–1 hp, 115V, single-phase = 16.00A FLC [Table 430.250]

(a) 4 AWG/100A (b) 4 AWG/110A
(c) 4 AWG/125A (d) 4 AWG/150A

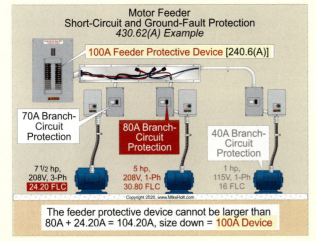

▶Figure 430–32

Solution:

Step 1: Determine the feeder conductor size [430.24]. Reminder; the 1 hp single-phase motor is not part of the largest group after balancing the motors on L1, L2, and L3 so its 16.00A FLC is not used in this calculation.

Feeder Conductor = (30.80A × 125%) + 24.20A
Feeder Conductor = 72.70A
Feeder Conductor = 4 AWG rated 85A at 75°C [110.14(C)(1)(a)(3) and Table 310.16]

Step 2: Feeder overcurrent protection [430.62(A)] is not greater than the largest branch-circuit ground-fault and short-circuit protective device plus the other motors' FLCs.

Determine the largest branch-circuit ground-fault and short-circuit protective device [240.6(A) and 430.52(C)(1) Ex].

7½ hp Motor = 24.20A × 250%
7½ hp Motor = 60.50; use the next size up, 70A

5 hp Motor = 30.80A × 250%
5 hp Motor = 77A; use the next size up, 80A

1 hp Motor—does not apply after balancing.

Determine the feeder protection size.

Feeder Protection = Not more than 80A + 24.20A
Feeder Protection = 104.20A; use the next size down, 100A [240.6(A)]

Answer: (a) 4 AWG/100A

Part VI. Motor Control Circuits

430.72 Overcurrent Protection for Control Circuits

(A) Class 1 Control Conductors. Motor control conductors that are not tapped from the motor branch-circuit conductors are classified as a Class 1 remote-control circuit and must have overcurrent protection in accordance with 725.43.

> **Author's Comment:**
>
> ▸ Section 725.43 states that overcurrent protection for conductors 14 AWG and larger must comply with the conductor ampacity from Table 310.16. Overcurrent protection for 18 AWG conductors are not permitted to exceed 7A, and not more than a 10A device can be used to protect 16 AWG conductors.

(B) Motor Control Conductors

(2) Motor control circuit conductors that are tapped from the motor branch-circuit overcurrent protective device and extend beyond the tap enclosure must have overcurrent protection as follows:

Article 430 — Bonus Material: Article 430—Motors, Motor Circuits, and Controllers

Table 430.72(B) Maximum Rating of Overcurrent Protective Device in Amperes

Conductor Size Copper	Column C Overcurrent Protection
18 AWG	7A
16 AWG	10A
14 AWG	45A
12 AWG	60A
10 AWG	90A
>10 AWG	(Note 3)

Note 3: 300 percent of the value specified in Table 310.16 for 60°C conductors.

430.75 Disconnect for Control Circuits

(A) Control Circuit Disconnect. Motor control circuit conductors must have a disconnect. Where the control circuit conductors are tapped from the controller disconnect, the controller disconnect can serve as the disconnect for the control circuit conductors [430.102(A)]. Where control circuit conductors are not tapped from the controller disconnect (supplied by a Class 1 control circuit), a disconnect located adjacent to the controller disconnect is required. ▶Figure 430-33

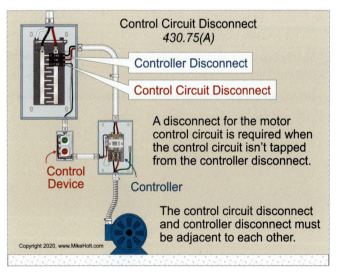

▶Figure 430-33

Part VII. Motor Controllers

430.83 Motor Controller Horsepower Rating

(A) General. The controller for a motor must have one of the following ratings:

(1) Horsepower Rating. For other than circuit breakers and molded case switches, the controller for a motor must have a horsepower rating not less than that of the motor. ▶Figure 430-34

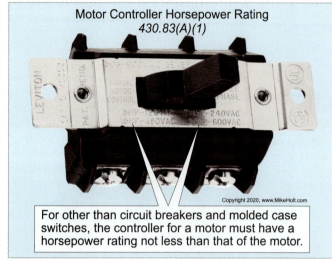

▶Figure 430-34

(2) Circuit Breakers. A circuit breaker can serve as a motor controller.

Author's Comment:

▸ Circuit breakers are not required to be horsepower rated.

(3) Molded Case Switch. A molded case switch, rated in amperes, can serve as a motor controller.

Author's Comment:

▸ A molded case switch is not required to be horsepower rated.

(C) Stationary Motors of Two Horsepower or Less. For stationary motors rated at 2 hp or less and 300V or less, the controller can be:

(2) General-Use Snap Switch. The motor controller can be a general-use snap switch for motors rated 2 hp or less where the motor FLC is not more than 80 percent of the ampere rating of the switch.
▶Figure 430-35

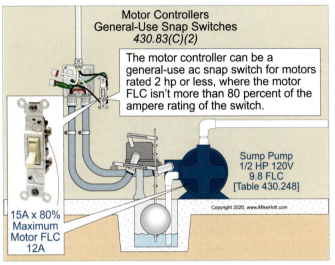

▶Figure 430-35

Part IX. Disconnecting Means

430.102 Disconnect Location

(A) Controller Disconnect. A disconnect is required for each motor controller and must be located within sight from the controller. ▶Figure 430-36

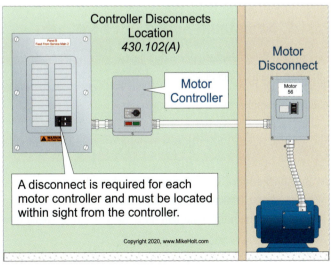

▶Figure 430-36

Author's Comment:

▸ According to Article 100, "Within Sight" means that it is visible and not more than 50 ft from the location of the equipment.

(B) Motor Disconnect. A motor disconnect must be provided in accordance with (B)(1) or (B)(2). ▶Figure 430-37

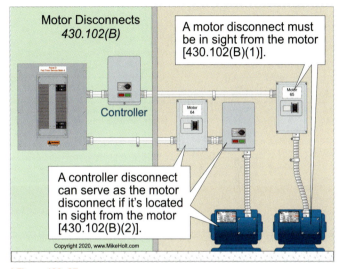

▶Figure 430-37

(1) Separate Motor Disconnect. A disconnect is required for each motor and be located within sight from the motor location.

(2) Controller Disconnect. The controller disconnect (if located within sight from the motor location) can serve as the disconnect for the motor.

430.107 Readily Accessible

Either the controller disconnect or the motor disconnect required by 430.102 must be readily accessible. ▶Figure 430-38

Article 430 — Bonus Material: Article 430—Motors, Motor Circuits, and Controllers

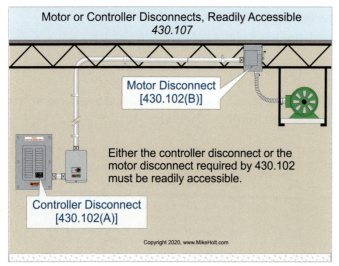

▶Figure 430–38

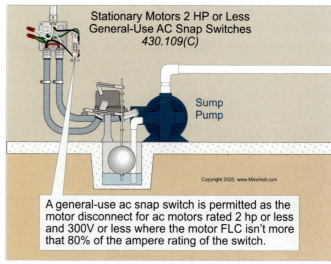

▶Figure 430–39

430.109 Type of Disconnecting Means

(A) General. The disconnect for the motor controller and/or the motor must be one of the following:

(1) Motor-Circuit Switch. A listed horsepower-rated motor-circuit switch.

(2) Molded Case Circuit Breaker. A listed molded case circuit breaker.

(3) Molded Case Switch. A listed molded case switch.

(6) Manual Motor Controller. A listed manual motor controller marked "Suitable as Motor Disconnect."

(B) Stationary Motors of 1/8 Horsepower or Less. For stationary motors of 1/8 hp or less, the branch-circuit overcurrent protective device can serve as the disconnect.

(C) Stationary Motors of Two Horsepower or Less. For stationary motors rated 2 hp or less and 300V or less, the disconnect can be a general-use ac snap switch (not a general-use ac-dc snap switch) where the motor's full-load current (FLC) as listed in Tables 430.248 and 430.250 is not more than 80 percent of the ampere rating of the switch. ▶Figure 430–39

Author's Comment:

▸ Section 430.83(C) has similar requirements for controllers for stationary motors rated 2 hp or less. In some cases, the switch is used for both the controller and motor disconnect.

(3) A listed manual motor controller marked "Suitable as Motor Disconnect."

(F) Cord-and-Plug-Connected Motors. A horsepower-rated attachment plug and receptacle, flanged surface inlet and cord connector, or cord connector having a horsepower rating not less than the motor rating can be used as a motor disconnect. ▶Figure 430–40

Part X. Adjustable-Speed Drive Systems

430.120 General

The installation provisions of Part I through Part IX are applicable unless modified or supplemented by this part.

430.122 Conductor Sizing

(A) Branch/Feeder-Circuit Conductors. Circuit conductors for an adjustable-speed drive system must have an ampacity of not less than 125 percent of the rated input current of the adjustable-speed drive system. ▶Figure 430–41

Bonus Material: Article 430—Motors, Motor Circuits, and Controllers | Article 430

▶Figure 430–40

▶ **Motor Branch-Circuit for Adjustable-Speed Drive System Example**

Question: What size branch-circuit conductors are required for an adjustable-speed drive system with a rated input of 25A and terminals rated 75°C? ▶Figure 430–42

(a) 14 AWG (b) 12 AWG (c) 10 AWG (d) 8 AWG

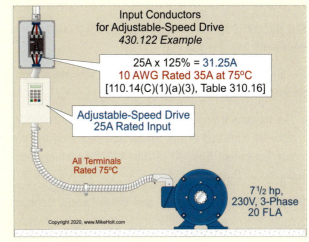

▶Figure 430–42

Solution:

Rated Input from Adjustable-Speed Drive = 25A

Branch-Circuit Conductor = 25A × 125%

Branch-Circuit Conductor = 31.25A

Use 10 AWG rated 35A at 75°C [Table 310.16 and 110.14(C)(1)(a)(3)].

Answer: (c) 10 AWG

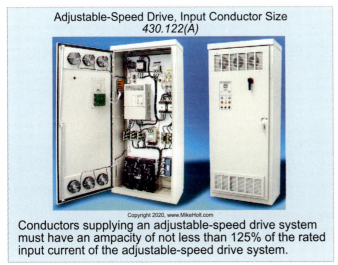

▶Figure 430–41

Note 1: Adjustable-speed drive systems can have multiple power ratings and corresponding input currents.

Note 2: Circuit conductors on the output of an adjustable-speed drive system are susceptible to breakdown under certain conditions due to the characteristics of the output waveform of the drive. Factors affecting the conductors include (but are not limited to) the output voltage, frequency and current, the length of the conductors, the spacing between the conductors, and the dielectric strength of the conductor insulation. Methods to mitigate breakdown include consideration of one or more of these factors.

(B) Output Conductors. The conductors between the power conversion equipment and the motor must have an ampacity equal to or greater than 125 percent of the motor's full-load current (FLC) as listed in Tables 430.248 and 430.250.

Ex: If the power conversion equipment is listed and marked as "Suitable for Output Motor Conductor Protection," the conductor between the power conversion equipment and the motor must have an ampacity equal to or greater than the larger of:

(1) 125 percent of the motor's full-load current (FLC) as listed in Tables 430.248 and 430.250

(2) The ampacity of the minimum conductor size marked on the power conversion equipment

Note: The minimum ampacity required of output conductors is often different than that of the conductors supplying the power conversion equipment. See 430.130 and 430.131 for branch-circuit protection requirements.

(D) Several Motors or a Motor and Other Loads. Conductors supplying several motors or a motor and other loads (including power conversion equipment) must have ampacity in accordance with 430.24, using the rated input current of the power conversion equipment for purposes of calculating ampacity.

> **Author's Comment:**
>
> ▸ 430.24 requires the ampacity of the feeder conductors to be the sum of 125 percent of the highest motor load or the power conversion equipment (drive) rated input current, the sum of the remaining full-load motor current (drive input current), 100 percent of the noncontinuous nonmotor loads, and 125 percent of the continuous nonmotor loads.

430.124 Overload Protection

(A) Included in Equipment. Where the adjustable-speed drive system is marked to indicate that motor overload protection is included, additional overload protection is not required.

430.128 Disconnecting Means

The disconnect for an adjustable-speed drive system must have a rating of not less than 115 percent of the rated input current of the conversion unit. ▸Figure 430–43

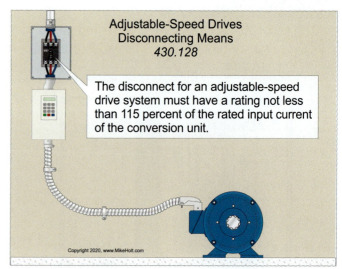

▸Figure 430–43

430.130 Branch-Circuit Short-Circuit and Ground-Fault Protection

(A) Circuits Containing an Adjustable-Speed Drive System. Circuits containing power conversion equipment must be protected by a branch-circuit short-circuit and ground-fault protective device in accordance with all of the following:

(1) The rating and type of protection must be determined by 430.52(C)(1), (C)(3), (C)(5), or (C)(6) using the motor's full-load current (FLC) rating as listed in Tables 430.248 and 430.250.

Ex: The rating and type of protection is determined by Table 430.52 using the power conversion equipment's rated input current where the power conversion equipment is listed and marked "Suitable for Output Motor Conductor Protection."

Note 1: Motor conductor branch-circuit short-circuit and ground-fault protection from the power conversion equipment to the motor is provided by power conversion equipment that is listed and marked "Suitable for Output Motor Conductor Protection."

Note 2: A motor branch circuit using power conversion equipment, including equipment listed and marked "Suitable for Output Motor Conductor Protection," includes the input circuit to the power conversion equipment.

(2) The maximum branch-circuit short-circuit and ground-fault protective ratings must be in accordance with the manufacturer's instructions.

Part XIV. Tables

Table 430.248 Full-Load Current, Single-Phase Motors

Table 430.248 lists the full-load current for single-phase alternating-current motors. These values are used to determine motor conductor sizing and branch-circuit and feeder protection, but not overload protection [430.6(A)(1) and 430.6(A)(2)].

The full-load currents (FLC) contained in this table are permitted for system voltage ranges of 110V to 120V and 220V to 240V.

Table 430.248 FLC Single-Phase Alternating-Current Motors				
	115V	200V	208V	230V
½ hp	9.80	5.60	5.40	4.90
¾ hp	13.80	7.90	7.60	6.90
1 hp	16.00	9.20	8.80	8.00
1½ hp	20.00	11.50	11.00	11.00
2 hp	24.00	13.90	13.20	12.00
3 hp	34.00	19.60	18.70	17.00
5 hp	56.00	32.20	30.80	28.00
7½ hp	80.00	46.00	44.00	40.00
10 hp	100.00	57.50	55.00	50.00

▶ **Example**

Question: What is the full-load current (FLC) of a 2 hp, 240V, single-phase motor? ▶Figure 430–44

(a) 12A (b) 13A (c) 14A (d) 16A

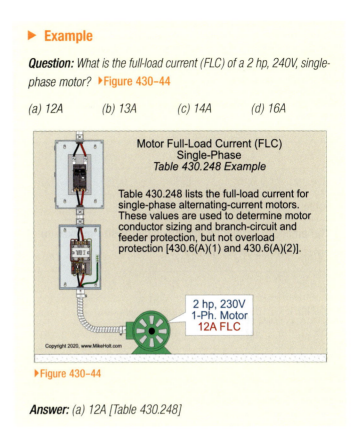

▶Figure 430–44

Answer: (a) 12A [Table 430.248]

Table 430.250 Full-Load Current, Three-Phase Motors

Table 430.250 lists the full-load current for three-phase alternating-current motors. The values are used to determine motor conductor sizing, ampere ratings of disconnects, controller rating, and branch-circuit and feeder protection but not overload protection [430.6(A)(1) and 430.6(A)(2)].

The full-load currents (FLC) listed in this table are permitted for three-phase system voltage ranges of 110V to 120V, 220V to 240V, 440V to 480V, and 550V to 600V motors. This means that the 115V column is used for any three-phase alternating-current motor rated 110V to 120V. The 230V column is used for any three-phase alternating-current motor rated 220V and 240V. The 460V column is used for any three-phase alternating-current motor rated 440V to 480.

Article 430 — Bonus Material: Article 430—Motors, Motor Circuits, and Controllers

Table 430.250 FLC Three-Phase Alternating-Current Motors				
	200V	208V	230V	460V
½ hp	2.50	2.40	2.20	1.10
¾ hp	3.70	3.50	3.20	1.60
1 hp	4.80	4.60	4.20	2.10
1½ hp	6.90	6.60	6.00	3.00
2 hp	7.80	7.50	6.80	3.40
3 hp	11.00	10.60	9.60	4.00
5 hp	17.50	16.70	15.20	7.60
7½ hp	25.30	24.20	22.00	11.00
10 hp	32.20	30.80	28.00	14.00
15 hp	48.30	46.20	42.00	21.00
20 hp	62.10	59.40	54.00	27.00
25 hp	78.20	74.80	68.00	34.00

▶ **Example**

Example: What is the full-load current (FLC) of a 10 hp, 208V, three-phase motor? ▶Figure 430–45

(a) 22A   (b) 31A   (c) 34A   (d) 36A

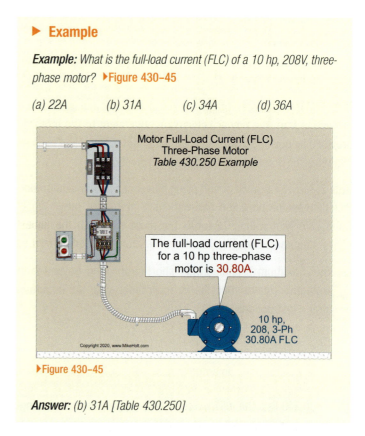

▶Figure 430–45

Answer: (b) 31A [Table 430.250]

Article 430 Practice Questions

CHAPTER 4—EQUIPMENT FOR GENERAL USE

1. In determining the highest rated motor for purposes of complying with 430.24, 430.53(B), and 430.53(C), the highest rated motor shall be based on the rated full-load current as selected _____.

   (a) from the motor nameplate
   (b) from Tables 430.247, 430.248, 430.249, and 430.250
   (c) by multiplying the horsepower by 746 watts
   (d) using the largest horsepower motor

2. Each motor used in a continuous duty application and rated more than 1 hp shall be protected against overload by a separate overload device that is responsive to motor current. The overload device for motors with a marked temperature rise 40°C or less, shall be rated at no more than _____ percent of the motor nameplate full-load current rating.

   (a) 80
   (b) 115
   (c) 125
   (d) 175

3. Where the motor short-circuit and ground-fault protection devices determined by Table 430.52 do not correspond to the standard sizes or ratings, a higher rating that does not exceed the next higher standard ampere rating shall be permitted.

   (a) True
   (b) False

4. A feeder supplying fixed motor load(s) shall have a protective device with a rating or setting _____ branch-circuit short-circuit and ground-fault protective device for any motor in the group, plus the sum of the full-load currents of the other motors of the group.

   (a) not greater than the largest rating or setting of the
   (b) 125 percent of the largest rating of any
   (c) equal to the largest rating of any
   (d) at least 80% of the

5. Motor control circuit conductors that extend beyond the motor control equipment enclosure shall have short-circuit and ground-fault protection sized not greater than _____ percent of the value specified in Table 310.16 for 60-degree C conductors.

   (a) 100%
   (b) 150%
   (c) 300%
   (d) 400%

6. A _____ shall be located in sight from the motor location and the driven machinery location.

   (a) controller
   (b) protection device
   (c) disconnecting means
   (d) all of these

7. If a motor disconnecting means is a motor-circuit switch, it shall be rated in _____.

   (a) horsepower
   (b) watts
   (c) amperes
   (d) locked-rotor current

8. A branch-circuit overcurrent device can serve as the disconnecting means for a stationary motor of 1/8 hp or less.

   (a) True
   (b) False

Notes

FINAL EXAM

What follows is the Final Exam for this textbook. There are 100 questions that will help you evaluate how well you understood the material that was covered.

Notes

Final Exam

Make sure you read all multiple choice selections for each question. Multiple choice selections such as "(d) all of these" or "(d) both a and b" indicate that more than one of the choices may be correct.

1. The circuit of a control apparatus or system that carries the electric signals directing the performance of the controller but doesn't carry the main power current is called a _____.

   (a) control circuit
   (b) service
   (c) feeder
   (d) branch circuit

2. In **Figure 1**, the auxiliary contacts are indicated by the letter _____.

   (a) A
   (b) B
   (c) D
   (d) M

3. In **Figure 1**, the power contacts in the magnetic starter are indicated by the letter _____.

   (a) A
   (b) B
   (c) C
   (d) D

4. In **Figure 1**, the letter D is the _____.

   (a) motor that's energized when the main power contacts close
   (b) overload relay for the contactor
   (c) coil that activates the auxiliary contacts and the main power contacts
   (d) stop-start station

5. In **Figure 1**, letter C is indicating a set of auxiliary contacts. Which of the following statements is(are) correct?

   (a) This is a set of normally open (NO) contacts.
   (b) The M over the auxiliary contacts indicates that coil M activates the contacts.
   (c) The NO auxiliary contacts have terminal numbers 2 and 3.
   (d) all of these

6. In **Figure 2**, the timing relay has _____ set(s) of contacts activated when it's energized.

   (a) 1
   (b) 2
   (c) 3
   (d) 4

7. In **Figure 2**, the timing relay in this ladder diagram has _____.

   (a) a set of NOTC contacts
   (b) a set of instantaneous contacts
   (c) a set of NCTC contacts
   (d) a and b

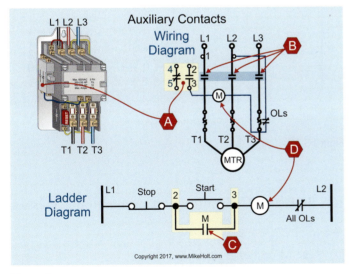

Figure 1

Final Exam

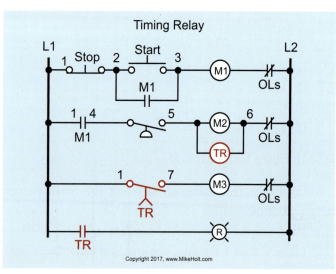

Figure 2

8. In **Figure 2**, when the timing relay is energized, a set of normally open, timed closing contacts _____.

    (a) close after a time delay
    (b) open after a time delay
    (c) open instantaneously
    (d) aren't activated by the timing relay

9. In **Figure 2**, the timing relay coil is connected to points _____.

    (a) 1-2
    (b) 1-4
    (c) 3-4
    (d) 5-6

10. In **Figure 2**, the timing relay contacts with a time delay feature are connected to points _____.

    (a) 1-2
    (b) 1-7
    (c) 3-4
    (d) 5-6

11. Motor control schematics are commonly called _____.

    (a) ladder diagrams
    (b) elementary diagrams
    (c) line diagrams
    (d) any of these

12. In **Figure 3**, there is(are) _____ momentary-contact pushbutton(s).

    (a) 1
    (b) 2
    (c) 3
    (d) 4

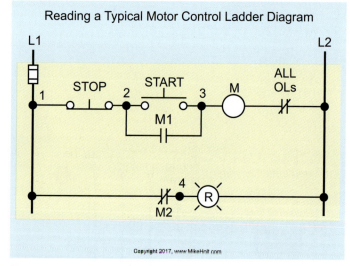

Figure 3

13. In **Figure 3**, when the start pushbutton is pressed, the _____.

    (a) M coil energizes
    (b) NO M1 contacts close
    (c) NC M2 contacts open
    (d) all of these

244 Mike Holt Enterprises | Understanding Basic Motor Controls

Final Exam

14. In **Figure 3**, the letter in the middle of the pilot light symbol represents _____.

    (a) the direction the motor turns
    (b) the color of the pilot light
    (c) which coil activates the pilot light
    (d) the terminal number to which the pilot light is connected

15. In **Figure 3**, the normally closed auxiliary contacts M2 are connected to points _____.

    (a) 1-2
    (b) 1-3
    (c) 1-4
    (d) 3-4

16. In **Figure 3**, the normally open auxiliary contacts M1 are connected to points _____.

    (a) 1-2
    (b) 1-3
    (c) 1-4
    (d) 2-3

17. _____ are devices using coils that can be used to facilitate remote-control functions.

    (a) Contactors
    (b) Magnetic starters
    (c) Solenoids
    (d) all of these

18. In **Figure 4**, the main power contacts are _____.

    (a) not shown in the ladder diagram A
    (b) shown in the wiring (connection) diagram B
    (c) not shown in either diagram
    (d) a and b

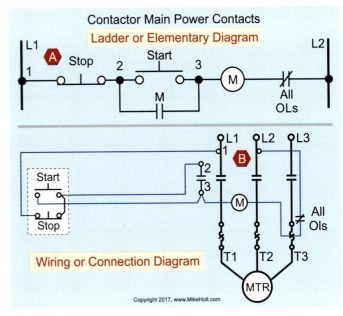

Figure 4

19. In **Figure 4**, the power for the control circuit is taken from _____.

    (a) L1 and L2 for both the ladder and wiring diagrams
    (b) L1 and L2 for the ladder diagram and from L1 and L3 for the wiring diagram
    (c) L1 and L3 for both diagrams
    (d) L2 and L3 for both diagrams

20. In **Figure 4**, when the start PB is pushed, the M coil _____.

    (a) closes the power contacts
    (b) closes the auxiliary contacts 2-3
    (c) energizes
    (d) all of these

Understanding Basic Motor Controls | Mike Holt Enterprises

Final Exam

21. In **Figure 5**, the mechanically held contactor has _____.

    (a) mechanically interlocked coil clearing contacts
    (b) a latch coil
    (c) an unlatch coil
    (d) all of these

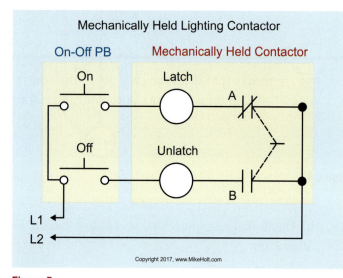

Figure 5

22. In **Figure 5**, when the On PB is pushed the _____.

    (a) latch coil stays energized until the Off PB is pushed
    (b) unlatch coil stays energized until the Off PB is pushed
    (c) latch coil momentarily energizes to close the contactor power contacts
    (d) unlatch coil momentarily energizes to close the contactor power contacts

23. In **Figure 5**, if the power contacts are closed when the Off PB is pushed, the _____.

    (a) latch coil stays energized until the Off PB is pushed
    (b) unlatch coil stays energized until the On PB is pushed
    (c) unlatch coil momentarily energizes, opening the contactor power contacts
    (d) latch coil is energized closing the power contacts

24. In **Figure 5**, after the On PB is pushed and released _____.

    (a) the mechanically held contacts A will be open
    (b) the mechanically held contacts B will be closed
    (c) neither of the coils will be energized
    (d) all of these

25. In **Figure 6**, the magnetic motor starter is designated by the letter _____.

    (a) A
    (b) B
    (c) C
    (d) D

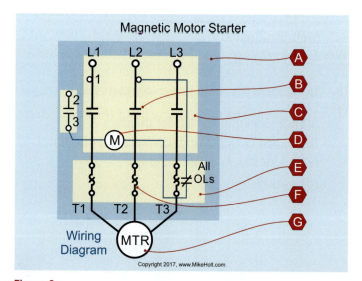

Figure 6

246 Mike Holt Enterprises | *Understanding Basic Motor Controls*

Final Exam

26. In **Figure 6**, the power contacts for the magnetic motor starter are designated by the letter _____.

    (a) A
    (b) B
    (c) C
    (d) D

27. In **Figure 6**, the coil for the magnetic motor starter is designated by the letter _____.

    (a) C
    (b) D
    (c) E
    (d) F

28. In **Figure 6**, the overload relay assembly for the magnetic motor starter is designated by the letter _____.

    (a) C
    (b) D
    (c) E
    (d) F

29. In **Figure 6**, the motor that's supplied by the magnetic motor starter is designated by the letter _____.

    (a) D
    (b) E
    (c) F
    (d) G

30. In **Figure 6**, the thermal overload (heater) is designated by the letter _____.

    (a) C
    (b) D
    (c) E
    (d) F

31. A 2-wire control circuit doesn't have low-voltage protection.

    (a) True
    (b) False

32. A 3-wire control circuit has built-in low-voltage protection.

    (a) True
    (b) False

33. _____ means that if power goes off to the control circuit, the equipment won't automatically restart when power is restored.

    (a) Sequence of operation
    (b) Low-voltage protection
    (c) Operation from rest
    (d) Operation for stop

34. Based on **Figure 7**, which of the following statements is true?

    (a) As the liquid rises the NC contacts will open.
    (b) As the liquid rises the NC contacts will close.
    (c) Wire A indicates a sump-pump type application.
    (d) Wire A causes the auxiliary contacts to close.

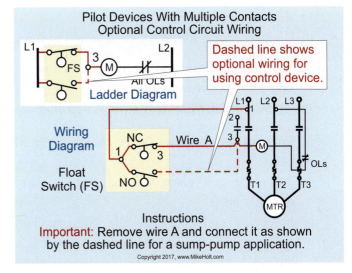

Figure 7

Final Exam

35. Based on **Figure 7**, which of the following statements is(are) true?

    (a) Coil M won't function since all of the contacts have been bypassed.
    (b) Coil M will function directly from the float switch.
    (c) Coil M is in parallel with the overload contacts.
    (d) all of these

36. Based on **Figure 7**, which of the following statements is(are) true?

    (a) The NC float switch contacts are open when the tank is full.
    (b) The NC float switch contacts are closed when the water level drops.
    (c) The NC float switch contacts control the M coil of the magnetic motor starter.
    (d) all of these

37. Based on **Figure 7**, which of the following statements is(are) true about wiring the float switch for a sump-pump application?

    (a) Wire A must be connected to the M coil, which is point 3 of the auxiliary contact if a jumper is installed.
    (b) Remove wire A from the NC FS contact and reconnect it to the NO FS contact.
    (c) Connect wire A to the NC float switch contact.
    (d) a and b

38. In **Figure 8**, if the motor isn't running, which of the following statements is true?

    (a) Pressing the start NO PB de-energizes the M coil.
    (b) After the coil energizes, the NO auxiliary contacts open.
    (c) After the coil energizes, the NO auxiliary contacts will stay closed when the start PB is released.
    (d) Pressing the stop PB energizes the M coil.

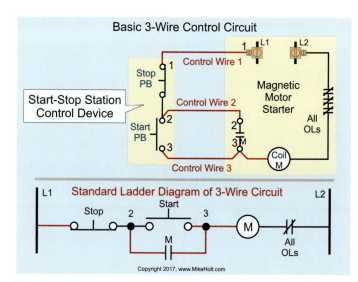

Figure 8

39. In **Figure 8**, if the motor is running, which of the following statements is true?

    (a) Pressing the NO start PB will start the motor.
    (b) NO auxiliary contacts are closed providing a holding circuit to keep the motor running after the start PB is released.
    (c) The motor will continue running if the NC stop PB is pressed.
    (d) The motor will only run if the NO start PB is held closed.

40. In **Figure 8**, if the motor is running, and the power to the magnetic motor starter is interrupted, the _____.

    (a) motor will automatically restart when power is restored
    (b) NO auxiliary contacts will remain closed
    (c) motor won't restart automatically
    (d) stop PB must be pressed to restart the motor

248 | Mike Holt Enterprises | *Understanding Basic Motor Controls*

Final Exam

41. In **Figure 9**, letter E from the green pilot light is connected to point _____.

    (a) 1
    (b) 2
    (c) 3
    (d) L2

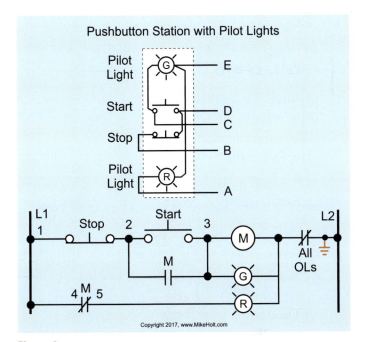

Figure 9

42. In **Figure 9**, letter D from the start PB is connected to point _____.

    (a) 2
    (b) 3
    (c) 4
    (d) 5

43. In **Figure 9**, letter C from the start PB is connected to point _____.

    (a) 1
    (b) 2
    (c) 3
    (d) 4

44. In **Figure 9**, letter B from the stop PB is connected to point _____.

    (a) 1
    (b) 2
    (c) 3
    (d) 4

45. In **Figure 9**, letter A from the red pilot light is connected to point _____.

    (a) 2
    (b) 3
    (c) 4
    (d) 5

46. In **Figure 9**, the red pilot light is on when the motor isn't running.

    (a) True
    (b) False

47. In **Figure 9**, when the start PB is pushed _____.

    (a) the NO auxiliary contacts close and the green pilot light comes on
    (b) the NC auxiliary contacts open and the red pilot light goes out
    (c) the M coil remains energized because the M contacts 2-3 are closed
    (d) all of these

48. In **Figure 10**, letter C from the selector switch is connected to point _____.

    (a) 1
    (b) 2
    (c) 3
    (d) L2

Understanding Basic Motor Controls | Mike Holt Enterprises   249

Final Exam

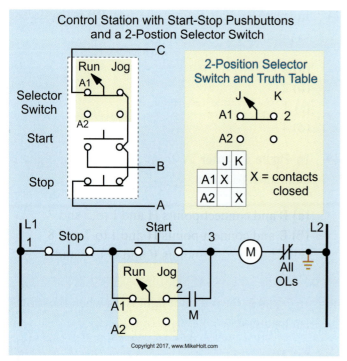

Figure 10

49. In **Figure 10**, letter B from the start PB is connected to point _____.

   (a) 1
   (b) 2
   (c) 3
   (d) L2

50. In **Figure 10**, letter A from the stop PB is connected to point _____.

   (a) 1
   (b) 2
   (c) 3
   (d) L2

51. In **Figure 10**, when the A2 contacts are closed, the 3-wire circuit _____.

   (a) is in the jogging mode
   (b) is in the normal run mode
   (c) won't function in any mode
   (d) will start the motor if the stop PB is pressed

52. In **Figure 10**, when the selector switch contacts A1 are in the closed position, pressing the start PB will _____.

   (a) start the motor normally
   (b) jog the motor
   (c) create a short circuit
   (d) stop the motor

53. In **Figure 11**, if the motor is running in reverse, the electrical interlocks that prevent the F coil from energizing are the _____.

   (a) auxiliary contacts 5-7
   (b) auxiliary contacts 3-6
   (c) auxiliary contacts marked F2
   (d) forward PB

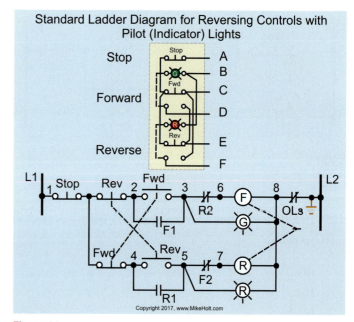

Figure 11

250 Mike Holt Enterprises | *Understanding Basic Motor Controls*

Final Exam

54. In **Figure 11**, letter A from the stop PB connects to point _____.

    (a) 1
    (b) 2
    (c) 3
    (d) 4

55. In **Figure 11**, letter B from the forward pilot light connects to point _____.

    (a) 1
    (b) 4
    (c) 6
    (d) 8

56. In **Figure 11**, letter C from the forward PB connects to point _____.

    (a) 1
    (b) 2
    (c) 3
    (d) 4

57. In **Figure 11**, letter D from the forward PB connects to point _____.

    (a) 1
    (b) 2
    (c) 3
    (d) 4

58. In **Figure 11**, letter E from the reverse PB connects to point _____.

    (a) 1
    (b) 2
    (c) 3
    (d) 4

59. In **Figure 11**, letter F from the reverse PB connects to point _____.

    (a) 3
    (b) 4
    (c) 5
    (d) L2

60. In **Figure 12**, the instructions state that in order to install LS-1, remove jumper _____.

    (a) B and connect points H and I to 5 and 7
    (b) B and connect points H and I to 7 and 8
    (c) A and connect points F and G to 3 and 6
    (d) A and connect points F and G to 4 and 5

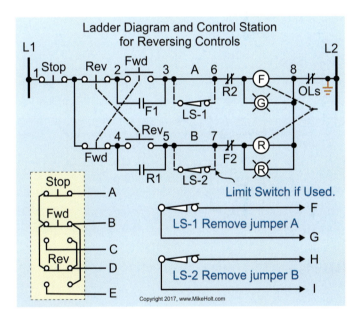

Figure 12

61. In **Figure 12**, if the optional limit switches are installed as shown, and the motor is running forward, when the NC LS-1 opens, the _____.

    (a) motor will run in a reverse direction
    (b) R coil will energize
    (c) stop PB will open
    (d) motor will stop

Final Exam

62. In **Figure 12**, the red pilot light will be on if the _____.

    (a) motor is running in the forward direction
    (b) motor is running in the reverse direction
    (c) stop PB is pressed
    (d) motor protection device opens

63. In **Figure 13**, there are _____ limit switches.

    (a) four different
    (b) two double-circuit
    (c) two single-circuit
    (d) four NC

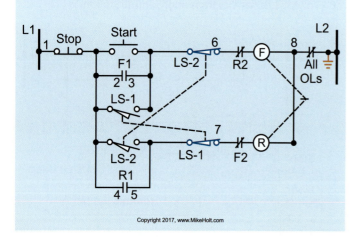

Figure 13

64. In **Figure 13**, if the motor is running forward, and LS-2 is activated, the motor will _____.

    (a) continue running in the forward direction
    (b) stop running
    (c) run in the reverse direction
    (d) energize the F coil

65. In **Figure 13**, if the motor is running in the reverse direction, the motor will stop if the _____.

    (a) stop PB is pressed
    (b) overloads open
    (c) power goes off
    (d) all of these

66. In **Figure 13**, when the motor is running in the reverse direction, contacts _____ will be open.

    (a) F1
    (b) R2
    (c) R1
    (d) both a and b

67. In **Figure 14**, letter A of the up PB is connected to point _____.

    (a) 1
    (b) 2
    (c) 3
    (d) L1

68. In **Figure 14**, letter B of the up PB is connected to point _____.

    (a) 1
    (b) 2
    (c) 3
    (d) 4

69. In **Figure 14**, letter C of the down PB is connected to point _____.

    (a) 2
    (b) 3
    (c) 5
    (d) L2

Final Exam

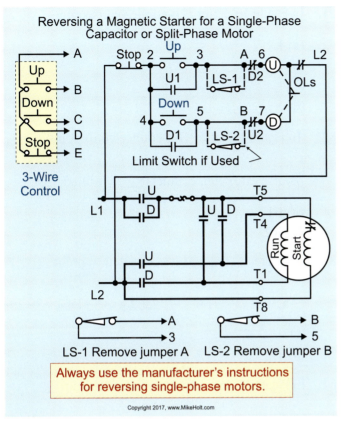

Figure 14

70. In **Figure 14**, letter D of the down PB is connected to point _____.

    (a) 1
    (b) 2
    (c) 3
    (d) 4

71. In **Figure 14**, letter E of the stop PB is connected to point _____.

    (a) L1
    (b) L2
    (c) L3
    (d) B

72. In **Figure 14**, pressing the up PB causes L1 to energize motor leads _____.

    (a) T1 and T5
    (b) T1 and T8
    (c) T2 and T3
    (d) T4 and T5

73. In **Figure 14**, pressing the up PB causes L2 to energize motor leads _____.

    (a) T1 and T4
    (b) T1 and T5
    (c) T2 and T3
    (d) T4 and T8

74. In **Figure 14**, pressing the down PB causes L1 to energize motor leads _____.

    (a) T1 and T5
    (b) T1 and T8
    (c) T2 and T3
    (d) T4 and T5

75. In **Figure 14**, pressing the down PB causes L2 to energize motor leads _____.

    (a) T1 and T4
    (b) T1 and T8
    (c) T2 and T3
    (d) T4 and T8

76. In **Figure 15**, letter A is connected to point _____.

    (a) 1
    (b) 2
    (c) 3
    (d) 4

77. In **Figure 15**, letter B is connected to point _____.

    (a) 2
    (b) 3
    (c) 4
    (d) 5

Understanding Basic Motor Controls | Mike Holt Enterprises 253

Final Exam

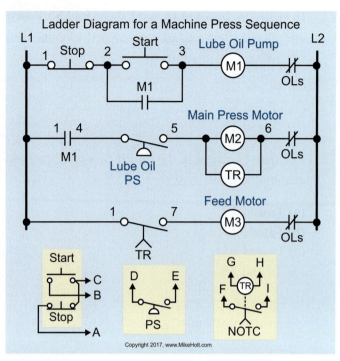

Figure 15

78. In **Figure 15**, letter C is connected to point _____.

(a) 2
(b) 3
(c) 4
(d) 5

79. In **Figure 15**, letter D is connected to point _____.

(a) 1
(b) 2
(c) 3
(d) 4

80. In **Figure 15**, letter E is connected to point _____.

(a) 1
(b) 4
(c) 5
(d) 6

81. In **Figure 15**, letter F is connected to point _____.

(a) 1
(b) 2
(c) 4
(d) 5

82. In **Figure 15**, letter G is connected to point _____.

(a) 1
(b) 2
(c) 4
(d) 5

83. In **Figure 15**, letter H is connected to point _____.

(a) 1
(b) 2
(c) 6
(d) 7

84. In **Figure 15**, letter I is connected to point _____.

(a) 4
(b) 5
(c) 6
(d) 7

85. In **Figure 15**, which coil needs to be de-energized in order for all of the motors to stop running in the machine press?

(a) Coil M1.
(b) Coil M2 or TR.
(c) Either coil M2 or M3.
(d) any of these

Final Exam

86. Based on **Figure 16**, which of the following statements is correct?

    (a) The controller disconnecting means is shown on the wiring diagram.
    (b) A 2-wire control circuit won't work with this motor controller.
    (c) The controller disconnect is provided by the user or installer.
    (d) The main power contacts aren't shown in this wiring diagram.

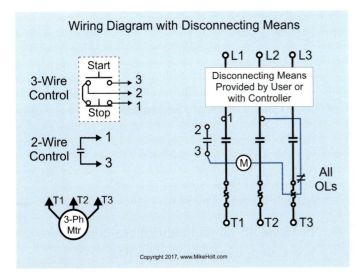

Figure 16

87. In **Figure 16**, if a 2-wire control circuit is used, which of the following statements is correct?

    (a) The auxiliary contacts 2-3 are necessary for the 2-wire circuit to operate.
    (b) The auxiliary contacts 2-3 will remain open after the contacts on the 2-wire circuit close.
    (c) The 2-wire circuit is connected to L1 and one side of the coil (point 3).
    (d) The 2-wire circuit is connected to both sides of the auxiliary contacts.

88. In **Figure 16**, the start-stop PB station with a 3-wire circuit can be used as the motor disconnecting means required by the *NEC*.

    (a) True
    (b) False

89. In **Figure 16**, the start-stop PB station with a 3-wire circuit can be used as the motor controller disconnecting means required by the *NEC*.

    (a) True
    (b) False

90. In **Figure 17**, letter A is connected to point _____.

    (a) 2
    (b) 3
    (c) L1
    (d) L2

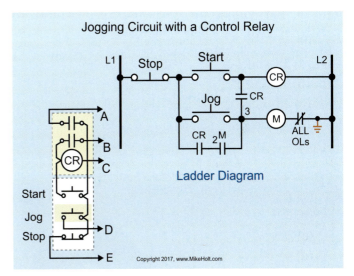

Figure 17

91. In **Figure 17**, letter B is connected to point _____.

    (a) 2
    (b) 3
    (c) 4
    (d) L1

Understanding Basic Motor Controls | Mike Holt Enterprises

Final Exam

92. In **Figure 17**, letter C is connected to point _____.

    (a) 3
    (b) 4
    (c) L1
    (d) L2

93. In **Figure 17**, letter D is connected to point _____.

    (a) 2
    (b) 3
    (c) L1
    (d) L2

94. In **Figure 17**, letter E is connected to point _____.

    (a) 2
    (b) 3
    (c) L1
    (d) L2

95. In **Figure 18**, if the low-voltage connections are being used, L1 will be connected to _____.

    (a) T1 and T2
    (b) T1 and T7
    (c) T1 only
    (d) T3 only

96. In **Figure 18**, if the low-voltage connections are being used, L2 will be connected to _____.

    (a) T1 and T7
    (b) T2 and T3
    (c) T2 and T8
    (d) T2 only

97. In **Figure 18**, if the low-voltage connections are being used, L3 will be connected to _____.

    (a) T3 and T4
    (b) T3 and T6
    (c) T3 and T9
    (d) T3 only

98. In **Figure 18**, if the low-voltage connections are being used, which motor leads not connected to the branch circuit are tied together?

    (a) T1, T2, and T3
    (b) T2, T3, and T4
    (c) T3, T4, and T5
    (d) T4, T5, and T6

99. In **Figure 18**, if the high-voltage connections are being used, L1 will be connected to _____.

    (a) T1 and T7
    (b) T1 only
    (c) T2 and T3
    (d) T2 only

100. In **Figure 18**, if the high-voltage connections are being used, L2 will be connected to _____.

    (a) T2 and T3
    (b) T2 and T6
    (c) T2 only
    (d) T3 only

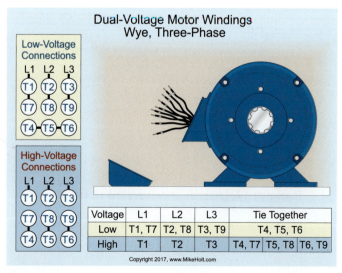

Figure 18

INDEX

Description	Page
2-Wire Control Circuits	81
3-Wire Circuit in a Wiring (Connection) Diagram	87
3-Wire Control Circuits	84

A

Description	Page
A Simple Control Circuit	45
Adding Forward and Reverse Pilot Lights	141
Auxiliary Contacts	23
Auxiliary Contacts	75

C

Description	Page
Coil Applications	55
Combined Interlock Methods for Reversing Starters	134
Combining Devices and Functions for Motor Control Circuits	191
Common (Tapped) versus Separate Control Circuits	99
Common Abbreviations Used for Electrical Terms and Devices	18
Control Conductor Sizes 16 AWG and 18 AWG	100
Control Devices with Multiple Contacts	48
Control Transformer Protection	102
Controls for Sequencing Multiple Motors	170

D

Description	Page
Definitions of Control Terminology	11
Disconnect for Separate Control Circuit	187
Doorbells	209
Drum Switch	25
Dual-Voltage, Nine Lead, Three-Phase Motors	200

E

Description	Page
Electrical Interlock for Magnetic Reversing Controls	131
Electromagnetic Control	53

F

Description	Page
Feeder Disconnect Contactor with Automatic Control	64
Float Switch	26
Flow Switch	26
Forward and Reverse Contactors	129
Forward-Reverse Control With 2-Wire Circuits	153

I

Description	Page
Illuminated Pushbuttons	112
Interlocking Devices	130

L

Description	Page
Lighting Contactor	61
Limit Switch—Mechanical	27
Limit Switch—Optical	28
Limit Switch—Proximity	28

M

Description	Page
Magnetic Motor Starters	69
Master or Emergency Stop Controls for Multiple Motors	177
Motor Control Basics	8
Motor Control Language	4
Motor Controllers and Disconnects	183
Multiple Start-Stop Pushbutton Stations	89

Index

Description	Page
O	
Option of Using a 2- or 3-Wire Circuit in One Diagram	92
Other Overload Protection Methods	75
Other Standard Control Circuit Overcurrent Protection Arrangements	103
P	
Pilot (Indicator) Lights	107
Power Sources for the Coil and Control Circuit	54
Pressure Switch	28
Protection for Control Circuits	99
Pushbutton Switch	29
R	
Reading a Motor Control Schematic	37
Relays	24
Remote Control—Introduction	59
Reversing Controls and Limit Switches for Garage Door Applications	150
Reversing Controls with Limit Switches Used to Automatically Stop a Motor	147
Reversing Controls—Limit Switches for Automatic Forward and Reverse	148
Reversing Three-Phase Motors	129

Description	Page
S	
Selector Switches—Variations	120
Sequencing Control	167
Single-Phase, Dual-Voltage Motors	204
Solenoid	31
Standard Symbols	19
Switch Operations	31
T	
Temperature Switch	34
Thermostats for Air-Conditioning and Heat	211
Three-Phase Motors	199
Three-Position Selector Switch	118
Timing Relay Terminology	36
Timing Relay with Instantaneous Contacts	35
Timing Relay—Pneumatic	35
Timing Relay—Solid-State	36
Truth Tables	117
Two-Position Selector Switch	117
Types of Motors	157
Typical Applications for Pilot Lights in Control Circuits	108
W	
Wiring a Reversing Control Pushbutton Station	136
Wiring a Reversing Control with a Selector Switch	136